Fool for Love

Fool for Love
F. Scott Fitzgerald

Scott Donaldson

University of Minnesota Press

Minneapolis | London

THE FESLER–LAMPERT MINNESOTA HERITAGE BOOK SERIES
This series is published with the generous assistance of the John K. and Elsie Lampert Fesler Fund
and David R. and Elizabeth P. Fesler. Its mission is to republish significant out-of-print books that
contribute to our understanding and appreciation of Minnesota and the Upper Midwest.

Frontispiece: F. Scott and Zelda Fitzgerald in Dellwood, Minnesota, the month before Scottie's birth,
1921. Photograph by Kenneth Melvin Wright. Photograph collection 9/1921. Courtesy of Minnesota
Historical Society.

Portions of this book appeared, in slightly or substantially different form, as "Money and Marriage
in Fitzgerald's Stories," in *The Short Stories of F. Scott Fitzgerald*, ed. Jackson R. Bryer (Madison:
University of Wisconsin Press, 1982), 75–88; "The Crisis of Fitzgerald's *Crack-Up*," *Twentieth-
Century Literature* 26 (Summer 1980): 171–88; and "F. Scott Fitzgerald, Princeton '17," *Princeton
University Library Chronicle* 40 (Winter 1979): 119–54.

Photographs of Emily Vanderbilt (opposite page 60) and Sheilah Graham (opposite page 201, top) are
from Bettman Archive. All other photographs are reprinted courtesy of Frances Fitzgerald Smith.

First published in 1983 by Congdon & Weed, Inc.

First University of Minnesota Press edition, 2012

Copyright 1983, 2001, 2012 by Scott Donaldson

Preface copyright 2001 by Scott Donaldson

Published by the University of Minnesota Press
111 Third Avenue South, Suite 290
Minneapolis, MN 55401-2520
http://www.upress.umn.edu

LIBRARY OF CONGRESS CATALOGING-IN-PUBLICATION DATA
Donaldson, Scott, 1928–
Fool for love : F. Scott Fitzgerald / Scott Donaldson. — 1st University of Minnesota Press ed.
p. cm. — (Fesler–Lampert Minnesota Heritage Book series)
Includes bibliographical references and index.
ISBN 978-0-8166-7820-4 (pbk. : acid-free paper)
1. Fitzgerald, F. Scott (Francis Scott), 1896–1940. 2. Authors, American—20th century—Biography.
I. Title.
PS3511.I9Z59 2012
813'.52—dc23
[B]   2012016943

Printed in the United States of America on acid-free paper

The University of Minnesota is an equal-opportunity educator and employer.

20 19 18 17 16 15 14 13 12   10 9 8 7 6 5 4 3 2 1

To Andrew

Dolly Bartlett walked to the auto and looked back at him, pert exultant and glowing. What he felt was like fright—appropriately enough for one of the major compulsions had just taken place in his life. Fool for love was Terrence from now, and not just at a distance but as one who had been summoned and embraced, one who had tasted with a piercing delight and had become an addict within an hour.

—F. Scott Fitzgerald, "That Kind of Party"

Contents

Preface

WITH FITZGERALD as with no one else in American literature save Poe, the biography gets in the way. Never mind that F. Scott Fitzgerald is the author of one exquisite short novel as perfect as anything in our literature and of another longer, more chaotic novel of tremendous emotional power. Never mind that he has written a couple of dozen stories that by any standard deserve the designation of "masterful." Ignoring those legacies, much of the general public still tends to think of him in connection with the legends of his disordered and difficult life, and to classify him under one convenient stereotype or another. So diminished in stature, Fitzgerald becomes the Chronicler of the Jazz Age, or the Artist in Spite of Himself, or—most prevalent stereotype of all—the Writer as Burnt-Out Case: a man whose tragic course functions as a cautionary tale for more commonsensical aftercomers. His saga offers an almost irresistible temptation to sermonizers, overt or concealed. *It is not right* to ride on top of taxicabs or disport oneself in the Plaza Hotel's fountain, *not right* to drink to excess or abuse a "lovely golden wasted talent." Go thou and do otherwise.

This warning usually remains implicit, of course. It is not the homily but the tale of star-crossed lovers that commands attention—handsome brilliant erratic Scott married for good or ill to beautiful willful unstable Zelda. There is an arresting poignancy in the way the two of them (Scott more than Zelda, perhaps) considered the alternatives and chose the sweet poison. Somehow, in the repeated retellings of this tale, the Fitzgeralds have come to stand for a kind of generic nonspecific glamour, now sadly departed. In 1980 the opening party for an exhibit of Fitzgeraldiana at the National Portrait Gallery drew an enormous crowd determined to celebrate a vanished past. The band played Glenn Miller and Benny Goodman numbers from the 1940s, the decade following Fitzgerald's death. A few women attempted flapper costumes, but for the most part the clothes were as anachronistic as the music. One chap, aiming for colonial elegance, danced in a pith helmet. The details that mattered so much to Fitzgerald, a man precisely in tune with his times, mattered very little to those come to the party to memorialize his legend. Zelda and Scott—they are fixed so securely in the collective mind as lovable reckless youths for whom it all went disastrously wrong that it has been difficult to set that image aside and concentrate on the work that established him as one of the major literary artists of the twentieth century.

Instead of ignoring Fitzgerald's story, this book attempts to draw lines of connection between his experience and his fiction. This is a risky endeavor. Lying underbrush is the biographical trap of assuming that events in a novel coincide with what actually happened. As the poet Donald Junkins has nicely observed, authors do not write *about* their experience, they write *out* their experience. Still, when Fitzgerald told and retold the story of the poor boy seeking the favor of the rich girl, and further explained that the theme kept recurring "because I lived it," the boundary between the real and the imagined blurs. So I have moved back and forth between the life and the work, tiptoeing and looking for patterns. Henry James, himself a biographer as well as a novelist, understood that the entire truth could never be told. "We can only take what groups together," he said.

What most grouped together in Fitzgerald's work and life, I came to realize over several decades in the classroom and five years of intensive research, was an overweening compulsion to please. He wanted to please other men, but did a poor job of it. His Princeton classmates considered him overinquisitive and friv-olous. Zelda's father thought him unreliable. Ernest Hemingway, the closest of friends in the mid-1920s, eventually came to regard him with something like scorn. Fitzgerald was far more successful in pleasing women. Readers of his fiction might expect as much, for he is one of our more androgynous writers, with a rare capacity to put himself in the place of characters of either sex. "All my characters are Scott Fitzgeralds," he acknowledged. "Even my female characters are feminine Scott Fitzgeralds." The set of instructions Fitzgerald drew up, at eighteen, for his younger sister Annabel provides convincing evidence along these lines. In this remarkable document he coached his sister in the finer points of attracting boys: how to groom herself, how to dance, what to talk about, how to flatter. And the androgyny is everywhere evident in the stories and novels, too, which is probably why most female college students are attracted to his fiction.

Equipped with this sensitivity, Fitzgerald played the game of courtship well. As a youth he was a notoriously successful flirt. "I've got an adjective that just fits *you*," he would tell a dancing partner early in the evening, and then withhold the laudatory word to build up her expectations. He was good-looking and at ease in the company of girls. He listened to them as few other boys did, and made it clear that he cared tremendously what they thought of him. Later, as a married man, he continued to woo women. He couldn't help it. He needed their approval, which is to say their love and adoration. Zelda Sayre Fitzgerald may have been the most important woman in his life, but she was not and could not be the only one.

To an extent, *Fool for Love* demythologizes the Scott and Zelda story by concentrating on other relationships. His passion to please, for example, clearly derived from his mother, as did his profound sense of social insecurity. Mollie McQuillan Fitzgerald was ambitious for her only son and made a habit of producing him, all dressed up, to recite or sing for company. But neither his well-to-do but dowdy mother nor his well-born but unsuccessful father gave him a sense of belonging to a particular place or class. His parents were forever moving from one rented apartment or row house to another, teetering on the edge of the social eminence occupied so comfortably by most of their son's boyhood companions. His first word as a baby, his mother recorded, was "up," and that was where she expected him to go. One way to rise, he discovered, was through beguiling young girls of higher social standing than his own.

Fitzgerald thus suffered a tremendous setback when Ginevra King of Lake Forest, north of Chicago—of the wealthiest and most beautiful debutantes of her day—spurned him in order to marry a young man of her own class. The rejection devastated Fitzgerald, even as it supplied him with the basic subject matter of much of his fiction. There are probably more characters in his stories and novels modeled on Ginevra than on Zelda, who caught him on the rebound. By altering the circumstances of the plot, Fitzgerald played variations on the age-old theme of the battle of the sexes.

What is unusual about Fitzgerald's treatment of this theme is its escalation—in the work as in the life—from the courting game of his adolescence to the fierce battle of his young manhood to the outright war of his maturity. Perhaps, we are inclined to think, Amory Blaine will not suffer unduly from his jilting by Rosalind Connage in *This Side of Paradise* (1920), Fitzgerald's first novel. But Gatsby *dies* for Daisy in his 1925 masterpiece, and Dick Diver is stripped of his vitality and tossed aside by Nicole and her family in *Tender Is the Night* (1934). In Fitzgerald's fictional treatment of the war between the sexes, it is almost always the man who ends up defeated. By repeatedly depicting the downfall of his male figures, Fitzgerald was imagining what might well have happened (had not Zelda been afflicted with schizophrenia) and also, it seems to me, excoriating himself for his weaknesses. *Tender*, in particular, is a novel about the enervating effects of charm. Compelled to please everyone around him (and particularly women), Diver dissipates away his life's work and his usefulness as a human being. The real Fitzgerald, like his invented protagonist, came to despise himself for his "fatal pleasingness," a self-disgust that characteristically emerged under the influence of alcohol. Drinking runs like an inner malaise through Fitzgerald's life and that of many of his male characters.

In the late 1920s and early 1930s, Scott Fitzgerald waged his own private war with his wife. Eventually he came to think of himself and Zelda as locked in a deadly struggle from which only one of them could emerge alive and whole. In plans that never came to pass, he laid the legal groundwork for divorce and for gaining custody of his daughter, Scottie. He even set down on paper his strategy for confrontations with Zelda. Hidden among the Fitzgerald archives at Princeton is a chilling document wherein he sketched out a secret plan to "attack [Zelda] on all grounds" although doing so might precipitate "another breakdown." The chapters devoted to Zelda and Scott in *Fool for Love* rely on much previously unused evidence in the Fitzgerald papers at Princeton, including a number of poignant letters she wrote him from the institutions where she was undergoing treatment.

During a six-month visiting fellowship I read through the memoirs, letters, and notes in the Princeton collection. There reposes, for example, the extremely revealing journal that Laura Guthrie, Fitzgerald's amanuensis, kept during the summer of 1935 in Asheville, North Carolina. This journal unveils the writer touching bottom: enslaved to drink, carrying on a reckless affair, unable to write coherently, unsure of himself, verging on suicide. Also at Princeton is the other half of the correspondence, the letters Fitzgerald saved not only from Zelda but from such other women as Marie Hersey and Beatrice Dance and Dean Stewart, the last a fascinating and otherwise ignored correspondent, and from a wide range of people reacting to his fiction and to "The Crack-Up" essays of 1936.

Fool for Love is also based on interviews and correspondence with a number of people, chief among them Scottie Fitzgerald Smith, who was generous, helpful, candid, and engaging throughout; Sheilah Graham, who made it clear that she never considered herself a victim trying to cope with a drunken has-been in Hollywood but instead a "second wife" who loved and enjoyed her life with a vital, intelligent, and (when sober) altogether appealing man; Budd Schulberg, who told me among other things about Fitzgerald's feeling toward Hemingway at the End; Norris and Betty Jackson, who grew up with Scott in St. Paul; and Margaret Egloff, a Jungian psychiatrist and intimate friend of Fitzgerald whose interpretation of a "big dream" about his mother is crucial to the argument of this book. In addition, I profited from the information and insights of biographers such as Arthur Mizener, Henry Dan Piper, Andrew Turnbull, Nancy Milford, and Matthew J.

Bruccoli. Mizener and Piper kindly let me examine the materials they accumulated in the process of writing their books.

There is much in this biography that was new when it was first published, and what was most different about it then—its interpretation of Fitzgerald—continues to remain so. It presents a man only hinted at in other books, a man driven to earn the approval and admiration of others, particularly of women, who crippled his self-image and his relationships as a consequence. Yet at the same time *Fool for Love* concludes with a celebration of Fitzgerald at the end of his lamentably brief life, shaking off his debilitation compulsion along with the drinking that was symptomatic of it and emerging at last with dignity as "a writer only."

This approach to Fitzgerald's life and work hardly represents an exclusive path to understanding. As he himself warned, there could never be an entirely effective biography of a major novelist, for "he is too many people if he is any good." But this biography does collect "what group[ed] together," as I came to see the evidence, and offers an angle of vision catching at the heart of this wonderful writer's life and fiction.

Scott Donaldson
March 2001

1

A Man with No People

As a boy Scott Fitzgerald tried to persuade himself that he wasn't the son of his parents at all but the son of "a king who ruled the whole world." When his parents refused to be conjured out of existence, he repudiated their plans for him. Father thought his only son should go into business, Mother thought the army, neither thought writing. Fitzgerald resented their lack of faith as he resented their financial control. Many children have felt such resentments. He felt them with unusual vehemence. Publicly, he announced his independence in his fiction and in interviews where, posing as spokesman for the Younger Generation, he attacked the incompetence and ignorance of the Older. Privately, he proclaimed the shortcomings of Edward and Mollie Fitzgerald.

"Why shouldn't I go crazy?" he wrote Max Perkins, his editor. "My father is a moron and my mother is a neurotic, half insane with pathological nervous worry. Between them they haven't and never have had the brains of Calvin Coolidge."

Fitzgerald condemned Mother and Father alike for their lack of intelligence and for its deleterious effect on him. "If I knew anything I'd be the best writer in America," he once remarked. More often, though, he stressed the difference between them, particularly the social difference.

His father bequeathed to him a heritage he might have been prouder of, had not the man himself turned out so poorly. Edward Fitzgerald was descended on his mother's side from prominent

1

Maryland families who had settled in the colony in the seventeenth century. Francis Scott Key was the second cousin, twice removed, of the boy born in St. Paul on September 24, 1896, and christened Francis Scott Key Fitzgerald. Scott's mother took special pride in the connection and liked to talk about it. So did her son. Both of them got the facts wrong, and claimed a closer relationship to the famous Key than was actually the case. "My great grandmother visited Dolly Madison," Scott observed in his notebooks. It mattered to him. He betrayed a measure of pride even in the mock genealogical chart he sent Edmund Wilson, wherein he traced the family tree of "F. Scott Fitzgerald (drunkard)" back to "Duns Scotus (philos.)," "Mary, Queen of Scotts (Queen)," "Edward Fitzgerald (The Rubiat)," "Sir Walter Scott (Ivanhoe)," and "Duke Fitzgerald (Earl of Lienster)" in addition to "Francis Scott Key (hymnalist)."*

On his mother's side there was money but no social distinction. Philip Francis McQuillan, Scott's maternal grandfather, had started from scratch and built a small fortune in the wholesale grocery business. The McQuillans also became pillars of the Catholic church. When Scott and Zelda Fitzgerald went to Europe in 1921, Archbishop Dowling of St. Paul tried to arrange an audience for Scott with the Pope. The archbishop confessed that he had not met young Mr. Fitzgerald himself, but pointed out that "none have merited more of the Church in this city" than his family "through several generations—staunch, devout, generous." Scott Fitzgerald was unimpressed. To him his mother's family remained "straight 1850 potato famine Irish." (Actually, Philip Francis McQuillan emigrated in 1843.) In a letter to John O'Hara, another American writer with Irish roots, Fitzgerald vividly drew the contrast:

> I am half black Irish and half old American stock with the usual exaggerated ancestral pretensions. The black Irish half of the family had the money and looked down upon the Maryland side of the family who had, and really had, that certain series of reticences and obligations that go under the poor old shattered word "breeding" (modern form "inhibitions"). So being born in

---

*Author's Note: Here, as elsewhere, I have reproduced Fitzgerald's occasional errors in spelling.

that atmosphere of crack, wisecrack and countercrack I developed a two-cylinder inferiority complex. So if I were elected King of Scotland tomorrow after graduating from Eton, Magdalene to Guards, with an embryonic history which tied me to the Plantaganets, I would still be a parvenu. I spent my youth in alternately crawling in front of the kitchen maids and insulting the great.

In short, Fitzgerald did not know how to act socially. Lacking social confidence, he felt he had to justify himself wherever he went. Often he tried too hard to impress people. Occasionally he refused to try at all.

"Mollie just missed being beautiful," Edward Fitzgerald used to say of his wife, but then he was a Southern gallant. Mollie was not beautiful nor close to it. In photographs she looks forthrightly at the camera, but the dark circles under her eyes dominate the picture. Her hair appears frizzy and unkempt, and her clothing drab. She seemed, to one of Scott's contemporaries, to have "worn the same dress all her life," and she was given to extravagantly droopy hats. Sometimes her shoes did not quite match, for she used to break in a new pair one at a time. She went to the beauty parlor for a manicure of her right hand only; she could do the left herself. She looked rather like a peasant, her son used to say. Others thought her more witchlike in appearance. Betty Jackson recalls watching Mrs. Fitzgerald walk to daily Mass, frumpy and unsmiling, toting her invariable umbrella and "followed by a lot of little glooms. You didn't get a lift when she went by."

In conversation Mollie was eccentrically outspoken. Whatever came into her head came out of her mouth. "Why did you have your house painted that awful color?" she'd ask. "Lorena," she demanded of her sister-in-law, "why do you put your table over there? We keep ours here." Once she was riding a streetcar with a woman whose husband was ill. What are you thinking about, the woman asked. "I'm trying to decide," Mollie Fitzgerald replied, "how you'll look in mourning."

In St. Paul Mrs. Fitzgerald was regarded as rather literary, since she was often seen carrying an armload of books home from the library. In fact she read eclectically in popular books of the day, and especially admired the uplifting poems—so Scott wrote in "An Author's Mother"—of Alice and Phoebe Cary. She sent her son religious books to read. When he began to publish his own books, she did not know what to make of them. For his part Scott relentlessly pilloried her taste. "It's a masterpiece, Mother," he scrawled in her copy of *The Great Gatsby*. "Write me how you like it." He assured Alfred Dashiell, editor of *Scribner's* magazine, that *Tender Is the Night* "must have *some* merit" since his mother "wasn't interested in it." Scott did dedicate *Tales of the Jazz Age* "Quite Inappropriately To My Mother"—inappropriately on at least two grounds. First, she hardly belonged to the Jazz Age herself. Second, she possessed little or no understanding of the stories in the collection, which included "The Camel's Back," "May Day," and "The Diamond as Big as the Ritz." "I wish," he told Margaret Turnbull, the mother of his biographer Andrew Turnbull, "I had had the advantage when I was a child of parents and friends who knew more than I did."

Mollie McQuillan was in her thirtieth year when she married Edward Fitzgerald in February 1890. The fine-featured, small Fitzgerald, then 36, looked a better catch than he turned out to be. Dapper in his Vandyke beard and well-cut clothes, Fitzgerald had beautiful manners but not much drive. He had come west from Maryland to run a wicker-furniture manufacturing business of his own in St. Paul. When it went under in 1897, Fitzgerald took a salesman's job with Procter & Gamble, a post that moved the family to Buffalo and Syracuse, New York. When Scott's father was fired ten years later, the Fitzgeralds returned to St. Paul to be supported by the McQuillan money. As a businessman Edward Fitzgerald failed twice, and it was characteristic of his son to take the emotional impact of his father's failure personally, yet to admire the manner in which he confronted it.

To a sensitive boy like Scott Fitzgerald, it must have seemed that everyone in St. Paul knew of his father's failure. Edward went regularly to an office in his brother-in-law's real estate firm, where he presumably functioned as a wholesale grocery salesman. But he barely earned enough to pay the rent, and his personal credit was so shaky that he had to charge his postage stamps to Mrs. Fitzgerald's account at the drug store. Besides, he drank. "He couldn't get anywhere with that fault," as C. N. B. Wheeler, the headmaster of St. Paul Academy, put it. Scott was perfectly aware of his father's fondness for alcohol. "Father used to drink too much and then play baseball in the back yard," he recorded in his ledger for August 1905. But he refused to make the connection between drinking and business failure.

In a passage excised from "Early Success," an article written in 1937, Scott Fitzgerald simultaneously celebrated his father's unwillingness to make excuses for his lack of success and supplied him with excuses of his own. Never, the younger Fitzgerald wrote, did he hear his father "blame his failure on anything but his own incompetence, yet he might have since he was caught once in a panic... and once in the first rush to weed older men out of business." Here he characterized his father as the victim of economic forces beyond his control. Elsewhere, he cited genetic forces. In his essay on "The Death of My Father" he described Edward Fitzgerald as the product of "tired old stock," unaccommodated to the bustling world of business. In effect, Scott was trying to convert his father's weakness into a virtue.

Such defensiveness testifies to a wound that refused to heal. Scott Fitzgerald grew up at the turn of the century reading the Alger books and believing in the gospel of success. Nothing he wrote or said could obliterate the fact of his father's failure. Scott liked his father enormously, and proudly remembered dressing up in long trousers and a short cane and walking downtown with his father on a Sunday morning to get his shoes shined. He absorbed from Edward Fitzgerald a taste for romantic poetry, especially Poe and Byron. "Tell Father," he wrote home from Lausanne in 1930, "that I visited the

'—seven pillars of Gothic mould
in Chillon's dungeons deep and old'

and thought of the first poem I ever heard, or was [it] 'The Raven?'" He also acquired from him a sentimental attachment to the lost cause of the Confederacy, for though his father was brought up in Rockville, Maryland, technically Union territory, his sympathies lay with the South and he loved to tell his enthralled son tales of the Civil War, drawing on his own childhood recollections.

Like the fictional Dick Diver and his father, Scott attempted to emulate Edward Fitzgerald's good manners—manners that were more the product of temperament than of calculation. And to the best of his ability, Edward served as his son's "only moral guide." Only once did he strike Scott, when the boy called him a liar. Edward was inordinately proud of his handsome son: proud of his boyhood accomplishments, proud of his (undistinguished) Army service in World War I, proud of his becoming a famous writer. Scott's feelings toward his father remained forever ambiguous, however; for how could he respect a man who had failed so abjectly and was virtually emasculated through living off his wife's income?

Mrs. Fitzgerald dominated the household. When they traveled to Washington to visit relatives, she'd take the sleeper and Edward would follow on the day coach. The neighborhood kids were terrified of her. Once when Scott's friends Paul Ballion and Cecil Read came to lunch, Mr. Fitzgerald was having some difficulty cutting a pie that stuck to the tin. "Edward, let me cut the pie!" Mollie demanded, and snatched it away from him. "Where would we be," she'd say, "if it wasn't for Grandfather McQuillan?"

The ambivalence of Fitzgerald's feelings about his father emerges in a letter sent to his agent, Harold Ober, after Ober had escorted the elder Fitzgerald to the Broadway production of *The Great Gatsby*. "He misses me, I think," Fitzgerald wrote in acknowledging Ober's courtesy, and then went on to touch the nerve. "His own life after a rather brilliant start back in the seventies has been a 'failure'—he's always lived in mother's shadow and he takes an immense vicarious pleasure in any success of mine."

In his fiction, Scott Fitzgerald tended to depict fathers in hazy outlines. Often he disposed of the protagonist's father precipitously. "My father is very much alive at something over a hundred," he observed in his notebooks, "and always resents the fact that the fathers of most of the principal characters in my books are dead before the book begins. To please him I once had a father stagger

The dapper Edward Fitzgerald and son Scott, c. 1899

Mollie Fitzgerald, dark-browed and forbidding

in and out at the end of the book but he was far from flattered." That must have been Henry Gatz, who appears briefly near the close of *The Great Gatsby*. But Mr. Gatz was clearly ignorant and declassé, hardly a character modeled on Edward Fitzgerald. Moreover, his values were blatantly materialistic. It is the father of Nick Carraway who serves as a kind of moral touchstone in that novel, as it is the minister with roots in old Virginia, Dick Diver's father, who stands for honor and courage and courtesy in *Tender Is the Night*. Scott idealized the best of his father in the Reverend Diver; in that novel the parallels run closest. Like Dick Diver, Scott Fitzgerald sailed across the Atlantic to attend his father's funeral. And like Diver he felt that with his father's death an era had passed, and a sense of honor and duty, as well as a generation. "Good-by, my father—good-by, all my fathers": Dick said it for them both.

Shadowy though the fathers are in Fitzgerald's novels, the mothers are still more wraithlike. Only once did he portray a protagonist's mother with any vividness. Beatrice Blaine, Amory's mother in *This Side of Paradise*, was almost exactly the kind of mother Fitzgerald would have chosen for himself. But Beatrice Blaine and Mollie Fitzgerald have little in common. Beatrice possesses wit and charm derived from "a brilliant education." Her beauty is accentuated by "the exquisite delicacy of her features" and complemented by "the consummate art and simplicity of her clothes." She is not merely rich, like Fitzgerald's mother, but "a fabulously wealthy American girl" whose name is known to cardinals and queens. When Amory's ineffectual father dies, Beatrice and her only child become boon companions, traveling around Europe together while she gaily drinks rather more than she should. Amory inherits this weakness, as he inherits his charm and his snobbery, from Beatrice Blaine. On one occasion he feels "a sudden great pride" in her and fears he will not be able to measure up to the standards she has established.

Amory Blaine represents a glamorized version of Scott Fitzgerald in *This Side of Paradise*, Fitzgerald's first and most openly autobiographical novel. One way Amory is glamorized is by eliminating his parents, even the engaging Beatrice. By the time Amory and Rosalind Connage fall in love, fate has orphaned him.

"I want to belong to you," the rich and beautiful Rosalind tells him. "I want your people to be my people. I want to have your babies."

"But I haven't any people," Amory replies.

Fitzgerald's own parents lived out a normal life span, but metaphorically he had "no people" from the age of social awareness on: none he would have wanted to introduce to the immensely wealthy parents of Ginevra King, the real-life Chicago–Lake Forest belle he courted in 1915 and 1916, none he would have wanted to present to the parents of Zelda Sayre, the Montgomery, Alabama, girl with ties to the Southern aristocracy he married a week after the publication of *This Side of Paradise* in the spring of 1920. The groom's parents did not come to the wedding in New York. Neither did the bride's.

Fitzgerald launched a novel tentatively titled *The Boy Who Killed His Mother* after finishing *The Great Gatsby* in 1925. He also composed and performed on festive occasions a humorous ballad about matricide, with lyrics that ran

> Just a boy that killed his mother
>   I was always up to tricks
> When she taunted me I shot her
>   Through her chronic appendix

While Mollie Fitzgerald could not be disposed of so easily, Scott kept her at a distance. By the time he was ten years old, he had apparently begun to be ashamed of his mother. During the summer of 1907, he went to Camp Chatham in Ontario and might have been expected to feel the pangs of homesickness. These were not strong enough to keep him from discouraging her visit. "I'd like very much" to have you come, the boy's letter began, but—he immediately added—"I don't think you would like it as you know no one here except Mrs. Upton and she is busy most of the time" and there were no good hotels and "about the only fare" in the boarding houses consisted of lamb and beef. Confronted by such elaborate signals, Mollie Fitzgerald stayed put. Neither then nor later did Scott want her around much.

He was annoyed by her gaucheries of dress and behavior, which included "majestically dripping her sleeves in the coffee" and flopping about in high buttoned shoes with the top buttons unfastened for comfort. Scott preferred not to look. "Never noticed mother's eyes after living with her 20 years," one of his notes reads. "Example of observation when I don't like to look at her."

Like many another youth he rebelled against his mother's overprotectiveness. Throughout his boyhood he was bundled up with hats and coats and scarves and overshoes at the least sign of outdoor chill. If he so much as hinted at a sore throat or cold, Mollie kept him home from school. Nor did her anxiety about his health lessen after he grew to manhood. "Report Here My Son Scott Fitzgerald very sick in Paris," she wired Scribner's in January 1926. Could his publishers supply any information? They could: the rumor was unfounded. Again in the spring of 1930, she wrote Maxwell Perkins seeking news of her son's well-being in Paris. Scott was all right, as it turned out, but Zelda had collapsed, an event that inspired Mollie Fitzgerald to send her son a moralistic poem and a check. Scott returned both, with the scornful comment that her poem contained "good rules for a man who wanted to be a chief clerk at 50."

Mollie was not only protective of her only son; she also spoiled him rotten. She may have been dowdy herself, but she saw to it that Scott wore the best. When he was two, she dressed him in bloomers and kept him in curls. Later there were silk bow ties to accompany his Eton collars and De Pinna suits. She liked to show him off in such finery, marching him around to the Convent of the Visitation in St. Paul to recite poetry for the nuns or producing him at home to sing popular ballads for visitors. "He used to sing for company—God!" Scott wrote in his ledger, stabbing the pen through the page in disgust. His mother could not bring herself to discipline her beautiful blue-eyed boy. "No matter what awful thing I did," Scott told Sheilah Graham, "I was just a bad brownie."

Perhaps the most permanent of the psychic difficulties his mother bequeathed to him, however, derived from her determined efforts to launch both Scott and his sister Annabel into St. Paul society. Scott went to Professor William H. Baker's dancing school with the sons and daughters of the city's leading families. He was invited to dances at the three-story houses on Summit Avenue and to parties at the University Club, Town and Country, and the White Bear Yacht Club. But his family's position was precarious. Grandfather McQuillan was respected for his success, but Edward Fitzgerald had never amounted to anything, and Mollie, though she attended the debutante teas, carried on no social intercourse with the Ordways and the Driscolls and the Clarksons.

He did not live there very long and never really had a home anywhere, but St. Paul, Minnesota, left its mark on Scott Fitzgerald. What sort of place was the St. Paul of Fitzgerald's youth? Most accounts characterized the city then as conservative, traditional, somewhat smug in its provincialism. "St. Paul presents to the eye," writer Thomas Boyd remarked in 1922, "the spectacle of a huge city clinging tenaciously to the east and alarmed over the danger of falling into the west." The word for St. Paul, writer Grace Flandrau concluded in a 1925 essay, was "complacent," and as a native daughter that was all right with her. "Complacency is what we need," she insisted with an eye on the Twin City of Minneapolis across the river. "Americans and American cities suffer from a disguised inferiority complex" called boosterism. If St. Paul got any bigger, its citizens might as well be living in Minneapolis.

When Fitzgerald characterized his home town, he emphasized something largely ignored by his friends, Flandrau and Boyd: the social hierarchy of the city. St. Paul felt itself superior to Minneapolis—and to Kansas City and Indianapolis and other Midwestern cities—because it was, by the first decade of the twentieth century, a three-generation town, while the others could claim only two. In an early draft of his story, "A Night at the Fair" (1928), Fitzgerald elaborated on the social structure those three generations had forged.

> There were the two or three nationally known families—outside of them rather than below them the hierarchy began. At the top came those whose grandparents had brought something with them from the East, a vestige of money and culture; then came the families of the big self-made merchants, the "old set-

tlers" of the sixties and seventies, American-English-Scotch, or German or Irish, looking down upon each other somewhat in the order named. . . . After this came certain well-to-do "new people"—mysterious, out of a cloudy past, possibly unsound. Like so many structures this one did not survive the cataract of money that came tumbling down upon it with the war.

Besides demonstrating Fitzgerald's social sensitivity and compulsion to rank people and places, this passage indicates where he felt he belonged in St. Paul's system of classification: not among the nationally known families, nor among those whose grandparents had brought money and culture from the East, but rather among the grandchildren of the "old settlers" who had come at mid-century to make their fortunes in the rude town on the banks of the Mississippi. One of these settlers was his Irish grandfather who took the steamboat upriver from Galena in 1857 and started his wholesale grocery business. "As Tarkington says," Fitzgerald observed, "American children belong to their mother's families," and Scott was thus Mollie McQuillan's son, even more so because his father had not achieved a successful career in business. Fitzgerald knew where he stood in St. Paul society, and since as a highly competitive youth he wanted nothing less than to reach the top, it troubled him.

As Mrs. C. O. (Xandra) Kalman—who with her husband remained the Fitzgeralds' lifelong friends—rightly asserts, Scott was certainly not "a little boy from the other side of the tracks." Edward Fitzgerald, wife Mollie, and Master Scott are all listed in the 1913 edition of the St. Paul Social Register. His father belonged to White Bear Yacht Club, and a few years later joined the new University Club in town. Nonetheless, young Fitzgerald understood that he did not rank with the elite. His parents were not included in either the 1909 or 1910 editions of the St. Paul Social Register (this may have been due to their recent return to the city from Buffalo). The family could not afford a second home at White Bear, so that Scott—and later, his sister Annabel—usually rode out on the trolley to visit friends at their summer houses. Money made in trade did not carry the same cachet as that accumulated through investment, though there was more than one kind of trade. A newspaper clipping in Fitzgerald's scrapbook refers to his grandfather as "a pioneer grocery dealer of St. Paul." In his own hand Fitzgerald added the word "wholesale."

The Fitzgeralds' position on the lower reaches of social prominence is neatly symbolized by their real estate habits. In a nostalgic passage in *The Great Gatsby*, Nick Carraway evokes his personal vision of St. Paul:

> That's my Middle West—not the wheat or the prairies or the lost Swede towns, but the thrilling returning trains of my youth, and the street lamps and sleigh bells in the frosty dark and the shadows of holly wreaths thrown by lighted windows on the snow. I am part of that, a little solemn with the feel of those long winters, a little complacent from growing up in the Carraway house in a city where dwellings are still called through decades by a family's name.

Scott Fitzgerald also rode the trains back at Christmastime for the parties and the sleighrides and the dances, but his St. Paul is nothing like Nick's. He did not feel complacent there. He lived in no one home, but rather a series of temporary domiciles. The city directories for 1909–19 list five different addresses for Edward Fitzgerald, broker, and the family is known to have occupied at least two other houses during this period. Brisk fall weather seemed to trigger their migration. In September 1909, the Fitzgeralds moved out of Grandmother McQuillan's apartment on Laurel into a duplex at 514 Holly Avenue. The following September, they packed up and moved across the street into a row house at 509 Holly. In September 1911, they rented a house at 499 Holly, their third home on the same street in three years, all within a block's compass.

In 1915 Scott's parents moved into a row house at 593 Summit Avenue and three years later into another one a few doors away at 599 Summit. (This, the house where Scott rewrote *This Side of Paradise*, has been officially designated as a National Historic Landmark.) But the Fitzgeralds established no permanent residence on Summit or anywhere else, no house that could be identified "through decades by a family's name."

Summit Avenue was once called (by an architectural historian) "the best-preserved American example of the Victorian monumental residential boulevard." Undoubtedly, it was and is St. Paul's "show street." On the eastern third of its course from the majestic Cathedral to the Mississippi River, Summit displayed the homes of its social and economic leaders, well set back from the street behind terraces of grass and canopies of fine old elms. Economic pressures have subsequently divided many of the old mansions into apartment warrens, and Dutch elm disease has stripped the street of its magnificent trees. But in Fitzgerald's youth, Summit reigned serenely. His family's residences on Holly and Laurel were respectable enough, but a house on Summit had special significance. Fitzgerald knew this, but he also knew that a rented row house hardly qualified as a family mansion. When he got word in September 1919 that Scribner's would publish his first novel, he wrote a letter headed

(599 Summit Ave.)
In a house below the average
Of a street above the average

The depth of Fitzgerald's antagonism toward his mother, and of the social insecurity she inspired in her ambitions for him, are suggested in a dream he set down on paper in the spring of 1931, shortly after returning to Switzerland from his father's funeral. He recorded the details for Margaret Egloff, at that time an intimate friend of his who was "working with the Jung group" in Zurich. Most of this dream, "a recent snooze by F. Scott Fitzgerald," follows:

I am in an upstairs appartment where I live with my mother, old, white haired, clumsy and in mourning, as she is today. On another floor are a group of handsome & rich, young men, whom I seem to have known slightly as a child and now want to know better, but they look at me suspiciously. I talk to one who is agreeable and not at all snobbish, but obviously he does not encourage my acquaintance—whether because he considers me poor, unimportant, ill bred, or of ill renown I don't know, or rather don't think about—only I scent the polite indifference and even understand it. During this time I discover that there is a dance downstairs to which I am not invited. I feel that if they knew better how important I was, I should be invited.

Mother and I have been quarreling—perhaps she had been trying to be my mother in the sentimental way (which in life made her hang in my room such texts as "The world will judge largely of Mother by you"), or perhaps I was merely taking out on her my ill-humour at being neglected by the people downstairs.

A parade begins outside in a great square not unlike the Place de la Concorde—columns of magnificently drilled troops in dress uniform move silently past in the blue twilight—men in dark blue, like British marines, but not exactly, then cadets like American cadets, then others, and, after an interval, Italian carbonierri with their big napoleonic hats. By this time it is quite dark, save for street illumination.

I go downstairs again, wander into the doorway of a sort of ballroom, see caterers at work and then am suddenly shamed by realizing this is the party to which I am not invited. Meeting one of the young men in the hall, I lose all poise and stammer something absurd. I leave the house, but as I leave Mother calls something to me in a too audible voice from an upper story. I don't know whether I am angry with her for clinging to me, or because I am ashamed of her for not being young and chic, or for disgracing my conventional sense by calling out, or because she might guess I'd been hurt and pity me, which would have been unendurable, or all those things. Anyway I call back at her some terse and furious reproach.

Nevertheless she follows me—I arrive a little after her at my Aunt Annabel's—(the real matriarch of my family, a dried up old maid, but with character and culture. She was rude and domineering to all the family but especially to my mother, but she had a secret love for all the men in the family—it was she who offered to pay my way if I'd go to Georgetown).

Mother and I were hungry. We wanted bacon and eggs, but mother was given only bacon and I was only given eggs. On being reminded that she'd only just had a collation a little before, my mother objected that the portion had been small, and was met with an austere, characteristic snub.

We returned home. On entering the house mother gave me a book, asking me pathetically (but remember her patheticness almost always repelled me) if it wasn't a particular book I'd loved and lost in my childhood. It was almost that book but not quite— after that she evidently gave up pleasing me for she passes, save for a last episode [in which she once more calls out to him and is answered angrily], out of the dream.

As Margaret Egloff observed, this "was a Big Dream." In it Fitzgerald reveals the humiliation his mother had caused him through such inappropriate actions as calling out to him too loudly, clinging too close, and demanding—but not getting—the best of service. He will not be placated, at least in the dream, by his mother's sentimental attempts to remind him of childhood joys. He tries to escape his bondage, to reject her as the aristocratic young men reject him. Yet no matter how nastily he speaks to her (another dream of Fitzgerald's concludes: "Blunder into Mother who nags me. My mean remarks."), she will not let him free. If Mollie Fitzgerald had been smart and well-bred and attractive, her son might have felt differently, for then, presumably, the young men would have welcomed him to their company and to the dance.

All of this connotes a strong sense of social inferiority. A continuing theme in Fitzgerald's life, Egloff commented, "was that the rich, powerful and the chic were the people to identify with, and become one with. The fact that he was not born into that society galled him, and he hated himself for his own and everyone else's snobbery. He hated his mother for her upward aspirations, and he despised his father for not setting his goal and his career in that direction. But with all his ambivalence his underlying value system was very similar to his mother's." The first word he uttered as a baby was "Up," which was where she wanted him to go. From her he inherited his compulsive drive for social success; from her he inherited "black Irish" roots that hardly facilitated such success. He had to make it on his own, through his own accomplishments. He had to prove himself over and over again, and there was always the danger that the right people—like the young men in the dream—would not take notice.

Lacking family background, he tried to achieve social acceptance through popularity, but his mother had ill equipped him for that route as well. She had given him "no habits of work," he lamented. And she had spoiled him so badly that with other boys he showed off and bragged and belittled and was desperately unpopular. Later in life Fitzgerald came to resent his mother's leniency, especially in contrast to his strict Aunt Annabel McQuillan, the "dried up old maid," who provided him with almost his "first taste of discipline." He felt fond of Aunt Annabel in a way he could not feel about the mother who let him have his way. "I didn't know till 15 that there was anyone in the world except me," he wrote his daughter.

That was an exaggeration, for in his ledger Fitzgerald recalled the boyhood traumas of repudiation by his peers. At seven, he "had a birthday party to which no one came." At nine, some boys at "a potato roast told him they didn't want him around." At ten, he was a "desperately unpopular camper." At St. Paul Academy he was known as the freshest boy in school. "If anybody can poison Scotty or stop his mouth in some way, the school at large and myself will be obliged," a letter in the school paper observed. It was the same story at Newman, the Catholic boarding school in Hackensack, New Jersey, where he finished his secondary education: "Bill Agar says I'm fresh." "Fight with Franciscus." "A new start. Poor marks and on bounds." "Growing unpopular." Almost everything in Fitzgerald's experience eventually found its way into his fiction, but it took 15 years to confront the painful recollection of his prep school unpopularity in "The Freshest Boy" (1928), the most moving of the Basil Duke Lee stories.

There was reason enough for Mollie Fitzgerald's spoiling her son and fussing over his health, as Scott well knew. "Three months before I was born," he wrote in "Author's House," "my mother lost her other two children. . . . I think I started then to be a writer." Perhaps so: certainly the death of his two older sisters affected the way he was brought up. In "A Baby's Biography," the scrapbook his mother kept, she refers only once to that tragedy. Baby Scott first crawled on May 30, 1897, she noted, and then went on, "Louise and Mary's little brother made his first attempt to walk and it seems as though they were nearer—" Three years later she gave birth to yet another girl who lived only an hour. Finally, Scott's sister

Annabel was born in July 1901, and survived. But her clever, handsome son was Mrs. Fitzgerald's favorite and her constant care. She kept his scrapbook until he was twenty-one, weighed 150 pounds, and stood five feet eight inches tall—or so she claimed in maternal exaggeration. Other accounts list Scott at five feet seven and rather less than 150 pounds.

2

Princeton '17

My father belonged all his life to Princeton.

—Scottie Fitzgerald Smith

No major American writer is so closely associated with his university as F. Scott Fitzgerald. Partly this is because Fitzgerald sticks in the public consciousness as a sort of perpetual undergraduate: charming, talented, and rather irresponsible. But the association is partly of Fitzgerald's making as well. Princeton bulks large in his first and immensely popular novel, *This Side of Paradise*, and serves as a setting for several stories. Like many another Old Grad, Fitzgerald became more devoted to his undergraduate college the older he grew. He also courted Princeton's approval, ardently and unsuccessfully.

He decided on Princeton, the nine-year-old Scott told his playmates in Buffalo, after attending a Princeton Glee Club concert in 1905. Or he made the choice, according to a note in his scrapbook, after watching Sam White race 95 yards with a blocked field goal to score the winning touchdown at the 1911 Princeton–Harvard game. Or he opted for Old Nassau, he told *Saturday Evening Post* readers, when he came across the Triangle Club score for "His Honor the Sultan" in the spring of 1913. Or, and this is most likely, there was no one determining occasion but instead an accumulating impression that Princeton would suit him better than either Yale or Harvard, the only alternatives he seems to have considered.

Of the two, Yale was the more formidable rival—too formidable,

18

for young Fitzgerald's taste. He conceived of Yale men as "brawny and brutal and powerful" (like Tom Buchanan in *The Great Gatsby*) and of Princeton men as "slender and keen and romantic" (like Allenby in *This Side of Paradise* and the Hobey Baker he was modeled on). In a letter Fitzgerald made pen-and-ink sketches of the typical graduate of Princeton (well turned out, Roman in profile), of Yale (an unshaven thug), and of Harvard (an aesthete in monocle and flowing tie). Yet "in preparatory school and up to the middle of sophomore year in college," Fitzgerald wrote in 1927, "it worried me that I wasn't going and hadn't gone to Yale." He regarded Yale as the breeding ground for success. But he wanted "something quieter, mellower and less exigent... a moment to breathe deep and ruminate" before plunging "into the clamorous struggle of American life."

So young Fitzgerald entered the college of his choice on his seventeenth birthday, determined to make his mark. He was too small for football, he soon found out, and turned instead to his literary talent as a path to success. By November of freshman year he was out for the *Tiger,* the campus humor magazine, and writing lyrics for the Triangle Club. Most of his freshman spring was devoted to composing book and lyrics for the 1914–15 Triangle show, "Fie! Fie! Fi-Fi!" The next year Edmund Wilson, Jr., '16, wrote the book for the Triangle's "Evil Eye," but come fall, Fitzgerald fashioned the lyrics for the show and took up his duties as Triangle secretary. A picture of him, dressed as a girl for the club's famous chorus line, ran in the *New York Times* and provoked a number of responses. One chap—"Ralph Hale, general delivery, Milford, Connecticut"—proposed a rendezvous. "Look him up and kindly poison him for me," Fitzgerald suggested to a girl friend.

In May of sophomore year, Fitzgerald was elected to the *Tiger,* a magazine he later characterized as not up to the standard of the (Harvard) *Lampoon,* (Yale) *Record,* and (Cornell) *Widow* "because most of the local wit was concentrated on producing the hullaballoo of the Triangle show." His most notable contribution to the *Tiger,* he reflected in 1935, was starting a series called "International Petting Cues," short takes acknowledging in print "that girls would be girls." When the *Tiger* was late to press, he and John Biggs, Jr., '18, sometimes slapped together an issue overnight.

In Fitzgerald's ledger for February 1916, the spring of his junior year, appears the notation, "Began Spires and Gargoyles, the beginning of mature writing." With his hopes for a leadership role at Princeton crumbling, he concentrated instead on writing serious fiction and poetry. This work appeared mostly in the pages of the *Nassau Literary Magazine*, the particular domain first of Wilson and then of John Peale Bishop, '17. Each of these men had read far more widely than Fitzgerald. Each became his lifelong friend.

In "The Spire and the Gargoyle"—the correct title of the story that eventually appeared in the February 1917 *Nassau Lit*—Fitzgerald attempted to come to grips with the academic troubles that prevented him from taking his place among the leaders of his class. The spire stood for aspiration and high hopes, dashed by the gargoyle, or instructor-preceptor. Matters came to a head in the fall of his junior year when he made up geometry with the aid of tutoring but failed makeup examinations in Latin and chemistry. In November he fell ill with malaria, dropped out of college, and did not return until the following fall. He watched from the audience when "The Evil Eye" played in St. Paul over the Christmas holidays. Early in January 1916, his friend Bishop, who had been on that trip, exhorted him: "For God's sake and your own get your conditions off and keep them off. I shall welcome you as next year's Managing Editor [of the *Nassau Lit*]. . . . You will also probably get a certain minor office in the P △ Club. Guess what? Oh, yes!"

Fitzgerald did nothing about making up his courses. On a February trip to Princeton he was formally set back into the class of 1918. During the spring he wrote a play for Triangle, but in May it was rejected, and though he once more wrote lyrics for the 1916–17 show and was again pictured as a "showgirl," Fitzgerald was no longer a strong candidate for Triangle president.

Considering his intelligence, Fitzgerald made a remarkably bad academic record. He did so poorly at Newman that he had to pass special entrance examinations before being admitted to Princeton. Once enrolled, he failed three subjects his first semester, took fifth groups (passing, but barely) in three others, and managed but one fourth group—a solid D. In the spring he earned his first 3, or C, and passed everything else except mathematics. For the year he finished in general group 5, on the brink of expulsion. As a consequence, he was declared ineligible to participate in extracurricular affairs in the fall of his sophomore year. Despite that warning, he finished in the fifth general group once again, failing three subjects and taking so many cuts that an extra course was added to his schedule as a penalty. Then came the disastrous fall of 1915, when the roof fell in despite his success at geometry:

> I'm off to the Math. School
> To pass it or bust,
> If Conics don't get me
> Then Politics must.

John Biggs, who roomed with Fitzgerald on his return in the fall of 1916, once commented that as long as Scott "could devote himself to the English courses, he, of course, did brilliantly." But even there his performance was far from brilliant. Fitzgerald never flunked an English course, but he never made a first group either. Here's the record by years. 1913–14: English 101, 4; English 102, 3. 1914–15: English 201, 3; English 202, 3. 1915–16: Dropped out. 1916–17, first term: English 301, 2; English 303, 3. During the fall 1916 semester, Fitzgerald also worked his way to a second group in Dean Christian Gauss's course in French literature, and seems to have earned an "A +" (if the transcript can be believed) in Philosophy 301. But he failed Chemistry 201 and History 301. Still, his lackluster performance in English courses—a third group average—may have bothered him more than actually failing subjects for which he had little affinity, like chemistry.

In his December 1927 sketch of Princeton for *College Humor* Fitzgerald praised the college administration, and then singled out for mention "a fine philosophy department, an excellent department of classics... and a surprisingly pallid English department, top-heavy, undistinguished and with an uncanny knack for making literature distasteful to young men." John Duncan Spaeth, who lectured on romantic poets and coached the crew, was an exception, but the interest Spaeth generated was "later killed in the preceptorial rooms where mildly poetic gentlemen resented any warmth of discussion and called the prominent men of the class by their first names." To Fitzgerald's way of thinking, his instructors were hopelessly behind the times. "No one of my English professors in college ever suggested to his class that books were being written in America." To a man they would have been startled to discover, in the Class of 1917 yearbook, that Fitzgerald intended to "pursue graduate work in English at Harvard."

He had learned more about poetry from John Bishop, he wrote his daughter in 1940, than from any of his professors. Some of them "really hated it [poetry] and didn't know what it was about." The lecturers were bad enough, according to the following bit of doggerel from *This Side of Paradise:*

> Good morning, Fool. . . .
>   Three times a week
> You hold us helpless while you speak
> Teasing our thirsty souls with the
> Sleek "yeas" of your philosophy. . . .
> Well, here we are, your hundred sheep
> Tune up, play on, pour forth . . . we sleep . . .

But the preceptors were worse, and particularly his preceptor for English 301, "The Renaissance," in the fall term of 1916–17. In the back of his copy of Sidney's *Defence of Poesie*, Fitzgerald lashed out with this judgment:

> Gee but this man Griffin is terrible. I sit here bored to death and hear him pick English poetry to pieces. Small man, small mind. Snotty, disagreeable. Damn him. "Neat" is his favorite word. Imagine Shakespeare being neat. Yesterday I counted and found that he used the expression "Isn't that so" fifty four times. Oh what a disagreeable silly ass he is. He's going to get married. God help his wife. Poor girl. She's in for a bad time. They say Griffin has made more men leave the English department than any other praeceptor in College The slovenly old fool! *I have the most terrible praeceptors.*

In a letter postmarked January 10, 1917, Fitzgerald again alluded to Griffin. "Just had a scrap with my English preceptor—he's a simple bone-head and I'm not learning a thing from him. I told him so!" Undoubtedly young Fitzgerald was here showing off for the benefit of the girl to whom he sent the letter. But his impatience with his preceptor may have been partly justified.

Nathaniel Edward Griffin (1873–1940) came to Princeton as one of 47 new men added to the faculty in 1905 when President Woodrow Wilson instituted the preceptorial system. According to Professor Louis A. Landa of the Princeton English department, Griffin's methods of instruction were somewhat eccentric. "In English 301 two weeks were allotted to the study of *Hamlet*. Griffin gave all of his time in the 'precept' to a line and a half describing the effect of the ghost on the watch: '. . . whilst they distill'd/ Almost to jelly with the act of fear. . . .' He spent the first meeting on 'distill'd' and the second on 'fear.'"

Griffin's technique sounds very much like "pick(ing) English poetry to pieces," yet it might be argued in his defense that Fitzgerald's own taste in poetry had hardly matured. He liked the romantic poets, especially Keats, he liked Shakespeare, and he liked Rupert Brooke. But he was totally unaware that Alfred Noyes—a member of the Princeton English department to whom he had been taking his own writing for criticism—was a poet at all. Furthermore, he produced a derogatory double limerick for the *Tiger* after hearing Robert Frost read his poems on campus:

> A rugged young rhymer named Frost
> Once tried to be strong at all cost
>   The mote in his eye
>   May be barley or rye
> But his right in that beauty is lost.

> Though the meek shall inherit the land,
> He prefers a tough bird in the hand,
>   He puts him in inns,
>   And feeds him on gins,
> And the high brows say, "Isn't he grand?"

"Aside from his literary talent," Glenway Wescott remarked, "I think Fitzgerald must have been the worst educated man in the world." Princeton was "probably as much to blame" for this state of affairs as Fitzgerald himself, critic Henry Dan Piper believes. In later years, however, Fitzgerald was quite forgiving toward the college. Only in letters to his daughter did he succumb to what *sounded* like bitterness: "It took them only four months [the fall of his junior year] to take it all away from me—stripped of every office and on probation—the phrase was 'ineligible for extra-curricular activities.'"

In fact, Fitzgerald exaggerated the maliciousness of the academic powers-that-be for daughter Scottie's benefit. If nothing else, his record at Princeton provided him with plenty of material for repeated lectures to Scottie. Even before she matriculated at Vassar, Fitzgerald was warning her by way of his own sorry example: "What an idiot I was to be disqualified for play by poor work while men of infinitely inferior capacity got high marks without any great effort." When Scottie went off probation in the spring of her freshman year, Fitzgerald once more resorted to argument by analogy: "*Don't* let it [the cloud] come down again! I was so happy when it lifted for me at Princeton and let me in for everything I'd wanted that I forgot. And the second time I never did manage to get out of a scholastic mess all the time I was in college. If you don't get *too* happy this spring, don't lose the ground you've gained—it's going to be all right." A year later, Scottie was busy writing book and lyrics for a Vassar musical modeled along Triangle club lines, and Fitzgerald could not resist the role of Jeremiah. "You are doing exactly what I did at Princeton. I wore myself out on a musical comedy...Result: I slipped way back in my work, got T.B., lost a year in college—and, irony of ironies, because of scholastic slip I wasn't allowed to take the presidency of Triangle."

Bad luck with preceptors aside, Fitzgerald was really blaming himself in these letters. As he wrote atop his ledger for 1915–16: "A year of terrible disappointments & the end of all college dreams. Everything bad in it was my own fault." When Scottie considered leaving Vassar at the beginning and during Christmas of her junior year, her father reacted with his warmest testimony to the value of his college education. "What on earth is the use of having gone to so much time and trouble about a thing and then giving it up two years short of fulfillment. It is the last two years in college that count." In his own case he had got nothing out of his first two years, while "in the last I got my passionate love for poetry and historical perspective and ideas in general (however superficially);

it carried me full swing into my career." Actually, Fitzgerald spent most of the 1915–16 year in St. Paul, but that hardly mattered, in retrospect. "The thing for which I am most grateful to my mother and father," he wrote Zelda two days before his death, "are my four years at Princeton, and I would be ashamed not to hand it on to another generation so there is no question of Scottie quitting. Do tell her this."

Meanwhile, he had been conducting his own "College of One" for Sheilah Graham. Her book on the subject makes it clear that Fitzgerald was largely self-educated, and that he "needed to play teacher as much as the pupil needed teaching." Fitzgerald, who had studied so little at college, had learned, somewhere along the line, to respect the process of learning. That may have been bequeathed to him by Princeton, but it was not the only item in the legacy.

Princeton was also responsible for sharpening that social sensitivity Fitzgerald had demonstrated as a boy. Several of his stories, the Basil stories particularly, document young Scott's awareness of his precarious status in the Midwestern pond of St. Paul. Back East, first at Newman and then at Princeton, he was thrown into much larger lakes, but learn to swim he did. Much of *This Side of Paradise* reads like a manual on how to succeed at Princeton, socially.

Education in the classroom takes on importance to Amory Blaine, the novel's protagonist, only as grades have a bearing on his social position. Fitzgerald's favorite scene in the book, according to *Esquire* editor Arnold Gingrich, occurs in the fall of Amory's junior year when he gets the results of a makeup examination. He knows that if he has failed the exam, he will be ineligible for the editorial board of the *Princetonian* and that his "stock will go down like an elevator at the club and on campus." The fateful envelope arrives and Amory stages a little drama for his friends. A blue slip, he tells them, will mean his name must be withdrawn from the *Princetonian* candidates; a pink one that he has passed and is eligible. He tears open the envelope; holds the slip to the light; then, after an extended pause, announces the results: "Blue as the sky, gentlemen." For Fitzgerald as for Amory, it was the devil-may-care gesture that counted. This makes highly suspect his protagonist's declaration, near the end of *This Side of Paradise*, that he "was probably one of the two dozen men in my class at college who got a decent education."

Though he knew that *This Side of Paradise* "rather damns Princeton," Fitzgerald was not prepared for the bitterness of the reaction against his novel. As he wrote years later, "Princeton turned on *This Side of Paradise*—not undergraduate Princeton but the black mass of faculty and alumni. There was a kind but reproachful letter from President Hibben, and a room full of classmates who suddenly turned on me with condemnation." Hibben objected to the impression the book gave "that our young men are merely living for four years in a country club and spending their lives wholly in a spirit of calculation and snobbery." Surely there was more to undergraduate life than mere social striving. As an admissions officer remarked long afterwards, "No one will ever know the damage Scott Fitzgerald did when he called this place a country club."

Fitzgerald's reply to President Hibben alternated wildly in tone. First the twenty-three-year-old groveled at the feet of the great man ("I...confess that the honor of a letter from you outweighed my real regret that the book gave you concern"). Then he attacked the lockstep curriculum, designed "for the average student," as responsible for his academic troubles. But he loved Princeton now and meant to capture its beauty in his book, Fitzgerald went on. If the picture was cynical, so was the author, having adopted from Theodore Dreiser and Joseph Conrad (writers *not* then taught in the Princeton English department, as unrespectably modern) the view "that life is too strong and remorseless for the sons of men."

Still, Fitzgerald admitted to President Hibben that he had "over-accentuate[d] the gayety and country club atmosphere....It is the Princeton of Saturday night in May. Too many intelligent classmates of mine have failed to agree with it for me to consider it really photographic any more, as of course I did when I wrote it." Which is to say, really, that most of his classmates—many of them products of Eastern prep schools far more prestigious than Newman—were less caught up in the struggle for social dominance than he was. As a reproduction of the Princeton inside Scott Fitzgerald's head, the photograph was accurate enough.

Fitzgerald's college career, like Amory Blaine's, reached its peak during the spring of his sophomore year. He was elected secretary of Triangle, made the *Tiger* board, and on the strength of those credentials was able to choose the eating club of his choice. These clubs marked the pinnacle of social success at Princeton, then and, to a lesser degree, now. Many sophomores spent months in nervous agitation before the annual spring bicker. But few underclassmen understood as thoroughly as Fitzgerald the character of the various clubs and their relative rank on campus.

In his essay on Princeton for *College Humor* (December 1927), he elaborated on the "big four"—Ivy, Cottage, Tiger Inn, Cap and Gown. Four years out of five, he wrote, Ivy was "the most coveted club in Princeton," but occasionally one of the other three mounted a challenge to its supremacy. Cottage was architecturally the most sumptuous, "with a large Southern following particularly in St. Louis and Baltimore." Unlike Ivy and Cottage, Tiger Inn cultivated "a bluff simplicity," placing its emphasis on athletics while maintaining "a sharp exclusiveness of its own." Cap and Gown had begun as an organization of "earnest and somewhat religious young men," but during the last decade "social and political successes have overshadowed its original purpose."

Clearly, Fitzgerald was an observant student of the club system. As he explained it, primer-fashion, to the readers of *College Humor*,

> There are no fraternities at Princeton; toward the end of each
> year the eighteen clubs take in an average of about twenty-five
> sophomores each, seventy-five per cent of the class. The re-
> maining twenty-five per cent continue to eat in the university
> dining halls and this situation has been the cause of revolutions,
> protests, petitions, and innumerable editorials. . . . But the clubs
> represent an alumni investment of two million dollars—the clubs
> remain.

In yet another part of the article, he discussed the social credentials of the college's undergraduates. "A large proportion of such gilded youth as will absorb an education drifts to Princeton. Goulds, Rockefellers, Harrimans, Morgans, Fricks, Firestones, Perkinses, Pynes, McCormicks, Wanamakers, Cudahys and duPonts light there

for a season. . . . The names of Pell, Biddle, Van Rensselaer, Stuy-
vesant, Schuyler and Cooke titillate second generation mammas
and papas with a social row to hoe in Philadelphia or New York."
The tone of such passages reflects that double vision so characteristic of Fitzgerald. On the one hand he stands back, the amused
observer commenting on the barely competent "gilded youth" who
like butterflies alight at Princeton "for a season." On the other
hand, the very recitation of prominent names suggests that like
the mammas in Philadelphia he was subject to titillation through
contact with the scions of famous families.

A similar doubleness pervaded his attitude toward the clubs
themselves. Though a snowstorm raged outside, it was a glorious
March day for Fitzgerald when he turned down bids from Cap and
Gown, Quadrangle, and Cannon in order to join Cottage with his
old friend from Newman, C. W. (Sap) Donahoe. The following
year, he made sure that the results of club elections were relayed
to him in his St. Paul exile. Arch-rival Ivy, he learned, had "signed
all they bid except Wilson," who happily went Cottage instead.
Yet by the spring of 1917 Fitzgerald was making sport of the whole
bicker procedure in a satirical piece for the *Tiger*. This approach
may have been encouraged by the anti-club movement of that year,
led by Henry Strater among others (in *This Side of Paradise*, Strater
appears as "Burne Holiday"). His own idealism "flickered out,"
Fitzgerald told President Hibben, with the failure of the anti-club
movement. But Fitzgerald never lost interest in his own club and
its fortunes. Recognizing the superficialities and cruelties of the
system, he nonetheless paid a full measure of loyalty to the University Cottage Club.

He maintained this loyalty through times when his relations with
Cottage were far from auspicious. In 1920, newly married and
newly famous as an author, Fitzgerald managed to get himself
suspended from the club. He and Zelda came down from New
York to chaperone houseparties the last weekend in April. As chaperones they were far from exemplary: "We were there three days,
Zelda and five men in Harvey Firestone's car, and not one of us
drew a sober breath." Zelda brought applejack to breakfast in order
to convert the eggs into *omelettes flambées*. She wore strong per-
fume. Scott introduced her as his mistress and was widely believed.

He got into brawls and acquired a very black eye. It was, he wrote a friend, "the damnedest party ever held in Princeton."

But he did not anticipate the humiliation that awaited him the following week, when he drove down with Stanley Dell, John Peale Bishop, and Edmund Wilson on May 1 for a banquet of former *Nassau Lit* editors. The men had costumed themselves for the occasion and when Fitzgerald presented himself at Cottage wearing a halo and wings and carrying a lyre, he was ejected from a rear window as a token of his suspension from the club. Drunk or sober, he was deeply hurt.

Fitzgerald next visited Cottage in an official capacity on January 19, 1928, when he returned as one of a series of distinguished alumni speakers. His fondness for Princeton had been stimulated the previous fall when he made several trips to the campus to watch football practice and do research for the *College Humor* piece. But the speech itself was a disaster, for Fitzgerald—overcome with nervousness—could only mumble a few sentences before admitting, "God, I'm a lousy speaker!" and sitting down. Once more he had disappointed others and embarrassed himself at his old club. "It was my first and last public appearance," he wrote Dean Gauss, who had been in the audience, "and the awful part of it was that I really did have something to say." Whether or not liquor affected his performance is in doubt, but after the debacle he did get properly drunk and insulted Edgar Palmer, '03, a Princeton trustee and the donor of Princeton's football stadium. He didn't like Palmer's looks, Fitzgerald told him; probably it was because Palmer had so much money.

Such behavior cost him considerable pain. Just how much can perhaps be suggested by Fitzgerald's account of a nightmare that plagued him in the spring of 1931. "Earlier in this night I'd woken in a dream where there was a Princeton banquet. They all yelled for me to come in, but I was very drunk, so didn't want to. To my intense embarrassment they turned a great spotlight on me which I tried to wobble out of."

Fitzgerald's attempts to sponsor candidates for Cottage were twice unsuccessful. On both occasions he wrote letters of support for potential club members. The first of these, dated February 12, 1929, is now on display in the club library. "I know this is a terribly busy time for you," Fitzgerald began, "but I want to give in the name of a sophomore and ask that he be called on or in some way looked over. His name is Whitney Darrow, Jr., his father is president of the University Press and very prominent in Princeton affairs, and the son was one of the first men on the Prince...." Fitzgerald had known the elder Darrow when he served as sales manager at Scribner's. The younger Darrow was to become one of the nation's best cartoonists. He did not join Cottage.

The second, more elaborate letter was on behalf of Andrew Turnbull, later Fitzgerald's biographer. It is reprinted below:

November
14
1939

Chairman of the Club Elections Committee
University Cottage Club
Princeton, New Jersey

Dear Sir:-

To many Cottage men of my generation it has been a source of regret that Baltimore (once almost as much a Cottage Town as St. Louis) now contributes so many of their boys to Ivy and Cap and Gown. This was frankly for several reasons—in the post war years a few prominent Baltimoreans, who were graduates of Princeton and of Cottage, succeeded in drinking themselves out of life and sight and Cottage was quite unjustly blamed for the business. The truth of the matter was that in those days the Baltimore boys were pretty sturdy drinkers before they headed northward. I'm told this has changed—but anyhow the origins of the charge are forgotten in Baltimore—but the prejudice remains.

Maryland will always be a great feeder for Princeton so I think such a prejudice is to be deplored. I lived in Maryland many years and made somewhat of a protegee of young Andrew Turnbull—used to take him and my daughter as moppets to the games from 1932 to 1935. I always took the children to the Cottage for lunch. Now, of course, if young Turnbull, a sophomore, is already tied up with some other group (I've never been really posted on the new system) then this letter is futile. But if he isn't, he might be an opening wedge to the Baltimore trade worthy of consideration. He was a brilliant kid and fearless, despite his small stature. He had strong convictions, not always popular ones, which kept him from being a leader at Gilman, but I believe he was very well liked at St. Andrews. He will make his mark somewhere, sometime, I believe, and carry on the tradition of a prominent Baltimore family. His father graduated from Johns Hopkins; his grandfather graduated from Princeton in the early seventies.

This kid should be a good organizer and a credit to any club. Will you kindly call on him? If he's sewed up for Cap, as might be the case, it's no use, because Pepper Constable was long his hero. Otherwise, I think it might turn out as valuable an interview for the club as for him.

Humbly—and with Softly-Falling Grey Hairs,

F. Scott Fitzgerald
1917

5521 Amestoy Avenue
Encino, California

Fitzgerald sent a copy of this letter to Andrew's mother, Mrs. Bayard (Margaret) Turnbull. (The Fitzgeralds had rented "La Paix," a house on the Turnbull family grounds outside Baltimore, during 1932 and 1933.) It would probably be "a little better for Andrew's future," he told Mrs. Turnbull, if Andrew joined "one of the so-called 'big clubs' at Princeton. . . . Only a few months ago Jimmy Stewart was telling me how it rankled throughout his whole Princeton career that he had joined Charter instead of Cottage, which had been his father's club." And he relied on daughter Scottie to let him know "the fate of Turnbull and other Baltimorians" the following spring. In the end, Andrew went Colonial. Colonial was a good enough club, Fitzgerald wrote Scottie, "older than Cap and Gown" in fact. Still, it might be best not to talk to Andrew about the subject at all.

Though Turnbull's candidacy stimulated his special interest,

Fitzgerald regularly kept himself informed about the admissions competition between the "big clubs." Among the many lists in his papers in the Firestone Library at Princeton are detailed comparisons of the leading clubs' results for 1937 and 1938, with the prep school background of each admitted member duly noted. The list for 1937 confines its attention to Ivy and Cottage; the one for 1938 includes Tiger Inn and Cap and Gown as well. "I see, by the way," he wrote Scottie on March 11, 1938, "that a boy named James W. Huntley has been admitted to the Cottage Club at Princeton. Did you know him in Baltimore?"

Later, when Scottie herself went down from Vassar to Princeton weekends, she could see a memento of her father's work on display. During 1933 and 1934, Fitzgerald was briefly caught up in the activities of the Memorial Committee of the University Cottage Club, whose prime mover was W. F. Clarkson, '17. Clarkson thought it would be a fine idea if the club's walls were decorated with reminders of the achievements of former members. At his request Fitzgerald sent a sample of his work—the "Good morning, Fool" poem, manuscript page 289 from *This Side of Paradise*. "A piece of writing done in the club, which has subsequently attained national attention, should be an interesting exhibit," he wrote Clarkson on September 19, 1933, but don't mount it, he added, before "at least a dozen photographs of the boys making touchdowns and other successes, which in the republic are considered really worthy of mention." In due time Fitzgerald's contribution (he'd supplied the frame himself) was hung in the club library. Today it is proudly pointed out by members conducting informal tours of the premises at 51 Prospect. Fitzgerald could hardly have anticipated his posthumous fame, but in his last years it gave him pleasure to know that his old club, where he had so often failed, had recognized his importance in this modest way. "It seems like the fulfillment of something," he wrote Scottie, "that you should go up to the library of Cottage and see that old poem hanging there."

Fitzgerald was proud of his club, yet he often deplored the system as cruel and arbitrary and unfair. His comments on the subject reveal a tension between emotional commitment and intellectual disapproval. "I'm just as glad Cottage lost out," he wrote his daughter about the March 1939 elections. "The only healthy thing about the God-awful system is that no one of the four is triumphant for long." In his November 13, 1939 letter to Mrs. Turnbull, he found yet another justification for the clubs. "Nothing would please me better than that the whole snobbish system be abolished. But it is thoroughly entrenched there, as Woodrow Wilson saw." And since it was so strongly entrenched, the only thing to do was to aim for one of the leading clubs. He himself might have felt "more comfortable in Quadrangle" with the literary crowd, but he "was never sorry" about choosing Cottage. As in the larger arena of life, one should try for the best: "College like the home should be an approximation of what we are likely to expect in the world."

In the last analysis, however, Fitzgerald was in favor of the de-emphasis of the club system that eventually came to pass. "I hope," he wrote Ralph Church on December 17, 1940, three days before his death, "that the pictures and membership lists [of the clubs] will be eliminated from *The Bric-a-Brac* proper." Alternatively, the yearbook might "print in addition pictures of all the clubs who eat at tables in Commons." Princeton was slipping behind Harvard and Yale in its attitude "toward this monkey business." What must the non-club men feel when they bring *The Bric-a-Brac* "home with all that emphasis on Prospect Avenue" (where the eating clubs are located)? The Fitzgerald who wrote this letter would have agreed with Edmund Wilson's observation, in 1944, that the Princeton of the teens "gave us too much respect for money and country house social prestige." He might even have seen the wisdom in Wilson's further remark that "Both Scott and John [Bishop] in their respective ways, fell victim to this."

As with many another alumnus, a combination of appeals lured Fitzgerald's thoughts back to his Alma Mater. The Tiger football team provided a symbolic way of identifying oneself with the university, and Fitzgerald was no casual fan. He often attended games, considered himself something of a football expert, and in fact was reading the Princeton alumni magazine and making notes on the following year's football prospects when he suffered his fatal heart attack on December 21, 1940. In addition to football, the music, the setting, and the traditions he associated with the university also aroused his nostalgia.

Andrew Turnbull recalled watching the tears well up in Fitzgerald's eyes as he waved his hat and sang "Old Nassau" one football Saturday in the early 1930s. He also sought to make his own contribution to the roster of college songs. Back in 1915 he had written the lyrics to "A Cheer for Princeton," the prize-winning entry in a contest for a new football song. That effort, with music by Paul B. Dickey, '17, never caught on, but Fitzgerald was still thinking along similar lines twenty years later. On January 16, 1935, he wrote a letter to Brooks Bowman, who had composed the most famous Triangle song of all, "East of the Sun," for *Stags at Bay*, the 1934–35 show. He complimented Bowman on the show, which he'd just seen, and then came to the point.

> My suggestion is this; that your song "East of the Sun" with a few changes could be made into a fine piece for senior singing. The general line would be:
>
> > "East of the sun, west of the moon
> > > *Lies Princeton,*
> > South of the south, north of the north
> > > *Lies Princeton,*
> > Here in my heart, etc. etc.
> > > *Lies Princeton."*
>
> The idea being, of course, that Princeton to Princeton men lies outside of time and space. It's an over-sentimental conception but perhaps might mean something to the older alumni. If practical, you might try it out with the Glee Club quarter.

Bowman may have realized that his melody was ill adapted to such purposes. In any case, there is no record of his response. Among the Fitzgerald papers in the Firestone Library, however, is the fragment of a lyric apparently intended as yet another Princeton song:

Keep the watch:

> When-the-tread-of the many feet is still
> Hold our place on the heights until
> We-come-back-many thousand strong
>
>> Keep the watch
>> —At Princeton

Fitzgerald saw not only *Stags at Bay,* but the next two Triangle shows as well when they played in Baltimore. He went to a Triangle dance in December 1927. He attended Princeton dinners in London and Hollywood. He arranged for Maxwell Perkins to send him a copy of Day Edgar's book of stories, *In Princeton Town* (Scribner's, 1929), which he rather liked. He read but was unimpressed by David Burnham's *This Is Our Exile* (Scribner's, 1931), another book with a Princeton background. He had Don Swann's Princeton etchings framed to decorate his daughter's room at Vassar in 1940.

The physical beauty of the place, evoked by Swann's etchings, helped to arouse the lyrical strain in Fitzgerald. Especially in spring: he wrote longingly of April "and the first real Princeton weather, the lazy green-and-gold afternoons and the bright thrilling nights." Might they take a flat together in New York, Bishop asked Fitzgerald in a letter written on Armistice Day? "Shall we go wandering down to Princeton on fragrant nights in May?" Bishop had gone off to the service in 1917 "fighting simply to keep the old way of things... fighting for Princeton, I suppose, for in spite of all its faults it somehow represents all that I want to hold on to." But he understood that the old order must inevitably give way to the new. The same understanding pervades Fitzgerald's valedictory "Princeton—The Last Day," a 1917 poem of such "depth and dignity" that it persuaded Edmund Wilson to think of him "by way of becoming a genuine poet":

> The last light wanes and drifts across the land,
> The long, low land, the sunny land of spires.
> The ghosts of evening tune again their lyres
> And wander singing, in a plaintive band
> Down the long corridor of trees. Pale fires

Echo the night from tower top to tower.
Oh sleep that dreams and dream that never tires,
Press from the petals of the lotus flower
Something of this to keep, the essence of an hour!

No more to wait the twilight of the moon
In this sequestered vale of star and spire;
For one, eternal morning of desire
Passes to time and earthy afternoon.
Here, Heracletus, did you build of fire
And changing stuffs your prophecy far hurled
Down the dead years; this midnight I aspire
To see, mirrored among the embers, curled
In flame, the splendor and the sadness of the world.

Heraclitus was right. All things expire, nothing endures; least of all the essence of youthful hours.

In one of those articles written almost entirely by his wife Zelda and signed by both Fitzgeralds, "'Show Mr. and Mrs. F. to Number____,'" she referred to a 1927 trip up to Princeton where there was a new inn, but otherwise the campus "offered the same worn grassy parade ground for the romantic spectres of Light-Horse Harry Lee and Benedict Arnold[!]" Scott judiciously lined out Arnold and replaced him with Aaron Burr. Then he altered the end of the paragraph as well. His wife had written of the old brick of Nassau Hall and the elm walks of the campus and the meadows and the college windows open to the spring "which has inspired so much poetry." Fitzgerald kept the descriptive material but omitted those six quoted words in favor of some real poetry of his own. Brick and elm, meadow and window lay "open to the spring— open, open to everything in life—for a minute." Many alumni have felt similar sentiments about the evanescence of college days. Few have communicated them with such eloquence.

Fitzgerald's mature attitude toward his university resembled that of an ardent suitor. As a young man he had failed at Princeton: failed to graduate, failed to make the presidency of Triangle, and above all failed to impress his fellows as a man of promise. Consider

the votes he received in the "class elections" column of the 1917
Nassau Herald.

Most Brilliant	2 votes
Handsomest	2 votes
Prettiest	5 votes
Wittiest	7 votes
Thinks he is (Wittiest)	15 votes
Thinks he is (Biggest Politician)	8 votes
Thinks he is (Best Dressed)	2 votes
Favorite Dramatist	6 votes
tied with George M. Cohan and 54 votes	
behind Shakespeare	

The image is that of a young man of some wit and attractiveness
who seems to think he is rather cleverer than is actually the case.
Still more revealing than the actual election results was the way
Fitzgerald recalled them. He had been voted first in "the most
perfect gentleman category," he later claimed. "I had gone out of
my way to be nice to so many people who had nothing and were
nobodies and then they rewarded me by this vote." He was ranked
second as "best politician," Fitzgerald further disremembered, and
(less inaccurately), first in "prettiest," which he regarded less as an
honor than a slap.

Even in a literary way, Fitzgerald at Princeton was regarded with
some amusement. Edmund Wilson recalled Scott's saying to him,
not long after they got out of college, "I want to be one of the
greatest writers who have ever lived, don't you?" Wilson had not
set his sights so high, for he "had been reading Plato and Dante.
Scott had been reading Booth Tarkington, Compton Mackenzie,
H. G. Wells and Swinburne."

A Princeton Book of Verse II, published in 1919, got his name
wrong, listing three contributions from "*T*. Scott Fitzgerald." Almost no one who knew him in those days thought he would become
a famous writer, much less a great one. As classmate Gregg Dougherty remarked, "We never thought he was a great literary figure
around here.... We just didn't have the sense to spot him."

Such lack of respect may have been tolerable to Fitzgerald at 20, but it would hardly do at 35, when he had come to regard himself—and wanted others to regard him—as a serious man and a writer of consequence. Yet during his lifetime, and for some years afterward, Princeton refused to accept Fitzgerald on these terms and remained stolidly indifferent to his advances.

In September 1934, for example, he proposed to Gauss that he deliver a series of lectures at Princeton "on the actual business of creating fiction." He sought to forestall possible objections by pledging "to do no drinking... save what might be served at your table." He also knew "there might be a barrier to crash in regard to the English Department" and asked Gauss to sound out the powers-that-be. He had a hunch, Fitzgerald added, that Gerould (Professor Gordon Gerould) rather liked him. The hunch was off target, for it was Gerould who used to argue that anyone whose English grades were as bad as Fitzgerald's couldn't possibly be the author of *The Great Gatsby*. Gauss tried to smooth things over. Why didn't Scott talk to The Club, a group of undergraduates who met at the Nass? But Fitzgerald already knew about The Club, and had turned down an invitation from them. He wanted to come back under the university's umbrella. It was not opened for him.

Another overture took the form of a suggested underground library system. Fitzgerald sent his subterranean library proposal to Asa Bushnell on April 27, 1936, in response to a *Princeton Alumni Weekly* request for ideas, and even included an illustrative diagram. But as with the lecture series and the songs and the football schemes he used to send coach Fritz Crisler, his architectural suggestion was not adopted.

Despite such setbacks, Fitzgerald continued to seek his university's recognition. At least he could be heard through the humble medium of class notes. Thus in 1938 he wrote to the class secretary commiserating about how hard it was to get into Princeton these days, even for the children of loyal alumni. "I understand," he remarked, "because my offspring couldn't get into Princeton either—so this fall she went to Vassar instead." Two years later, on November 28, 1940, he once more responded to the 1917 class secretary's appeal for news, beginning with an untruth about the status of *The Last Tycoon* and continuing with a celebration of

Scottie: "Just finished a novel. My daughter is a junior at Vassar and for two years has written the 'OMGIM' show there which is trying to be the equivalent of the 'Triangle' at Princeton."

The members of University Cottage Club were not, apparently, impressed. The Club's official letter of condolence—duly signed by the chairman, treasurer, and secretary and dated February 14, 1941—demonstrates the point:

> While an undergraduate, Scott was an outstanding member of the Cottage Club, being interested in every phase of the University's social life, and his eagerness to dissect it on every occasion made him a rare companion—interesting, amusing, provocative, sometimes annoying, but never dull.
>
> Perhaps unconsciously, he was laying the ground work for the very stories which afterwards brought him fame. In the years immediately following the World War, his brilliant novels and short stories made Scott one of America's best known writers.

Fitzgerald had been an "outstanding" member of Cottage, a "rare" companion, but rather too outstanding and too rare. In fact, his annoying habit of dissecting the university's social mores stamped him as an outsider, a parvenu. It was precisely this viewpoint— at once within and without the social world—that made Fitzgerald so valuable and perceptive a writer. But the Cottage letter, while conceding his brilliance, concentrates on his celebrity (he was, one suspects, entirely *too* visible for the club's taste). The unkindest touch of all comes in the last sentence quoted, with its talk of his work in the years immediately after the war. The assumption is that Fitzgerald had written nothing worth mentioning since the early 1920s. Probably the authors of the letter had read nothing of his since those days. Almost certainly they were thinking back to *This Side of Paradise*, with its emphasis on the social side of Princeton.

Besides, to some members of Cottage he would always be remembered as the drunken Fitzgerald of the immediate postwar years. Even during the early to middle 1930s, Princeton sometimes served him as a place to get drunk on holiday from his troubles in Baltimore. His notebooks record the result of a 1933 sojourn: "Finally trip to Princeton in February, unfortunate because I ran into old friends & feeling like a celebration I celebrated for the first time over a year." On yet another occasion, a taxicab driver rang the bell of chemistry professor Gregg Dougherty's home in the wee hours of the morning. "I got something for you," the cabbie announced. It was Fitzgerald, who had taxied out from New York inebriated. He was crying, distressed about Zelda's condition, and in bad shape generally. But he wouldn't let his old classmate put him to bed, so Dougherty took him down to the Princeton Inn and went off to his classes and labs. When he returned at mid-afternoon, Fitzgerald had gotten up and left. Dougherty never saw him again.

Like an over-eager swain, Fitzgerald repeatedly made a hash of his courtship of his Alma Mater. Had she succumbed to his blandishments, he might have modified the idealized picture of Princeton that he carried in his heart. But the university kept its distance and so remained a hallowed place for him. "I hope," his daughter Scottie wrote in 1942, "that Princeton is as proud of [my father] as he was of Princeton." Only recently has that hope begun to be realized.

When, shortly after his death, Zelda Fitzgerald attempted to sell her husband's papers to Princeton for $3,750, the librarian declined the offer. The university had no obligation, he commented, to support the widow of a second-rate Midwestern hack who'd been lucky enough to attend Princeton. Similarly, Edmund Wilson's 1941 efforts to persuade the university to bring out a book honoring Fitzgerald were unsuccessful. Fifteen years later, when the Princeton University Library did publish *Afternoon of an Author,* a collection of Fitzgerald pieces, some sons of Princeton were less than pleased. The March 9, 1956 *Princeton Alumni Weekly* ran several articles about Fitzgerald in connection with the book's publication. By way of introduction, the editor called Fitzgerald "the greatest of Princeton authors, not only because of the distinction of his work but because he was the most Princetonian." That last observation provoked a few indignant responses. "Come, come," one alumnus wrote in protest, "how do you get that way in stating that he was 'A Princeton type'?" To characterize Fitzgerald as "most Princetonian" was ridiculous, another objected. "Let us not contribute unnecessarily to the charicature [sic] of ourselves."

Fitzgerald himself was tastelessly caricatured in the fall of 1959, when the Princeton band—in the midst of a halftime show at the Yale–Princeton game—played "Roll Out the Barrel" and reeled about in mock tribute to "Princeton's gift to literature, F. Scott Fitzgerald." The incident was especially ill-timed, since Sheilah Graham, who that morning had presented to university president Robert Goheen a sheaf of Fitzgerald manuscripts, happened to be in the stands. The editor of the alumni weekly rose to Fitzgerald's defense: "The mind boggles at the inane spectacle of publicly vilifying the memory of a Princeton alumnus—almost literally dancing on his grave—and especially of one so pathetically devoted to Princeton." In the early 1960s, John Kuehl, then a member of the English department, asked President Goheen to investigate awarding a posthumous degree to Fitzgerald. The suggestion, Goheen reported, met with opposition.

Only belatedly has the college he loved and assiduously courted come to recognize the accomplishment of F. Scott Fitzgerald, class of 1917. During its fiftieth reunion his class sponsored a faculty-alumni forum on "F. Scott Fitzgerald '17—The Man, the Myth, the Artist." Articles about him have appeared on several occasions both in the *Princeton University Library Chronicle* and in the *Princeton Alumni Weekly*. An award has been established in his name to recognize "student creative writing achievement." But Fitzgerald's ghost might best be pleased to know that his once-spurned papers, originally donated to the university in 1950 and supplemented by additions over the years, are examined more frequently than those of any other author in Princeton's vast manuscript collection. He built his own monument with words.

3

"I Love You, Miss X"

A MAN who feared, expected, and even dreamed of rejection, Scott Fitzgerald encountered it disconcertingly often. From the Princeton plutocrats who detected the intruder in their midst to Judge Anthony Dickinson Sayre who at death's door declined to tell his son-in-law that he believed in him, Fitzgerald suffered a series of repudiations from men. For consolation, for validation of his very worth as a person, he turned to women.

Perhaps because his own mother's approval was so easily won as to mean nothing, the young Fitzgerald coveted the approbation of his friends' mothers. He paid them the kind of attention they rarely encountered from adolescent boys. The mother of Norris Jackson, who went to Princeton with Scott, thought his manners were excellent, since he actually seemed to care what she had to say. Other St. Paul mothers, perhaps sensing a trace of calculation, were not so sure about Fitzgerald. Marie Hersey's mother had her doubts. So did Bob Dunn's. "If your mother lives," Fitzgerald wrote Dunn in the mid-1930s, "give her my eternal homage, unqualified by the fact that she was always skeptical of me." While on holiday from Princeton he talked by the hour with Ruth Sturtevant's mother. Mrs. Sturtevant thought him "a lonely boy, with strange ideas," and did not entirely approve of the pale young man with the brilliant eyes and the half grin who was to remind an acquaintance, years later, "of a little boy who wanted to play but wasn't quite sure of his welcome."

Fitzgerald had better luck with daughters than with mothers, and pursued them assiduously throughout his life. The quest was inextricably tied up with success. If he could win the heart of the girl—especially the golden girl over whom hung an aura of money, beauty, and social position—surely that meant that he had arrived, that he belonged.

In November 1905, Fitzgerald's ledger notes, he "went to dancing school and fell in love with Nancy Gardner." He was nine, and had already embarked on the ritual of courtship that was to become an obsession. At eleven the girl was Kiddy Williams in Buffalo. Scared silly, Scott gave her a box of candy for Christmas. Two months later he had his reward at a party where he kissed her "a great deal." Fitzgerald recorded such conquests laconically in his ledger, and at greater length in two extraordinary pre-puberty documents, "Girls I Have Known" written at twelve and his "Thoughtbook" written when thirteen and fourteen years old. Clearly, he saw the relations between the sexes in a competitive light. What counted were rankings. He felt a glow of triumph when he moved from third to first in the affections of the bewitching Violet Stockton, a Southern girl visiting St. Paul. He suffered the pangs of defeat when a rival supplanted him at the head of the list. Yet he understood that his real antagonists were not other boys but the girls themselves. One anecdote in "Girls I Have Known" ends as follows:

> I smiled, and she said admiringly, "What I wouldn't give to have your lovely teeth." But she didn't get them.

Fitzgerald's "Thoughtbook," a twenty-six page diary he kept between August 1910 and February 1911, noted his rise and fall in the teen-age sexual hierarchy of St. Paul. The entry for November 10 reads: "One day Marie Hersey wrote me a note which began either 'Dear Scott I love you very much/ or I like you very much' and ever since then she has been rather shy when she meets me." Marie Hersey was Scott Fitzgerald's first girl. Not the first he noticed, or the first he kissed, but his first "fixation," as he put it, certainly his "first love." In dancing school, that winter of 1911, Fitzgerald developed "two new Crushes. To wit—Margaret Armstrong and Marie Hersey." Margaret was the best talker, but Marie the prettiest and the most popular with other boys. "I am crazy about her," he wrote. "I think it is charming to hear her say, 'Give it to me as a comp-pliment' when I tell her I have a trade last for her."

Marie's popularity caused Fitzgerald a measure of concern. His ledger for March 1911 reads: "Dancing school. Marie. Love. The triangle." The next month he recorded a "Faint sex attraction" in connection with bicycling around the Ames's back yard on St. Paul's Grand Avenue. These two notes coalesced in "The Scandal Detectives," one of the Basil Duke Lee stories fashioned after Fitzgerald's own adolescence.

> Basil [Scott] rode over to Imogene Bissel [Marie] and balanced idly on his wheel before her. Something in his face then must have attracted her, for she looked up at him, looked at him really, and slowly smiled. She was to be a beauty and belle of many proms in a few years. Now her large brown eyes and large beautifully shaped mouth and the high flush over her thin cheekbones... offended those who wanted a child to look like a child. ... For the first time in his life he realized a girl as something opposite and complementary to him, and he was subject to a warm chill of mingled pleasure and pain.

In the story Hubert Blair (Reuben Warner) takes Imogene-Marie away from Basil-Scott, largely because of his natural grace of movement. Scott could not compete with Warner's physical gifts, but he was well-endowed for the competition in other ways.

According to a self-assessment at about this time, Fitzgerald considered himself physically handsome, mentally ingenious, and socially personable. He also believed that he "exercised a subtle fascination over women." Much later he summarized the situation in his notebooks: "I didn't have the two top things: great animal magnetism or money. I had the two second things, though: good looks and intelligence. So I always got the top girl." Or *almost* always.

Above all, Fitzgerald understood how to woo with words. At

dances he would cut in on a girl and tell her immediately, "God, you're adorable, you're so beautiful." He'd pique her curiosity by announcing, "I have an adjective for you." He'd hint darkly that he was a reprobate who could only be saved by the love of a good woman. Not many held out against such blandishments.

Then there was the written word, and Fitzgerald carried on a wide correspondence with a number of socially prominent sub-debutantes. The Fitzgerald–Marie Hersey letters were particularly lively, since she shared with him a fondness and talent for doggerel.

> My Very Very Dear Marie:
> I got your little note
> For reasons very queer Marie
> You're mad at me I fear Marie
> You made it very clear Marie
>   You cared not what you wrote

Fitzgerald sent this letter late in January 1915, and Marie's apparent annoyance with him may have traced to the previous Christmas vacation. Marie had asked her Westover schoolmate, Ginevra King, to visit St. Paul, and Fitzgerald had met her and fallen hard. Possibly in retaliation, Marie penned a satiric "Ode to Himself" in which Fitzgerald supposedly remarks,

> I am the *Great Heart Breaker*
> And I am the *Dreamer of Dreams*
> I am the *Great Love-Maker*
> 'Neath the moon's palest gleams
> Girl-fusser and girl-forsaker
> They come at my beck and call
> And I am the *Mover and Shaker*
> Of the whole world—after all!

Whatever its source, Marie's annoyance did not last long. She and Scott had too much in common. Both were enamored of the game of love, and both played it well. "Dear Playmate," she used to address him. At Westover, as she lamented in a mock-heroic ballad, her romantic inclinations were frustrated:

> The crucial moment is at hand
> Where is a hero to console?
> The knock-kneed furnace man is near
> I guess he'll have to play the role!

On the bright side, her father had promised her a new car, and she'd begun to plan a hundred schemes: "(1) To run over every good looking boy I see, bring him home to recuperate then—(2) To have punctures whenever adventure seems available."

They joked together about themselves and each other, yet remained the closest of friends. IF YOU ARE NOT MARRIED, she wired him in November 1919, WILL YOU GO TO THE ASSEMBLY WITH ME ON DECEMBER 12TH. The following spring, when Scott and Zelda *were* to be married, he sent his bride-to-be shopping with Marie for something more suitable to New York than her Southern frills and furbelows. And fifteen years later, when Fitzgerald published his "Crack-Up" essays in *Esquire*, Marie tried to rally his spirits with a cheering letter.

In the spring of 1915, however, Scott Fitzgerald was riding high. The academic axe had not yet fallen at Princeton, where he promised to become one of the leaders of his class. He also ranked first in the affections of Ginevra King, to whom he posted long, frequent, and intense letters. That did not prevent him—any more than it prevented her—from indulging in other flirtations. At Easter he met Ruth Sturtevant and Helen Walcott in Washington, and thereafter launched correspondence with both of them. Of the two, Scott was probably more interested in Ruth, a "tres bonne tonne" blonde who was attending Miss Porter's school. He was writing her, Scott once insisted, while Ginevra's letter lay unanswered on his desk. She was the only girl, he told her, who'd kept her color until the dance ended at 3 A.M. "If we both lived in St. Paul," he assured her, "we would have a desperate affair." Meanwhile, he was hoarding her special adjective. Ruth replied with some coolness. They hardly knew each other, she pointed out. Like her mother she thought Scott somewhat unsuitable. For one thing, he made it sound as if she were "the only *nice* girl" he'd run around with. Besides, he only stood to her shoulders and did not strike her as entirely masculine.

Helen Walcott, like Marie Hersey, understood how to play the game. When she'd visited Princeton in May 1915, Fitzgerald managed to monopolize her attention during a tea dance at Cottage. Apparently he was inveigled into revealing her special adjective (a word that invariably lost its magic upon revelation) and in atonement sent her one of the imitation Gilbert-and-Sullivan lyrics he'd twice turned out for Triangle shows:

> I called you "Miss" Helen, addressed you as "Hey"
> I hemmed and hawed and my accents I slurred
> Till you kidded me, winked at me, almost said "Say!"
> (But all in a highbrowish-Washington way)
> And then, tho' I'd known you only a day,
> I uttered the terrible, horrible word.

Once again, as with Ruth Sturtevant, Fitzgerald made a point of mentioning Ginevra in this letter. Perhaps he did so to seem more attractive in Helen's eyes; perhaps he simply wanted everyone to know. In any case, she responded with a highly flattering letter proclaiming Scott "a marvel" and reminding him of his promise to "look us up, next time you come thru Wash." Helen knew how to handle young men. If she could get a man talking about himself, she told Scott, she had him "cinched and harnessed." It was one of the lessons the nineteen-year-old Fitzgerald stressed when he instructed his younger sister Annabel in the art of attracting the opposite sex.

This remarkable ten-page document covered in detail such matters as conversation, posture, dress, personality, dancing, facial expression, smile, hair, and so on. Few young men could have written this set of instructions, which Fitzgerald later turned to fictional account in "Bernice Bobs Her Hair." Few men of any age could have imagined themselves so effectively in the position of the young woman. "Boys like to talk about themselves—much more than girls," he advised Annabel. "Here are some leading questions for a girl to use... (a) You dance so much better than you did last year. (b) How about giving me that sporty necktie when you're thru with it? (c) You've got the longest eyelashes! (This will embarrass him, but he likes it.) (d) I hear you've got a 'line'!

(e) Well who's your latest crush? Avoid (a) When do you go back to school? (b) How long have you been home? (c) It's warm or the orchestra's good or the floor's good...." Annabel had splendid eyebrows, her brother told her, but she ought to "brush them or wet them and train them every morning and night" as he'd advised her "long ago." Most men noticed such things subconsciously, he said. Fitzgerald noticed them, period.

Despite his expertise, Scott Fitzgerald could not compete with Ginevra King, for he was matched against a legend. It may seem foolish to use such terminology to describe a teen-aged girl, but there can be no doubt that the wide-eyed dark-haired beauty from Chicago appeared to Fitzgerald's eyes as more than simply mortal. Her very name, with the aristocratic and lovely Gi-nev-ra preceding the royal surname, partook of the legendary, and it was *the name* that Fitzgerald heard—doubtless from Marie Hersey—a full two years before he met the girl herself. By then the name had become associated with a reputation for what passed, in those days, as sexual daring. It was rumored that Ginevra had kissed dozens of boys, and that almost all of them had fallen desperately in love with her. Her beauty and wealth were not in doubt. Fitzgerald stayed in St. Paul an extra day during the Christmas vacation of 1914–15 expressly to meet the girl who embodied the name and the reputation. He hoped to win her favor and was fully prepared to be smitten. He did and he was.

The meeting took place January 4, 1915, during a dinner dance at the Town and Country Club near the Mississippi River in St. Paul. The next day Scott went back to college, and there commenced a flurry of twenty-page letters from Princeton to Westover, accompanied by pangs of jealousy. After Scott left St. Paul, Ginevra had struck up a flirtation with his old rival Reuben Warner. In a chillingly light-hearted letter, Reuben regaled Fitzgerald with his account of one afternoon when he and Ginevra had outwitted Mrs. Hersey and another chaperone. "Well when I saw those two I said, 'Reuben no fun for you this after-noon.'" But Ginevra put her muff in her lap, her hands inside, nudged Reuben with "her sweet elbow and...looked down at her muff—Well! I just slid my massive paw in there and enjoyed the rest of the show. When I would squeeze, she'd squeeze back—hmm!—Swell!" He and Ginevra had taken several rides together and every time, Reuben reported, he'd "loved hell out of her, but no kissing." Ginevra had even told Reuben she liked him best, but he was sure that she really preferred Scott. He wished he had the "drag" with Ginevra that Scott had, Warner wrote, and signed himself "Your downcast *contender in love*." But he sounded anything but downcast. It would be better not to say anything to Ginevra about his letter, he pointed out, for if she came to St. Paul next summer "you and I want to have a hell of a time."

It seems unlikely that Scott could have maintained silence about Reuben's letter. But whether he chastised Ginevra through the mails cannot be known for certain, since she did not preserve his letters (he kept hers, and had them typed into a 227-page portfolio). Of necessity their contacts in 1915 and 1916 came largely through correspondence, since Westover girls were rarely allowed off premises and Fitzgerald had no automobile. They made the most of their few opportunities—a night at the theatre in New York, a dinner in Waterbury, two football games, a brief encounter in Chicago, a longer one in Lake Forest—but for every hour together they spent months apart. During much of this time Fitzgerald imagined "his girl" in the company of "some 'unknown Chicagoan' with crisp dark hair and glittering smile" and conjured up visions of her riding regally in one young man's electric or another's Stutz Bearcat. The visions were accurate enough. At the time, as she later recalled, Ginevra "was definitely out for quantity not quality in beaux, and, although Scott was top man, I still wasn't serious enough not to want plenty of other attention!" Nor would she be reproached. It was not her fault, she pointed out, that Scott had idealized her.

In the spring of 1916, Ginevra was expelled from Westover for talking to boys at night from her bedroom window. According to Marie Hersey, Ginevra was no more to blame than twenty other girls who had done the same thing, but the headmistress "picked on G. K." and so her father came up to Connecticut and took her home. It wasn't the same as getting fired at all, Marie wrote Fitzgerald. In his ledger, however, he simply noted, "Ginevra fired from school." The incident did not diminish his ardor. That summer he visited her in Lake Forest, the summer home of Chicago's very rich and the playground, those years, of the debutantes who were known on Ivy League campuses as the "Big Four": Courtney Letts, Edith Cummings, Margaret Cary, and Ginevra. The visit was not entirely successful, Fitzgerald's ledger indicated:

> Lake Forest. Peg Carry. Petting Party. Ginevra Party.
> The bad day at the McCormicks. The dinner at Pegs.
> "Poor boys shouldn't think of marrying rich girls."

It is not clear who made the remark about poor boys and rich girls, but perhaps, as critic Richard Lehan has suggested, the speaker was stockbroker and horseman Charles King, Ginevra's imposing father and the likely model for Tom Buchanan in *The Great Gatsby*. By the standards of Mr. King and his neighbors in Lake Forest, Fitzgerald was a poor boy indeed. Certainly he felt that way himself. "Once I thought that Lake Forest was the most glamorous place in the world," he wrote his daughter Scottie in July 1940. "Maybe it was."

By the time Ginevra came down to Princeton for the Yale game in the fall, the rift between them was widening. "After the game," she recalled in 1974, "we all rode the train back to New York. My girlfriend and I had made plans to meet some other, uh, friends. So we said good-bye, we were going back to school, thanks so much.

"Behind the huge pillars in the station there were two guys waiting for us—Yale boys. We couldn't just walk out and leave them standing behind the pillars. Then we were scared to death we'd run into Scott and his friend. But we didn't. I think they'd just headed for the bar."

In January 1917, they met again but she was no longer interested. That summer, when Scott asked for his letters back, she told him she had destroyed them, adding that she "never did think they meant anything." And she wrote him again the following summer, when she was about to be married. "I'm surprised I remembered to write him," Ginevra recalled. "I had quite a few other letters to write, because I was engaged to two other people then. That was very easy during the war because you'd never get caught. It was just covering yourself in case of a loss."

Ginevra took no risks with Scott Fitzgerald. He was one of the many beaux of her youth, and when it came time she dropped him. In response to inquiries from biographers and others, Ginevra consistently referred to their romance in an offhand manner. She must have kissed Scott, but "it wasn't exactly a big thing" in her life. She was sorry she hadn't kept any letters, but she did "have his Triangle pin if that is any use to anyone." In 1947 she sent the pin, along with two undergraduate pictures of Fitzgerald, to biographer Arthur Mizener, and wiped the slate clean.

For Fitzgerald it was a very different story. Ginevra King was the love of his young life. The hurt of losing her never left him, and thinking about it invariably brought tears to his eyes. Furthermore, his rejection by Ginevra motivated much of his fiction. Time after time he attempted to exorcise—and, paradoxically, to keep alive—that pain in story and novel. In *This Side of Paradise,* she became Rosalind Connage (and, earlier, Isabelle Borgé). As he observed in 1938, in that novel he was writing "about a love affair that was still bleeding as fresh as the skin wound on a haemophile." He cast Ginevra as Judy Jones in "Winter Dreams" (inspired, so he observed, by the "fascination of a visit to... Lake Forest. Also my first girl 18–20 whom I've used over and over and never forgotten"). Ginevra sat for most of Daisy Buchanan in *The Great Gatsby* and for much of Nicole Diver in *Tender Is the Night*. She modeled for Josephine Perry in his Josephine stories. But the wound would not heal, no matter how often he cauterized it.

Ginevra King, in short, was the golden girl that Fitzgerald, like his male protagonists, could not have. When she wired him from Santa Barbara in 1937 to arrange a meeting, he fell half in love with her over lunch and off the wagon immediately afterwards. It was too bad, she thought. She'd found him amusing until he began to drink. He found her "still a charming woman," and still unavailable.

In pursuing Ginevra he had reached beyond his grasp, for she came from a different social world. A newspaper article Fitzgerald pasted in his scrapbooks suggests just how different. Headed "These Charming People" and datelined Chicago, the society page piece takes as its peg the portrait of Ginevra (then Mrs. William H. Mitchell, III) "by the great painter Sorine." The article goes on to describe Ginevra's "truly natural beauty. No tinting of eyelids, darkening of eyelashes, or rouging of cheeks in her line. Here is a fresh, radiant quality that does your heart good to see." Her eyes "are enormous, deep brown sparkling lights. Her lashes sweep downward and then abruptly up, giving her eyes a sparkling look which almost shocks you when she looks at you suddenly. She laughs a lot and her teeth are very white. . . . She is vibrant. She is energetic." What's more, Mrs. Mitchell was to be admired for managing "to run her life in a way which combine[d] a tremendously gay amusing time with a thoughtful organized existence." Ginevra drifted around the country on her way to Aiken or Palm Beach or Santa Barbara, but she was also "one of the props and stays" of St. Luke's Hospital in Chicago and a supporter of every worthy charity. In addition, she was "a grand and courageous horsewoman" and ran her house "to the queen's taste." How could a middle-class boy like Fitzgerald fit into that world?

In the summer of 1917, Fitzgerald visited his Princeton friend John Peale Bishop in Charles Town, West Virginia, and attempted to bolster his wounded ego by courting Fluff Beckwith. They swam in the Shenandoah, she saw him thrown by a livery-stable horse, and they danced the evenings away in her big ivy-walled house. Fluff did not especially like Fitzgerald's technique. "He was always trying to see how far he could go in arousing your feelings," but only with words, she observed in her memoir. Unlike the Southern boys she'd known, who were "more aggressive and physically satisfying," Fitzgerald just "wasn't a very lively male animal." Instead, he gave her a copy of a poem, "When Vanity Kissed Vanity," and declared he had written it for her. In 1945, she discovered the poem in *The Crack-Up*, dedicated, in print, to Fitzgerald's much-admired cousin Cecilia.

When Fitzgerald and Fluff (then Mrs. Paul MacKie) renewed their acquaintance in Baltimore during the early 1930s, he resumed the courtship. His talk had coarsened somewhat. "Are your breasts standing up like that for me?" he asked her. But still it was all words and no action. With the screendoor closed between them, he told her, "I have never had you, but I believe we get the things we most want." It was, she concluded, typical of his approach. Fluff particularly remembered a dinner party in the spring of 1932 at

Brian and Ida Lee Dancy's, for it seemed as if two Scott Fitzgeralds had come: the charming young man she'd known in Charles Town and the foul-mouthed drunk of the present. Fitzgerald brought along the actress Osa Munson, who was visiting him. As soon as dinner ended, he got up, announced he was going home to hug his pillow very tight, and departed with Miss Munson.

Through the years there was almost always someone besides Zelda. Jean Bankhead in Westport, Helen Buck in Great Neck, Olive Burgess in Paris, Sara Murphy and Marice Hamilton on the Riviera, Dorothy Parker there and in New York—these names like many others found their way into Fitzgerald's ledger of significant encounters during the 1920s. Just how significant these encounters were is difficult to determine, though Dorothy Parker in Denver once telegraphed Fitzgerald in New York: "DEAR SCOTT THEY JUST FORWARDED YOUR WIRE BUT LOOK WHERE I AM AND ALL MARRIED TO ALAN CAMPBELL AND EVERYTHING.... DEEPEST LOVE AND ALL THOUGHTS ALWAYS FROM BOTH OF US." If no fires were set, Fitzgerald certainly provided his share of smoke. During an evening in Paris with the James Joyces, he first humbled himself before the author of *Ulysses*, and then began expounding on the beauty of Nora Joyce. Finally Fitzgerald "darted through an open window to the stone balcony outside, jumped up on the eighteen-inch-wide parapet and threatened to fling himself to the cobbled thoroughfare below unless Nora declared that she loved him, too." She hurriedly complied, and later remarked—to produce a smile from her husband—"Ah, he's a good lad. I think I'll do a bunk with him some day." At a party in Hollywood, his approach was still more direct. "Miss X, meet Mr. Fitzgerald," Carmel Myers remembers introducing him. "I love you, I love you, I love you," Fitzgerald told Miss X.

Miss X could have been anyone, but Fitzgerald actually did fall in love with an actress during a Hollywood sojourn in the winter of 1927. He was thirty and the blonde Lois Moran only seventeen when they met. Despite her youth, Lois circulated in a crowd that included Carl Van Vechten, John Barrymore, and Richard Barthelmess, in addition to Carmel Myers. Still she was young enough to be amused by the outrageous behavior of both Scott and Zelda, who attended a "come as you are" party in their nightclothes and at another party collected everyone's jewelry and boiled it in tomato soup. HOLLYWOOD COMPLETELY DISRUPTED SINCE YOU LEFT, she wired the Fitzgeralds on their departure. BOOTLEGGERS GONE OUT OF BUSINESS COTTON CLUB CLOSED ALL FLAGS AT HALF MAST EVEN JOHN BARRYMORE HAS GONE OUT OF TOWN BOTTLES OF LOVE TO YOU BOTH.

Zelda knew who the bottles were meant for. Lois and her husband were obviously fascinated with each other. Lois had even arranged for Scott to take a screen test in hopes that they might make a film together. As Zelda wrote Scottie, putting the best possible construction on the situation, "Daddy was offered a job to be leading man in a picture with Lois Moran!! But he wouldn't do it. I wanted him to, because he would have made so much money and we could all have spent it, but he said I was silly." In fact, the relationship rapidly progressed beyond the stage of casual infatuation. One morning during the Hollywood visit Fitzgerald burst into Arthur W. Brown's room at the Ambassador, awakened him, and said, "Say hello to Zelda." But it was Lois Moran, and not Zelda, on his arm. Scott asked Brown to cover for him. If any questions were asked, Brown was to say that they'd spent the day together at First National Studios.

Fitzgerald also invited Lois to a weekend house party at Ellerslie, his house outside Wilmington. Come she did, "a young actress like a breakfast food"—so Zelda described her—"that many men identified with whatever they missed from life since she had no definite characteristics of her own save a slight ebullient hysteria about romance. She walked in the moon by the river. Her hair was tight about her head and she was lush and like a milkmaid." To please Lois and the other guests, Fitzgerald involved them in concocting a play. The rich and famous Tommy Hitchcock, a war hero and one of the world's premier polo players, was delighted by the proceedings and proposed a return engagement the following year. "I understand Lois Moran is coming East the end of July," he wrote Scott in May 1928. "Could we not have a weekend then at Sands Point, with you and Zelda, and write the second act of Polo Balls?"

For Lois Moran, as for Rosemary Hoyt in *Tender Is the Night*, an affair with an older man could be chalked up to experience. In fact, she seemed to regard Fitzgerald as a charming if somewhat

Ginevra King, debutante of Lake Forest and Chicago

Actress Lois Moran—"lush and like a milkmaid"

childish mentor. He recommended books for her: David Garnett's *The Sailor's Return*, Hemingway's *The Sun Also Rises*, and Paul Morand's *Open All Night*. In letters addressed to "Darling, dumbbell, upsetting, adorable Scott," she reported on her reading, stirred the coals by remarking on "the very satisfactory kisses" of her leading men, and signed off, "Au revoir, cher enfant."

What he wrote her in response is not known, but they did meet in New York, Hollywood, and Baltimore on several occasions prior to her marriage in 1935. Yet once the first flush of romance had passed, it was never the same, and the very words of love rang false. Lois telephoned him on the day of her marriage to airline executive Collier Young, and he sent her a congratulatory letter that concluded, "Anyhow I love you tremendously always." But losing Lois did not hurt as losing Ginevra had. Besides, it was not as if they were free to choose. In stories like "Magnetism" and "Jacob's Ladder" and "The Rough Crossing," as well as in *Tender Is the Night*, Fitzgerald sublimated his yearning by emphasizing the inappropriateness of a "middle-aged" man (and a married one as well, except in "Jacob's Ladder") falling heels over head for a girl about half his age.

Still, it was more than Lois's youth that attracted Fitzgerald, though at thirty he may have been especially vulnerable. It was more, too, than the prospect of intimacy with a girl whose image on the screen could thrill a million men.

The secret of Lois Moran's particular appeal to Fitzgerald was that she made him feel like a man of accomplishment who was also a gentleman of charm and distinction and social position. As Fitzgerald worked it out in a long self-analysis written in 1930, "with Zelda gone to the Clinique," he'd begun to think of himself during 1925 and 1926 in France as a man of the world and had decided "that everybody liked me and admired me for myself but I only liked a few people like Ernest [Hemingway] and Charlie McArthur and Gerald and Sara [Murphy] who were my peers." Then that euphoric mood faded. "I woke up in Hollywood no longer my egotistic, certain self but a mixture of Ernest in fine clothes and Gerald with a career—and Charlie McArthur with a past." Gerald Murphy belonged to a social elite, or Fitzgerald thought he did. Hemingway was a roughneck writer and MacArthur a playwright without family background, or so Fitzgerald believed. What he wanted was to combine the two, become a literary man of the world, a gentleman artist. "Anybody that could make me believe that, like Lois Moran did, was precious to me." It was not by accident that he invited Tommy Hitchcock to Ellerslie on the weekend Lois was visiting.

The Fitzgeralds left Delaware to spend the summer of 1928 in Paris, and abandoned Ellerslie entirely to move abroad the following May. By this time Scott's drinking was out of control, and friends of earlier expatriate days tended to avoid the Fitzgeralds. Scott found new companions in the sexual *demimonde* depicted in *Tender Is the Night*. These people followed but one rule: No Rules. Anything went. As Fitzgerald observed to Margaret Turnbull in 1932, a girl who had enough money could easily change husbands these days "or live in Paris and not even bother." On the fringes of this world, he came to know Emily Vanderbilt.

The daughter of a "New York banker, horseman and clubman," Emily Davies had married William H. Vanderbilt, son of Alfred Gwynne Vanderbilt, in 1923. When Fitzgerald saw her in Paris five years later, she was in the process of divorcing Vanderbilt. In December 1928, she married theatrical producer Sigourney Thayer, prominent figure in New York and Boston society, but that marriage lasted less than a year. When Fitzgerald lunched with her at Armenonville in the spring of 1930, Emily Vanderbilt (or Mrs. Davies Vanderbilt Thayer, as she then styled the name) was clearly in distress. Rebecca West, who had come to the same restaurant with her son, remembered the day vividly.

> ... very few people were there and we sat down by the lake. Presently Scott Fitzgerald appeared with a woman from New York whom I knew, called Emily Vanderbilt. She was very handsome, I think she had the most beautifully shaped head and the most cunningly devised hair-cut to show it off that I have ever seen. They sat down at a table still nearer the lake than we were, with their backs to us. She was telling him some long and sad story, and going over and over it. He was leaning towards her, sometimes caressing her hands, showing this wonderful gentleness and charity which I remember as his great characteristic. Finally he stood up and seemed to be saying, "You mustn't go

over this any more." His eyes fell on us, and he said to her, "Emily, look who's here," and they finished their lunch with us. I can't remember a thing we said. I think we did what is the great resort for people finding themselves in emotional crises near water, we fed some birds with bread. But he was gay and charming, and we all laughed a lot. And then he took her off to her car, her arm in his, jerking her elbow up, telling her to cheer up. I have always remembered this scene with emotion, for later Emily Vanderbilt committed suicide.

At the Val-Mont clinic, Zelda resented Scott's attentions to Emily Vanderbilt. "You know that I was much stronger mentally and physically and sensitively than Emily," Zelda wrote him, "but you said... that she was too big a *poisson* for me. Why? She couldn't dance a Brahm's waltz or write a story—she can only gossip and ride in the Bois and have pretty hair curling up instead of think-ing—*Please explain*—I want to be well and not bothered with poissons big or little and free to sit in the sun and choose the things I like about people and not have to take the whole person."

"Please explain." But couldn't Zelda see? Emily swam in the big pool. She was brought up in society. She belonged to the 400 in New York and had a cottage in Newport. In Pittsburgh, where her mother came from, her grandfather had published the *Dispatch*. *And she had walked out on a Vanderbilt.* Not even Ginevra could match that.

During the fall and winter of 1930 and 1931, while Zelda was confined to Dr. Oscar Forel's sanitarium at Prangins, in Switzer-land, Fitzgerald apparently carried on affairs with at least two other women. One of them, Bijou O'Connor, rather loudly confessed as much in 1975. "We had a roaring, screaming affair," the daughter of the English diplomat Sir Francis Elliott said. Fitzgerald was fascinated by Bijou's spy-story background. An entry in his note-books reads: "Bijou as a girl in Athens meeting German legacy people in secret. Representing her mother." The two met during September 1930 in Lausanne, where Fitzgerald was living to be close to the sanitarium. The next month they both moved to Lau-sanne's Hotel de la Paix, where—according to Bijou's recollec-tion—she used to watch him happily typing away "and consuming bottle after bottle of gin."

Bijou left Switzerland in November, and over the Christmas holidays in Gstaad Fitzgerald became interested in Margaret Egloff. They were naturally drawn together, for two reasons. Both were spending the holiday season as single parents with children in tow, Fitzgerald with Scottie and the young American with her two children from a marriage about to be dissolved. In addition, both were interested in psychiatry, Scott because of Zelda's illness and Margaret as a medical student about to launch a career in the field. After Christmas Margaret went to Zurich to study with Jung, while Fitzgerald stayed in Lausanne. But there were frequent meetings during the next six months when they spent long hours talking about literature and psychology and she came to know him "very intimately." The two of them also took trips together to the Italian lakes and to France, where they startled the John Peale Bishops by showing up on their doorstep as traveling companions. Then they went their separate ways, Margaret to remarry, and met only once more, surreptitiously, in the Washington train station in the mid-1930s.

Fitzgerald put both women into stories, Bijou as Lady Capps-Karr in "The Hotel Child" and Margaret as Emily Elliott in "Indecision." The second story was revealing because of the way Fitzgerald altered the facts to suggest his basic loyalty to Zelda, or at least to the Zelda Sayre he had fallen in love with in Montgomery, twelve years earlier. The most significant change he made had to do with age. Tommy McLane, the not especially likable Lothario of the story, is trying to carry on simultaneous flirtations both with Emily Elliott, twenty-five years old and divorced, and with eighteen-year-old Rosemary Merriweather, "a blonde, ravishing, Southern beauty" who flirted recklessly with European men and could not be persuaded to act sensibly. In the end Tommy makes his choice. He asks Rosemary (the Zelda of 1918, not 1931) to marry him and as he does so the image of Emily "faded from his mind forever."

In life if not in fiction, Scott Fitzgerald almost always carried around more than one woman's image inside his head. In the decade after Zelda's breakdown in 1930 he attracted the love and admiration of many women, including members of two particular professions. "Excepting for trained nurses," as he observed in one of his last stories, "an actress is the easiest prey for an unscrupulous male." It was a generalization based on experience. As his health declined and he tried to dry out from drinking, Fitzgerald frequently required nursing—in Baltimore, in Asheville, and in Hollywood. "Trained nurses on duty," he confided pointedly to his notebooks, "should not be allowed to talk in their sleep."

Fitzgerald needed the love of women, and the acceptance and approval that came with it. Ideally, the woman should have been Ginevra King or Emily Vanderbilt or another charter member of a club to which he was not vouchsafed admission. But any admiration he could command served to reassure him of his importance or, to use the existential term, his authenticity. At length the compulsion to attract love grew wearing. "Enough, Enough My Masters," he scrawled atop one of his last notebook entries. Below ran a list of seven women in his thoughts, including Zelda and Sheilah Graham.

In an early newspaper interview, Fitzgerald insisted that he thought men much nicer than women, "more open and aboveboard, more truthful and sincere. Wouldn't you a whole lot rather be with a bunch of men," he asked the interviewer, "than with a group of women?" In groups, Fitzgerald may have preferred men, but he was very much a ladies' man himself. He talked their language. He was sensitive to shades of meaning and half-concealed feelings. He knew how to flatter. He paid attention when women talked. He treated them with the courtly manners of an earlier age. And of course they responded. "He liked women," Zelda wrote after Scott's death, and they "usually lionized him, unless he was intolerably scandalous: which was rare; then they usually forgave him because he kept all the rites and sent flowers and wrote notes world without end and was most ingratiating when contrite." No one was in a better position to know.

4

Darling Heart

WHATEVER LEGEND may have made of it, the relationship between Scott Fitzgerald and Zelda Sayre hardly began as a romantic idyll. On the rebound from Ginevra King, Fitzgerald was playing the field. "My army experience," he commented, "consisted mostly of falling in love with a girl in each city I happened to be in." There were several cities and not much time. When he learned he was to be transferred to Camp Sheridan outside Montgomery, he wrote Lawton Campbell—an Alabaman he'd known at Princeton—asking for the name of the "fastest" girl in town. (The editors of the *Birmingham News*, doing their genteel part in myth-making, changed the adjective to "prettiest.")

Campbell supplied two or three names, but not Zelda's. She was too young, not yet eighteen to Fitzgerald's almost twenty-two when they met at the Montgomery Country Club's Saturday night dance early in July 1918. But the petite seventeen-year-old with the rose-pink coloring and red-gold hair immediately caught his eye. They danced. She refused a late date. They quarreled. She consented to a meeting a few days later. She reminded him of "Isabelle" in the novel he was writing, he told her. She was impressed. He did not tell her that Isabelle was modeled on Ginevra.

Scott and Zelda had begun their game of courtship, but neither of them ceased other maneuvers. Fitzgerald's ledger testifies to his involvement with at least three other girls during the summer and fall. July: "May Stiener [Steiner]. Zelda...Helen

Emily Vanderbilt, heiress—too big a poisson *for Zelda?*

Zelda Sayre of Montgomery, who did what she pleased

Dent... Ginevra married... May and I on the porch. Her visiting hours." August: "Zelda & May." September: "Fell in love [with Zelda] on the 7th... Zelda sick... Discovery that Zelda's class voted her prettiest & most attractive." October: "May Stiener... left for North on 26th. Helen Dent's Frenchman" November: "Wild letters... Return to Montgomery. Ruth [Sturtevant] in Washington. Zelda's friend Dent & the stolen kiss on the stairs."

In Zelda, Fitzgerald more than met his match. Much the youngest of Judge and Mrs. A. D. Sayre's five children, she became a free-spirited tomboy in childhood, leading the neighborhood girls in climbing trees, roller-skating on the Whitfields' paved-over backyard, and sneaking into the pool at Huntingdon College for a swim. "Any time she said frog, I jumped," one of her friends remarked. Zelda didn't like "sissy ladylike" girls. She liked boys instead, though she teased them unmercifully as she grew older. In high school English class she read a jingle about shy, handsome Charles Wolfork:

> I do love my Charlie so
> It nearly drives me wild
> I'm so glad that he's my beau
> And I'm his baby child

Poor Charlie reddened, everyone else howled.

Boys liked her anyway, as much for her daring as her beauty. The teen-aged Zelda brooked no authority. On occasion her father attempted to rein her in, but with little success. If he forbade her to leave the house, she'd puncture his dignity by calling him "old Dick" and go out anyway, often with the connivance of her mother. She did what she pleased and made sure that people noticed. At dances she reveled in attention, turning cartwheels or performing a solo Highland Fling. At Tuscaloosa, when the chaperones objected to her antics, she pinned a sprig of mistletoe to the tail of her flannel coat and flipped the coat tail at them as she danced by. In Atlanta, she "left the more or less sophisticated beaux and belles... gasping for air."

This was the girl—defiant, lovely, irresponsible, brave—that Fitzgerald fell in love with in Montgomery. Characteristically, she soon confounded his expectations by letting him seduce her. It may have happened as early as her eighteenth birthday on July 24, "a radiant night, a night of soft conspiracy" (as she later remembered) when the three pines on one side and four on the other "agreed it was all going to be for the best." Or it may have happened on another summer night—again, the recollection is Zelda's—

> when you invited me to dine and I had never dined before but had always just "had supper." The General was away. The night was soft and gray and the trees were feathery in the lamp light and the dim recesses of the pine forest were fragrant with the past, and you said you would come back from no matter where you are. So I said and I will be here waiting.
>
> . . .
>
> It was me who said:
> "I feel as if something had happened and I don't know what it is."
> You said:
> —"Well"—and you smiled—". . . if you don't know I can't possibly know."
> Then I said "I guess nobody knows—"
> And
>   you hoped and I guessed
>   Everything's going to be all right

Fitzgerald's feelings about the seduction were ambivalent: in 1920 he began and abandoned a novel in which he attempted to come to terms with the issue. But when he left Montgomery in October 1918, he felt committed to Zelda emotionally and apprehensive about her morally. He knew that she drank more than other girls: she'd been drinking the first night they met. He knew that she flirted wildly and was pursued by dozens of men. But he did not know how far she went with them, and she was not about to tell him. Years later, she confessed—and it is possible that the confession was contrived more to disturb Scott than to provide him with the truth—that she had "been seduced and provincially outcast" even before they met. Fitzgerald's notebook entry confirms her admission: "There was an elaborate self-consciousness about our seduction which told of deep intuition that you were playing a role, though my one-track mind didn't choose to notice it, and I should have guessed... there had been old emotional experience for you had learned to feel before I did." A letter he wrote but did not send to Zelda's sister Marjorie in December 1938 revealed something of the outrage he felt. "Your mother took such rotten care of Zelda," he wrote, "that John Sellers was able to seduce her at fifteen and she was so drunk the first time I met her at the country club that her partners were carrying her around in their arms." Probably Fitzgerald exaggerated here in the course of arguing against the Sayres' conviction that he'd driven Zelda insane. But the bitterness seems real enough, and must have been compounded by the years he'd spent wondering—and worrying— about Zelda's sexual behavior.

The wondering began almost at once. Zelda understood that her attractiveness to other men mattered a good deal to Fitzgerald and repeatedly let him know of her adventures. At a dance the week after they met, she dragged her escort into a lighted phone booth and began passionately kissing him. "What's the idea?" he asked. "Oh," she airily replied, "Scott was coming and I wanted to make him jealous." When Fitzgerald left Montgomery in the fall, she continued her efforts in correspondence. "In desperation, yesterday Bill LeGrand and I drove his car to Auburn and came back with ten boys to liven things up—Of course, the day was vastly exciting—and the night even more so—" "'Red' said last night that I was the pinkest-whitest person he ever saw, so I went to sleep in his lap— Of course, you dont mind because it was really very fraternal, and we were shaperoned by three girls—" "I'm just recovering from a wholesome amour with Aubern's 'startling quarterback' so my disposition is excellent as well as my health. . . . Please bring me a quart of gin—I haven't had a drink all summer, and you're already *ruined* along alcoholic lines with Mrs. Sayre—" Yet soon her mother was berating her about drinking, "all on account of a wine-stained dress—Darling heart [Fitzgerald's proposed novel about seduction was to be called "Darling Heart"]—I won't drink *any* if you object—Sometimes I get so bored—and sick for you— It helps then—"

In nearly every letter Zelda provoked Scott's jealousy. He responded frantically, making repeated trips to Montgomery from his advertising job in New York and suggesting in correspondence that she might moderate her amorous activities. In March 1919 he sent her an engagement ring as a consequence of which, she wrote him, the "whole dance was completely upset last night." Then she added that the 37th Ohio Division was apparently coming down to Montgomery in May, and it would seem "dreadfully peculiar not to be worried over the prospects of the return of at least three or four fiancees."

Engaged or not, Zelda did not intend to give up her social life. Fitzgerald came to Montgomery in April, in May, and in June 1919, but she would not set a wedding date and continued to torment him through the mails. She was "damned tired" of being told that he "used to wonder why they kept princesses in towers," which he'd written, verbatim, in his "last *six* letters!" If he had to strain so hard for something to say, maybe they ought to correspond less often. When he proposed a June visit she advised him to come "any time except the week of June 13. I'm going to Georgia Tech to try my hand in new fields—You might come on the 20th and stay till we go to North Carolina—or come before I go to Atlanta, only I'll be mighty tired, and they always dance till breakfast." But now there was more than coquetry involved. When Scott did arrive in Montgomery, she broke things off. "I've done my best and I've failed," he wrote Ruth Sturtevant on June 24. "It's a great tragedy to me and I feel I have very little left to live for. . . . Unless someday she will marry me I will never marry."

Zelda's decision was largely a practical matter. As of June 1919 Fitzgerald's prospects were dim. He had not graduated from Princeton. He did not like his job in advertising and was not doing particularly well in it. His novel had been rejected by Scribner's. His parents were well off but not wealthy, while the Sayres had very little money indeed. It made excellent sense for Zelda, as a belle of good family, to seek a husband whose financial success was assured. Mama Sayre made the point clear to Zelda, and Zelda made it more subtly to Scott. "All the material things are nothing," she told him, yet she'd "hate to live a sordid, colorless existence" for he would surely soon love her less and less.

Fitzgerald got the message, and resented it. Despite her customary recklessness, he confided to his notebooks, "Zelda was cagey

about throwing in her lot with me before I was a money-maker."
Moreover, she withheld the sexual favors she had earlier granted.
"After yielding," he wrote in his plan for the 1934 "Count of Darkness" stories, "she holds Phillipe at bay like Zelda & me in Summer
191[9]." Such behavior smacked of calculation, and the romantic
side of Fitzgerald objected. By the time she finally said *yes*, some
of the magic had dissipated.

One effect of his broken engagement was to send Fitzgerald back
to St. Paul to rewrite his novel. When Scribner's changed *its* mind
about *This Side of Paradise* and offered to publish it in the fall of
1919, he decided to try to change Zelda's mind as well. Not only
did he have a contract for a novel to show, but his stories had
started selling for good prices. By November he was ready to go
to Montgomery and woo Zelda once again. "I may be a wreck by
the time I see you," he wrote Princeton classmate Ludlow Fowler
in New York. "I'm going to try to settle it definitely one way or
the other." He didn't succeed. Zelda slept with him but would not
promise to marry him. "I'll tell you what the situation is now," he
told Edmund Wilson. "I wouldn't care if she died, but I couldn't
stand to have anybody else marry her."

Zelda married Scott soon enough, but not before they were both
convinced that she had become pregnant. In January he secured
some pills that were supposed to solve the problem, but Zelda
refused to take them:

> I wanted to for your sake, because I know what a mess I'm
> making and how inconvenient it's all going to be—but I simply
> *can't* and *won't* take those awful pills—so I've thrown them
> away; I'd rather take carbolic acid. You see, as long as I feel that
> I had the right I don't much mind what happens—and besides,
> I'd rather have a *whole family* than sacrifice my self-respect.
> They just seem to place everything on the wrong basis—and
> I'd feel like a damned whore if I took even one, so you'll try to
> understand, please Scott—and do what you think best—but
> don't do ANYTHING till we *know* because God—or some-
> thing—has always made things right, and maybe this will be.

God, or something, did make things right, and the crisis passed.
Meanwhile, Mama Sayre kept leaving "stories of young authors,

turned out on a dark and stormy night," on Zelda's pillow. But all the Sayres capitulated when the movie studios began buying film rights to Fitzgerald stories for four-figure sums. "Darling Heart, our fairy tale is almost ended," Zelda wrote him then, "and we're going to marry and live happily ever afterward just like the princess in the tower who worried you so much—and made me so very cross by her constant recurrence." She was sorry for the times she'd been "mean and hateful," Zelda added, but Fitzgerald didn't expect her to change simply because they were getting married. He knew that "any girl who gets stewed in public, who frankly enjoys and tells shocking stories, who smokes constantly and makes the remark that she has 'kissed thousands of men and intends to kiss thousands more'" would be widely criticized and even thought immoral. But he'd fallen in love with Zelda's "courage, her sincerity and her flaming self-respect" and that was the only thing that mattered. Scott went up to New York to find an apartment. Zelda went to the country club, where—she wrote her husband-to-be—one man tried to elope to New York with her and told her she'd "make a fortune Shaking-It thusly up Broadway." On March 20 the engagement was announced in the Montgomery newspapers. On March 26 *This Side of Paradise* came out to good reviews and excellent sales. On April 3 Scott and Zelda were married in the rectory of St. Patrick's Cathedral on Fifth Avenue.

The week before his wedding, Fitzgerald wrote Ruth Sturtevant that he wanted her to meet Zelda "because she's very beautiful and very wise and very brave as you can imagine—but she's a perfect baby and a more irresponsible pair than we'll be will be hard to imagine." He was right to stress their mutual immaturity. Like an insecure child he needed approval. Like a willful one she demanded attention. Both sought to occupy the center of the stage, sometimes in collaboration but often in competition. It made for incessant quarreling, and always had. "When Zelda Sayre and I were young," Fitzgerald remarked, "the war was in the sky." Between them they brought it down to earth too, to the dance floor of the country club and the Sayres' front porch. These arguments distressed Scott, but Zelda rather enjoyed them. "I love your sad tenderness—when I've hurt you," she wrote Scott in 1919. "That's one of the reasons I could never be sorry for our quarrels—and they bothered you so—Those dear, dear little fusses, when I always tried so hard to make you kiss and forget."

Almost always sexual jealousy was at the root of the trouble. Fitzgerald might call it something else: "The most enormous influence on me in the four and a half years since I met her has been the complete, fine and full-hearted selfishness and chill-mindedness of Zelda," he wrote Edmund Wilson in January 1922. But the selfishness usually expressed itself in a search for amusement involving other men. In his notebooks of the mid-1930s, Scott outlined a sample plot:

> A person perfectly happy succumbing to the current excitement and looking for trouble. Each time he or she is rescued. . . . Begin with her attempt to achieve a real point with her husband—and with her losing it because of this superimposed excitement hunting. One scene where she's pathetic Zelda-Gemma natural—another where you want to wring her neck for ignorant selfishness.

Actually, he had already depicted that girl many times in his earlier fiction, as, for example, in the reckless trouble-making of the title character in "Gretchen's Forty Winks" and of the hopelessly selfish Luella Hemple in "The Adjuster." In fact, as critic Milton Hindus has pointed out, almost all of Fitzgerald's leading female characters, from Rosalind Connage through Gloria Patch and Daisy Buchanan to Nicole Diver, are intensely self-centered. And yet if his readers condemn these women, they do so without any warrant from Fitzgerald himself, who seems to have admired them despite their failings.

"It is one of the many flaws in the scheme of human relationships that selfishness in women has an irresistible appeal to many men," he commented in "The Adjuster." Such women might be exasperating at times, but they had their charm. "I wish I was dead—God forbid!" Fitzgerald has a character remark in a 1924 article. Then he adds: "In the same spirit I have often wished that I had never laid eyes on my wife—but I can never stand for her to be out of my sight for more than five hours at a time." Zelda well understood this attitude. In one of her courting letters to Scott, she speaks of the woman's function as providing a "disturbing element" to men. Given her willfulness and beauty and thirst for adventure, she found it easy to keep her husband disturbed.

Soon after their marriage, Zelda told him "a terrible thing...that if he were away she could sleep with another man and it wouldn't really affect her, or make her really unfaithful to him." This thought stayed with him while she continued the flirtations that had become a way of life. In the summer of 1920 they moved up to Westport from New York, and Zelda became restless. "Scott's hot in the middle of a new novel, and Westport is unendurably dull," she observed in inviting Ludlow Fowler to visit, "but you and I might be able to amuse ourselves—and both of us want to see you dreadfully." The major flirtation of the summer was with George Jean Nathan, not Fowler. Nathan bantered gaily with her, in person and by mail:

> Dear Misguided Woman:
>
> Like so many uncommonly beautiful creatures, you reveal a streak of obtuseness. The calling of a husband's attention to a love letter addressed to his wife is but part of a highly sagacious technique.... It completely disarms suspicion. I refer you, by way of proof, to cases of Beethoven, General McLellan and Gaby Deslys...
> Why didn't you call me up on Friday? Is it possible that your love is growing cold?

In comparison with Montgomery standards this was high-style courting, and Zelda was flattered and amused. Scott was not, and angrily broke off the friendship with Nathan.

The Fitzgeralds were back in New York by fall, where they saw a good deal of former Princetonian Alec McKaig. Out of loyalty to Scott, McKaig refused to kiss Zelda during a taxicab ride and tried to persuade her to lead a less "extravagant" life. But as his diary attests, she bewitched him nonetheless. "She is without doubt the most brilliant & most beautiful young woman I've ever known," he noted in April 1921.

By that time she was three months pregnant, and the Fitzgeralds decided to take their first trip to Europe before the baby arrived.

On board the *Aquitania*, they encountered the Howard MacMillans and Crawford Johnstons, couples from Minneapolis on their honeymoons, and liquid reunions took place. Several days out at sea, the newlywed ladies came upon Zelda huddled in a robe in a deck chair and looking rather the worse for wear. Gently, they said they hoped she'd feel better soon. "You wouldn't look so good, either," Zelda responded, "if you were seasick, hungover, and pregnant." Upon returning to St. Paul to await the birth, she put on a great deal of weight. "Who's your fat friend?" someone asked Xandra Kalman about her, and Zelda did not forget. Pregnancy did not agree with her.

Scottie was born in October. Three months later Zelda discovered she was pregnant once more, and though both she and Scott had wanted a son, it was just too soon. In March 1922 she had an abortion. Perhaps something of her attitude may be gleaned from the fragment of Gloria's diary Fitzgerald quotes in *The Beautiful and Damned*, published the month after the abortion. "I refuse to dedicate my life to posterity," the fictional Gloria wrote. "Surely one owes as much to the current generation as to one's unwanted children. What a fate—to grow rotund and unseemly, to lose my self-love." Later in the novel, when she thinks she's pregnant, Gloria determines to have an abortion, but it turns out to be a false alarm.

But it may also be true, as Nancy Milford suggests, that Fitzgerald was attempting in *The Beautiful and Damned* to transfer any guilt he may have felt to Zelda (or her fictional counterpart). What did he have to feel guilty about? His attitude toward his wife's abortion in 1922 is not on record, though in *The Beautiful and Damned*, Anthony Patch goes along with the idea. But Fitzgerald had secured miscarriage-inducing pills for Zelda a few months before their marriage and an abortion may actually have taken place at that time. "Do you think Zelda's abortions could have had anything to do with her illness?" her sister Rosalind inquired in 1930. The plural reference probably was to a time before March 1922, since during the fall of 1924, in Rome, Zelda underwent "a minor operation" to *enable* her to become pregnant and—in her words— she "became horribly sick from trying to have a baby." She could not do so, and apparently suffered more than one miscarriage trying in the years immediately thereafter. But the attempt in late 1924 had a special significance, for it came on the heels of her affair with the French naval aviator Edouard Jozan.

Whatever it was that drove Zelda into her romance with the young French officer, it marked a turning point in the Fitzgeralds' marriage. They had sailed for Europe in May 1924, and by June were settled in St. Raphael, where Scott was working with concentrated intensity, "living in the book," on *The Great Gatsby*. Bored by lack of company, Zelda spent long afternoons on the beach with Jozan, who with his air of military command and physical hardness represented everything her husband did not. At the beginning she may have intended only a casual flirtation. It did not stay that way. Both in *Save Me the Waltz*, the novel she wrote in 1932, and in *Caesar's Things*, the fragment of a novel she worked on in subsequent years, Zelda recreated her lover in sensual terms. "He drew her body against him till she felt the blades of his bones carving her own. He was bronze and smelled of the sand and sun; she felt him naked underneath the starched linen." Eventually Scott found out—"The Big Crisis" came on the "13th of July"—and took immediate action. "So she told her husband that she loved the French officer and her husband locked her up in the villa," as Zelda described it.

According to Fitzgerald's ledger, he and Zelda grew close together in the aftermath of the affair and the trouble cleared away with a last sight of Jozan in October. But Zelda did not stop feeling her loss: "Whatever it was that she wanted from [Jozan, he] took with him." Nor would her marriage be the same again. "That September 1924," as Scott wrote with the advantage of hindsight, years later, "I knew something had happened that could never be repaired." It marked the beginning of a permanent rift between them. "Her affair with Edouard [Jozan] in 1925 and mine with Lois Moran in 1927, which was a sort of revenge shook something out of us," he wrote her psychiatrist in 1932, "but we can't both go on paying and paying forever."

Fitzgerald paid most agonizingly through not knowing exactly what had happened. Interviewed by Nancy Milford for her book on Zelda Fitzgerald, Jozan maintained that his relationship with Zelda had not resulted in adultery. That denial may have been

Gallic gallantry, but perhaps not. Certainly Fitzgerald never knew. Eleven years after the Jozan summer, he came to grips with his lingering doubt in a story called "Image on the Heart." Tom, the male protagonist, is about to marry Tudy, though he realizes that she has been deeply attracted to Riccard, a young French aviator. Immediately after their wedding Tom discovers that Tudy and Riccard had taken a train trip together the previous day. She tells him it hadn't been her idea, that she'd been furious with Riccard, and offers Tom an annulment. But he decides to accept her story and promises not to reproach her. Then they ride off on their honeymoon, "silent for a while each with a separate thought. His thought was that he would never know—what her thought was must be left unfathomed—and perhaps unfathomable in that obscure pool in the bottom of every woman's heart."

There are some things, clearly, that men and women can never know about each other, and a confession—true or false—would hardly have eased Fitzgerald's torment. But unlike Tudy of "Image on the Heart," Zelda would neither deny nor confirm her unfaithfulness. His imagination took over and conjured up visions—like Dick Diver's of Rosemary being seduced in a Pullman car—more vivid and terrifying than reality. When critic and biographer Henry Dan Piper went to see Zelda in 1947, she told him she regretted having flirted so much with other men and never telling Scott how far she'd gone with them, letting him guess the worst and neither denying nor correcting his suspicions.

Scott tended to internalize his jealousy, Zelda to express hers histrionically. But both, as accomplished competitors in the struggle between the sexes, knew how to retaliate when wounded. Thus while Zelda aroused her husband's jealousy during the early and mid-1920s, he carried on various flirtations—according to Zelda's recollections—with a number of women and especially, after they had returned to the United States from their long trip abroad late in 1926, "further apart than ever before," with the young actress Lois Moran (in Hollywood, Delaware, and New York). The previous year, Zelda had flung herself down a flight of stone steps when Isadora Duncan had called Fitzgerald to her dinner table at St. Paul de Vence and begun a public wooing. Confronted by her husband's infatuation with the seventeen-year-old Lois Moran, she burned her clothes in the bathtub and threw from the window of a train the platinum and diamond wristwatch Scott had given her during their courtship.

Such gestures commanded attention, but did not stop Fitzgerald from inviting the affection and admiration of other women. With exquisite insensitivity he traveled to Hollywood alone in November 1931, leaving Zelda behind to cope with her own lingering malady, her father's severe illness and death, and the demon of suspicion. It troubled her to think of him in Hollywood "with all those beautiful women," and he did little to reassure her through the mails. "I had the most horrible dream about you last night," she wrote Scott. "You came home with a great shock of white hair and you said it had turned suddenly from worrying about being unfaithful." The dream had made her angry all day, she added. In another letter she treated the matter humorously.

> D.O. [for Dear One] if you will come back I will *make* the jasmine bloom and all the trees come out in flower and we will eat clouds for desert bathe in the foam of the rain—and I will let you play with my pistol and you can win every golf game and I will make you a new suit from a blue hydrangea bush and shoes from pecan-shells and I'll sew you a belt from leaves like maps of the world and you can always be the one that's perfect. But if you write me about Lily Dalmita and Constance I will go off to Florida for a week and spend our money and make you jealous of my legs à la Creole when you get home.

Soon after he did return, Zelda suffered a serious relapse and they took the train north to Baltimore, where she was treated at the Phipps clinic of Johns Hopkins University. Only then did he begin to grasp the power he held over her. In fifteen minutes of "well-planned conversation," he told Dr. Thomas A. C. Rennie, he could bring on her insanity again. "I would only need intimate that I was interested in some other woman." For whatever it was worth, he had won their battle for sexual supremacy.

During 1928 and 1929, as Scott drank more and more heavily and Zelda threw herself into the discipline of the ballet, physical relations between them virtually ceased. Her appeal as a woman challenged, she lashed out with accusations. He had never satisfied her, she said. His penis was too short. In *A Moveable Feast* Hemingway wrote a wickedly funny account of how Fitzgerald asked him about his sexual equipment at lunch, and how Hemingway then used the lavatory mirrors and works of painting and sculpture in an attempt to reassure Scott. To many this anecdote rings false, and Hemingway may well have elaborated on the truth, but there is no reason to doubt that Fitzgerald told him about the supposed deficiency in the size of his penis. He told many people that he was worried about it, women as well as men. The problem seems to have been imaginary; Sheilah Graham found him perfectly normal.

In 1929 Zelda assigned another reason to her husband's lack of interest in her. He was, she decided, a homosexual. The accusation struck a nerve, not because it was true but because he recognized in himself certain indications—his appearance, his cast of mind, even his latent tendencies—that might lead others to believe it was true. In boyhood Scott had been thought "too pretty, too feminine" by many observers. He was cast as a chorus girl for two Princeton Triangle shows. On his own he dressed up as a woman and attended a dance at the University of Minnesota. This was all in good fun, but as he grew older the humor palled. When told that he looked like someone else, he ruefully remarked in 1935, it usually turned out that the someone else was a fairy.

Not only did the fine-featured Fitzgerald rather look like a woman, he often thought like one too. "I'm half feminine—at least my mind is," he observed. Like Anthony Patch in *The Beautiful and Damned*, his mind was "Not strongly gendered either way." For example, he took a rather prudish attitude toward sex. He was shocked by the talk of his fellow undergraduates at Princeton. He disapproved of explicit sex in novels. He told John Peale Bishop that he'd devoted far too much space to "sex-in-the-raw" in *Act of Darkness*. He refused to send a blurb about *Butterfield Eight* to John O'Hara's publishers: O'Hara should have used sex more sparingly, he thought. Frank Harris's pornographic memoirs disgusted him. "It's the kind of filth your sex is often subjected to," he told a woman.

In his own fiction, Fitzgerald's tendency was either to write around the issue, as in Gatsby's seduction of Daisy, or to invest sex with overtones of revulsion, as in young Amory Blaine's sudden loathing for Myra St. Claire, the girl he has just kissed, in *This Side of Paradise*. He deleted a phrase about "making love to dry loins" from *Tender Is the Night*. Only once, in *The Last Tycoon* episode involving Stahr and Kathleen at the beach house, did he write an adult sex scene, and—as it turns out—he had left that scene understated as well until Sheilah Graham showed him how to make it provocative.

If Fitzgerald evaded depicting heterosexual acts in his fiction, he was far from condoning any less conventional behavior. Homosexuals like Royal Dumphry, Luis Campion, and the unfortunate Chilean Francisco are portrayed satirically in *Tender Is the Night*, while a long passage excised from the novel served to segregate the author firmly from the world they inhabited. Dick and Nicole are in a hotel that houses a virtual "battalion of the Boys":

> She saw the males gathered down at the bar, the tall gangling ones, the little pert ones with round thin shoulders, the broad ones with the faces of Nero and Oscar Wilde, or of senators— faces that dissolved suddenly into girlish fatuity, or twisted into leers—the nervous ones who hitched and twitched, jerking open their eyes very wide, and laughed hysterically, the handsome, passive and dumb men who turned their profiles this way and that, the pimply stodgy men with delicate gestures, or the raw ones with very red lips and frail curly bodies, their shrill voluble tones piping their favorite word "treacherous" above the hot volume of talk; the ones over-self-conscious who glared with eager politeness toward every noise; among them were English types with great racial self-control, Balkan types, one small cooing Siamese. "I think now," Nicole said, "I think I'm going to bed."
> "I think so too."
> —Goodby, you unfortunates. Goodby, Hotel of Three Worlds.

Zelda provoked her husband's anger by accusing him of homosexuality. She outraged him by naming Ernest Hemingway as the man he loved. Here she struck very close to home, for Fitzgerald not only made a hero of Hemingway—a job Ernest said he'd gladly renounce—and worked with vigor to promote his career, but obviously felt a deep affection for him. The much-repeated story of

Scott and Ernest's friendship hardly bears further repeating, but one quotation from Fitzgerald's notebooks is apropos. "I really loved him, but of course it wore out like a love affair. The fairies have spoiled all that."

When Zelda suffered her mental breakdown and was hospitalized in the spring of 1930, she was housed in three different institutions within a month's time. At each of them she related the same tale. Her husband was a homosexual, in love with a man named Hemingway. Scott did not want to see her again until she disabused herself of such notions, he insisted by letter. She knew what she knew, Zelda responded. She'd like him to come see her, "but there's no good telling lies."

He was especially troubled by her conviction, which served to make her story more credible. For the first month after she moved to Prangins, he later maintained, Zelda "had Dr. [Oscar] Forel convinced that I was a notorious Parisian homosexual." She almost convinced Scott as well. "My instinct," he commented, "is to write a public letter to the Paris Herald to see if any human being except yourself and Robert McAlmon [who characterized Hemingway the same way] has ever thought I was a homosexual. The three weeks after the horror of Valmont when I could not lift my eyes to meet the eyes of other men in the street after your stinking allegations and insinuations will not be repeated."

Zelda's delusions about him, Fitzgerald believed, were intimately bound up with her own homosexual leanings. The "idea began," he wrote, "in an attempt to implicate me in what you thought were your own tendencies (i.e. your first accusation about Ernest occurred exactly one month after the Dolly Wilde matter)." One cause of her breakdown was her inability to confront those tendencies. As her first doctor at Malmaison reported, "she believes herself in love with her dance teacher (Madame X), she already believes herself to have been in love with another woman." The other woman was probably a "friend in the Paris Opera" whom Zelda admitted she loved. Dolly Wilde was the niece of Oscar Wilde, and a libertine who practiced her lesbianism publicly in Paris. In a fragment cut out of *Tender Is the Night,* she appears as the wicked Vivian Taube. "Zelda & Dolly Wilde," Scott's ledger for May 1929 reads. Whatever happened then was enough that he rebuked Zelda for it, but he was wrong to do so, she thought, since he'd sat her beside Dolly in the first place and then "disparaged and belittled the few friends" she had "whose eyes had gathered their softness at least from things that I understood." Besides, in "all that horror Dolly Wilde was the only one who said she would do anything to be cured." Dolly Wilde was the particular friend of the notorious Natalie Barney, whose salon the Fitzgeralds attended at least twice during 1928 and 1929. They also were taken to visit the studio of lesbian artist Romaine Brooks, whose paintings depicted men in women's attire and vice versa. A self-portrait revealed the artist in riding coat and top hat; Natalie Barney was portrayed brandishing a whip. Zelda described the studio as "a glass-enclosed square of heaven swung high above Paris."

Madame X was Madame Lubov Egorova, head of the ballet school for the Diaghilev troupe. Gerald Murphy had recommended Egorova to Zelda as an excellent coach and technician. In the summer of 1928 the lessons—and the attraction—began. On the boat going back to the United States in September, Zelda was to remind Scott, "I told you I was afraid there was something abnormal in the relationship and you laughed." When they returned to Paris in May she "became dependent on" her teacher. There were group lessons in the morning, individual ones in the afternoon. Daily she stopped at the flower stall to take Egorova a fresh bouquet. Zelda invited her teacher and her husband to dinner, and became annoyed when Scott flirted with her inamorata.

When the Fitzgeralds went to North Africa in February, Zelda could not get Egorova out of her head and felt miserable, nervous, and unhappy. Back in Paris once more, she drove herself past the limits of exhaustion at her lessons. As she later tried to explain matters, she felt an "intense love" for Egorova:

> I wanted to dance well so that she would be proud of me and have another instrument for the symbols of beauty that passed in her head that I understood, though apparently could not execute. I wanted to be first in the studio so that it would be me that she could count on to understand what she gave out in words and . . . I wanted to be near her because she was cool and white and beautiful.

She loved Egorova more than anything in the world, she told Dr. Forel. Egorova "had everything of beauty in her head, the brightness of a greek temple, the frustration of a mind searching for a place, the glory of cannon bullets." To Scott she wrote that she could not sleep and was going through hell and could not grasp why God had imposed this torture on her "except that it was wrong, of course, to love my teacher when I should have loved you. But I didn't have you to love—not since long before I loved her."

Whatever the accuracy of Zelda's accusations about Scott, she was not imagining about herself. At Val-Mont in April 1930 one of her nurses was forced to repulse her "overly affectionate" gestures. At Prangins in October 1930 she conceived an "infatuation for [a] red-haired girl." Nor did she obliterate the image of her ballet teacher. She painted a portrait of Egorova, in fact, and displayed it at her 1934 show in New York. But, she instructed Scott, that was one painting she did not want sold.

5

Genius and Glass

ZELDA'S OBSESSION with the dance could not have been predicted from a youth in which she demonstrated some artistic precociousness but not much ambition. Probably she sensed that such a drive would be out of place in the makeup of the well-bred Southern girl. She was exposed to the arts, but not expected to excel at them. "I hope I'll never get ambitious enough to try anything," she wrote Scott in 1919. "It's so *much* nicer to be damned sure I COULD do it better than other people—and I might not could if I tried—that, of course, would break my heart—" Instead she played the lead role of "Folly" in Montgomery's *Les Mystérieuses* ball, and much the same role in her own young life.

For the first seven years of her marriage she was content to maintain this attitude. Everyone who met her was struck with her brilliance, for she was a remarkably impressive person. The actress Louise Brooks has described meeting the Fitzgeralds at the Ambassador hotel in Los Angeles in 1927. "They were sitting close together on a sofa, like a comedy team, and the first thing that struck me was how *small* they were." The next was Zelda herself. She "had come to see the genius writer," Brooks said, "but what dominated the room was the blazing intelligence of Zelda's profile...the profile of a witch." Shortly afterwards, the Fitzgeralds' marriage turned moribund. Only then did Zelda try seriously to establish herself as an artist. She had already written and published stories (and done some dabbling with paints), but now she decided

Dour Zelda, impish Scottie, discouraged Scott
en route to France, April 1928

An inspired amateur, brilliant and fragile

to proceed in a direction where her husband had not led. At twenty-seven, she undertook to shape herself into a first-rate ballerina.

"Daddy loved glamour and so I also had a great respect for popular acclame," Zelda wrote her daughter in 1944, and then implied that such acclaim might have come to her if she'd stuck to a single field. "I wish that I had been able to do better one thing and not so given to running into cul-de-sacs with so many." This is an extremely accurate self-analysis of Zelda Fitzgerald's artistic career. In ballet she could not equal the skill of those who dedicated their entire lives to the craft. In fiction she lacked the economy of language, the sense of construction, and the gift for drama of the best writers. As a painter she was perhaps most successful, for here her curious use of proportion and unusual color palette fit into the expressionistic mode, yet her paintings remain more interesting biographically than intrinsically.

In all three pursuits she achieved the level of the inspired amateur, not that of the top-flight professional. It was this point that her husband made to her, over and over, often with a brutality and tactlessness that betrayed his own insecurity. Yet even in 1944 Zelda was unpersuaded. "I have always held a theory," she continued in her letter to Scottie, "that one who does one thing superlatively could transfer his talents successfully to others. One never knows about genius."

Zelda was not Blake or Leonardo, however. Nor was she destroyed by her husband's insensitivity. As Scottie has observed, it is wrong to think that her father contributed to her mother's mental problems by preventing her from pursuing her career. The upsurge of interest in her mother's plight she attributes to the women's liberation movement. "They had their consciousness raised and they needed a martyr." Zelda Fitzgerald was it.

Fitzgerald did not object to his wife's dancing until the ballet—and Egorova—became all that she could talk or think about. In her obsession Zelda pared down to a dangerous thinness and bruised herself through overexercise. Moreover, she stretched mind as well as body to the breaking point. "There's no use killing yourself," Scott objected. "You'll never be any good." He underestimated her progress. In September 1929, Zelda received an invitation to join the school of the San Carlo Opera ballet company in Naples.

Madame Julie Sedova, head of the company, promised her a solo in *Aida* or another opera as a debut. The management of the theater would give her a monthly salary if she stayed the whole season, Sedova pointed out, and it would be "very useful" for Zelda to dance on the stage. One could get room and board in Naples for 35 lire a day, she added.

Zelda did not go, possibly because she was unwilling to leave Paris and Egorova, possibly because Scott prevented her. In *Save Me the Waltz*, David Knight attempts to stop Alabama from taking a similar position in Naples, but she goes anyway and makes a critical success. "She had promise and should be given a bigger role, the papers said. Italians like blondes; they said Alabama was as ethereal as a Fra Angelico angel because she was thinner than the others." That was fiction; in actuality Zelda did not know how good she was.

In June 1930, two months after her hospitalization, she persuaded Scott to write Egorova and secure a professional opinion about her competence. "*Please* write immediately to Paris about the dancing," she pleaded, adding that if the recommendation was that she should continue her studies, she would go to another school. "I know Egorova would not want to be bothered with me," she reassured her husband. On July 9, Egorova wrote her assessment. Zelda could never become a dancer of the first rank, she said. She had started too late to become a star like Nemtchinova. Yet she had been a good, hard-working student, and could now dance important roles with success in the Ballet Massine in New York. In concluding, Egorova extended the best regards of her husband and herself to Fitzgerald and their sincere wishes for the recovery of Zelda, "que j'embrasse tendrement."

In the light of what Scott knew about Zelda's dancing, it is difficult to account for the way he belittled her accomplishments. He denigrated her to Harold Ober, for example, by inventing the tale that she had thought visitors to Egorova's studio were scouting her for Diaghilev, while in reality—he said—they were looking her over as a possible "shimmy dancer" for the Folies-Bergère. Fitzgerald had told her she would never be any good; therefore, his reasoning· must have gone, she never *had* been any good. As a way of proving superiority, this was cruel enough. When it came to Zelda's writing, Scott was even crueler.

During their courtship Zelda wrote Scott that she hoped to help him with his writing. She did. From the beginning she supplied him with story ideas, as for "The Ice Palace," for example. Further, he appropriated her writings as well as her ideas. In *The Beautiful and Damned,* Zelda reported in a tongue-in-cheek review, she "recognized a portion of an old diary... which mysteriously disappeared" shortly after her marriage and "scraps of letters which... sound... vaguely familiar. In fact, Mr. Fitzgerald—I believe that is how he spells his name—seems to believe that plagiarism begins at home." Clearly, he considered everything in their experience, Zelda's as well as his own, as grist for the mill of his fiction.

More questionable financially was his habit of publishing her actual stories or articles as his own or as joint ventures. In 1923 she wrote her first story, "Our Own Movie Queen," or wrote two-thirds of it anyway, with Scott adding a climax and revisions. The story appeared under his name, and earned $900. Later in the 1920s she wrote more fiction and published a series of stories in *College Humor* at prices ranging from $500 to $800. When one of these, "A Millionaire's Girl," was sent to the *Saturday Evening Post* as his work rather than hers, the price went up to $4,000. At this stage Scott was far from opposed to her writing, and not only for reasons of finance.

"A Millionaire's Girl" appeared in the May 17, 1930, issue of the *Post*. With Zelda in the sanitarium, Scott tried to interest Scribner's in bringing out a book of her short pieces to take her mind off the ballet and give her a sense of accomplishment. He also sent Max Perkins three "haunting and evocative" stories she'd written "in the dark middle of her nervous breakdown," for possible publication in *Scribner's* magazine.

Upon returning to the States in 1931, Zelda gave up ballet but continued work on her fiction. She also adopted a tone of humility toward Scott that sounded a new note in their relationship. "I *wish* you could teach me to write," she implored. "*I* want to write like you some day..., I want to do everything like you—" Within months, however, she suffered a second breakdown and while at Phipps Clinic in Baltimore early in 1932 produced *Save Me the Waltz* in a burst of energy. It marked the beginning of the end of Scott's tolerance for her writing.

For one thing, she sent the novel directly to Perkins without consulting Scott as mentor. He was outraged by this attempt to bypass him, since he'd specifically asked to see the novel before anyone else. In fact, as Dr. Mildred Squires at Phipps indicated in a telegram, the novel had been addressed to Fitzgerald originally, "but patient changed address last moment."

The manuscript was mailed to Perkins on March 9, 1932. That same day Zelda wrote Scott that she knew Scribner's wouldn't take it but thought Knopf might. She was going to put his copy in the mail on Monday, as soon as she knew the other one had reached New York safely. Whatever happened to her novel, she was now seeking a writing career of some kind. "Please let me ask somebody for a job on the paper somewhere," she concluded.

Why didn't she send the ms. to Fitzgerald first? Perhaps she wanted Perkins' opinion on her work, unmediated by her husband's revisions or comments. "Also," as she explained herself to Scott, "feeling it to be a dubious production due to my own instability I did not want a scathing criticism such as you have mercilessly—if for my own good given my last stories, poor things." But the principal reason, surely, was that she had written about herself and Scott, material he regarded as exclusively his province, and that in doing so she had depicted him in unfavorable terms. "You will like it," she had predicted early in the composition process. "It is distinctly École Fitzgerald, though more ecstatic than yours." But it was far too much of the school of Fitzgerald to suit him.

When he did read the novel, on March 14, he was furious and shot off letters demanding that some sections be cut and others revised. For one thing, the name "Amory Blaine" had to go. Not only had Zelda appropriated the name of his protagonist in *This Side of Paradise*, he wrote Dr. Squires, but "one whole section" of her novel imitated the book he'd been unable to finish "*because of the necessity of keeping Zelda in sanitariums.*"

In irritation Zelda wrote back that she would make some changes but only on aesthetic grounds. Apparently he also had accused her of fishing around in their past. If so, she answered, her fish-nets

> ...were beautiful gossamer pearl things to catch the glints of the sea and the slow breeze of the weaving seaweed and bubbles at dawn. If a crab filtered in and gnawed the threads and an octopus stagnated and slimed up their fine knots and many squids shot ink across their sheen and shad laid comfortable row on their lovely film, they are almost repaired once more and the things I meant to fish still bloom in the sea. Here's hope for the irridescent haul that some day I shall have. What do you fish with, by the way? that so puts to shame my equipment which I seriously doubt that you have ever seen, Superior Being—

She could not bring herself to feel guilty about his having to interrupt *his* novel to write stories that would pay for the treatment that gave her time to write *her* novel. She couldn't help her illness and, besides, he wouldn't have wanted her to fold her hands during her long unoccupied hours. Later, in a more plaintive tone, she added, "I hope you'll like my book—or something that I do some-time—"

He was willing to like her work as long as he could control its direction. Once he took charge of *Save Me the Waltz,* guiding Zelda through revisions and negotiating with Perkins himself, Scott became an advocate of the novel. "If you like it," he instructed Perkins, "please *don't* wire her congratulations, and please keep whatever praise you may see fit to give *on the staid side*—I mean, *as you naturally would,* rather than yield to a tendency one has with invalids to be extra nice to cheer them up." Also, he cautioned his editor, "don't discuss contract with her until I have talked with you." In mid-May he sent the revised book to New York with his endorsement. "It is a good novel now, perhaps a very good novel—I am too close to it to tell." If Perkins decided to refuse it, he should write Scott directly. If he accepted the novel, he could write Zelda, and Scott withdrew "all restraints" on praise. Scribner's decided to publish *Save Me the Waltz.* The contract stipulated that half the royalties would be credited against "the indebtedness of F. Scott Fitzgerald" up to $5,000. Zelda's novel, which sold very few copies, had no effect on her husband's debt to Scribner's.

Fitzgerald remained keenly sensitive to any encroachment on the autobiographical material he transformed into fiction. When, a year after completing *Save Me the Waltz*, Zelda began to plan a novel dealing with insanity, it seemed to Scott that she was covering some of the same ground as *Tender Is the Night* in order to justify herself and make him look bad. "Possibly she would have been a genius if we had never met," he acknowledged in an April 1933 letter to Dr. Adolf Meyer. But as matters stood, she was only hurting him and his work by continuing to invade his territory in her own writing. The next month brought the issue to a head in a May 28 session organized by Dr. Thomas A.C. Rennie, Dr. Meyer's colleague. The ostensible purpose was to talk out their differences. Scott's real goal was to put a stop to Zelda's fiction and redirect her energies elsewhere.

In advance of the confrontation, he planned to make this point in forceful but subdued fashion. He even devised an elaborate strategy—"Prepare physically," he reminded himself, "begin with apology for repetition," and so on through seven more points of debater's notes—but when they faced each other the discussion became bitter.

"You are a third-rate writer and a third-rate ballet dancer," Scott told Zelda, while he was "a professional writer with a huge following... the highest paid short story writer in the world."

"It seems to me," she replied, "that you are making a rather violent attack on a third-rate talent, then." Why should he care what she wrote about?

Because, he said, "she was broaching at all times on [his] material," she was picking up the crumbs he dropped at the dinner table and putting them into books. It was bad for her to undertake a novel about insanity (a point Dr. Rennie agreed with) but also bad for him, since as the professional writer in the family that was his material, the material he was going to use in *Tender Is the Night*.

At this stage Zelda struck back where it hurt the most, at her husband's long procrastination over finishing this novel he had been working on intermittently since completing *Gatsby* eight years earlier. If he ever got it written, she said, he wouldn't feel "so miserable and suspicious and mean towards everybody else." Meanwhile, he was so "full of self-reproach" that he'd stooped to the device of accusing her.

Things were said between the Fitzgeralds that afternoon that could not easily be unsaid. Both of them insisted that they could not stand living together without a change in their relationship. Zelda recounted what had happened the previous fall when Scott had come back from New York drunk: "You sat down and cried and cried...you said I had ruined your life and you did not love me and you were sick of me and wished you could get away." She could not live under such conditions, Zelda said; she'd rather live in an insane asylum. The basic trouble lay in his drinking, she insisted. The basic trouble lay in her defiance about the novel, he insisted. They'd had no sex for three or four months, he revealed, though before that time their relations were pleasant enough. Then he posed the crucial question: "Would you like to go to law about it?" and she answered that she would, that she thought "the only thing is to get a divorce because there is nothing except ill will on your part and suspicion." That was probably not what he had expected to hear, for he ignored the topic of divorce as the long afternoon of their confrontation waned. Finally he gave his ultimatum. Zelda was to stop writing about their lives in any form, novel or otherwise. "If you write a play, it cannot be a play about psychiatry and it cannot be a play laid on the Riviera, and it cannot be a play laid in Switzerland, and whatever the idea is it will have to be submitted to me." Zelda reluctantly agreed to put aside her writing until he finished his book. After that, she said, "I think we'd better get a divorce and any decision you choose to make with regard to me is all right because I cannot live on those terms, and I cannot accept them."

Soon after this session, Scott consulted Edgar Allan Poe, his lawyer in Baltimore, who reported that there were sixteen states that permitted divorce on the ground of insanity, with the most lenient law in Nevada. Fitzgerald also considered the issue of custody, and outlined his case in notes apparently prepared for a legal argument on the subject (the words, "KEEP COOL BUT FIRM," are written in red capitals across the first page):

> As I got feeling worse Zelda got mentally better, but it seemed to me that as she did she was also coming to the conclusion she had it on me, if I broke down it justified her whole life—not a very healthy thought to live with about your own wife. . . . Finally four days ago told her frankly & furiously that had got & was getting rotten deal trading my health for her sanity and from now on I was going to look out for myself & Scotty exclusively, and let her go to Bedlam for all I cared.

"Either she gives up completely this attitude," the memo concludes, "or I'm going to law to get Scotty." In the end there was no divorce, though Fitzgerald—and, possibly, Zelda—repeatedly considered the idea, and no battle over custody.

He also considered at least one other way of dealing with what he came to regard as a mortal contest between them. Among Fitzgerald's papers at Princeton resides the chilling document reproduced below. It was probably written late in 1933 or early in 1934.

Plan—To attack on all grounds

Play (suppress), novel (delay), pictures (suppress), character (showers??), child (detach), schedule (disorient to cause trouble) no typing

Probably result—new breakdown

Danger to Scotty (?)
   ″   ″ herself (?)

All this in secret

Presumably he did not carry out this diabolical plan. Meanwhile, though restricted from writing about the subject matter of his novel-in-progress, there were other things Zelda could do. In his notes for the meeting with Dr. Rennie, Fitzgerald set down two such alternatives:

to try to write instead of self-justification (& working always
on schedule) a series of short observations on things & facts,
observed things which she can sell & make money if she wants
that
   go to art school or to learn commercial design & try to combine
talent for art with etc. into some unit ? like cartooning & leave
my field to me

In fact it was art she turned to—oils, watercolors, and drawings
instead of cartoons. "I am not trying to make myself into a great
artist or a great anything," she wrote Scott in March 1934. It wasn't
the will to power or exaggerated ambition that drove her, but other
"motivating elements." She did not say what these elements were,
for good reasons. Her husband would hardly have wanted to hear
that her artistic pursuits helped to fill up the vacuum left by the
collapse of their marriage. Nor was he tolerant of any talk of "self-
expression," since he was convinced that there was no such thing
in the realm of art. Here his opinion ran counter to those of Zelda's
doctors. "I do not think she will ever be happy without some
creative work," Dr. Squires wrote to him in March 1932. Painting
provided that creative outlet without driving her into dangerous
depths, like her dancing, or invading Fitzgerald's territory, like
her writing. And, as in everything she tried, Zelda immediately
demonstrated considerable talent and worked with dedication on
her canvases.

From March 29 to April 30, 1934, the results were exhibited at
Cary Ross's studio in New York, with Scott once again organizing
matters. As of May 4, Ross reported to him that sales totalling
$328.75 had been made. Purchasers included the Gerald Murphys,
Dorothy Parker, Mrs. Thomas Daniels, Tommy Hitchcock, Adele
Lovett, Muriel Draper, and Mrs. Maxwell Perkins, all friends or
prominent artists themselves. Another famous figure, Mabel Dodge
Luhan, wrote from New Mexico expressing interest in the oil,
"Portrait in Thorns," that Zelda did not want sold.

Prior to her own show, Zelda came to New York and was so
excited by seeing the Georgia O'Keeffe paintings at the American
Place that she "felt quite sick afterwards." She loved O'Keeffe's
"rhythmic white trees winding in visceral choreography about the

deeper green ones" and "the voluptuous tree-trunk with a very pathetic blue flame shaped flower growing arbitrarily beneath it." Diaghilev had a theory that successful art should shock the emotions, Zelda wrote, and that had happened to her; a "person could not walk about that exhibition and maintain any dormant feelings." O'Keeffe, she decided, "was the most moving and comprehensible painter" she'd ever seen. It made sense that Zelda should have been so affected by O'Keeffe's paintings, since her own work treated the natural world, and especially flowers, with similar extravagance.

Zelda had no more exhibitions, but both Dr. Rennie and Dr. Robert S. Carroll, head of the hospital near Asheville where she was to spend much of her life after 1936, encouraged her painting as therapy. To allow her to earn money, Dr. Carroll commissioned her to paint screens for the patients' bedrooms. She was not pleased, considering the project a waste of her professional talent, "the cumulate result of years of effort, aspiration, and heart-break...do you think I am socially obliged to undertake an oil painting of 3 panels each for every room in this hospital?" she asked Scott. Eventually she did the screens in tempera, a less exacting process, but still felt resentful.

Not until after Scott's death did Zelda turn back to writing, but by then she was incapable of producing coherent fiction. The result, a disorganized manuscript called *Caesar's Things*, covered much of the autobiographical material in *Save Me the Waltz*, now mingled with religious visions and fantasies. It was the work of a fragmented mind.

Zelda's malady was variously described, by her doctors, as schizophrenia and dementia praecox. Whatever the technical designation, both Fitzgeralds regarded her troubled mind metaphorically as a fragile house of thinly spun glass or as a broken eggshell. In *Save Me the Waltz*, for instance, Alabama feels "the essence of herself pulled finer and smaller like those streams of spun glass that pull and stretch till there remains but a glimmering illusion." Once the house of glass—or the eggshell—fissured, the job of reconstruction became terribly difficult. As Scott wrote the Sayres in December 1930, "Humpty Dumpty fell off a wall and we are hoping that all the king's horses will be able to put the delicate eggshell together." The psychiatrists tried to patch up the shatterings and failed. Instead, as Zelda wrote in 1932, they presented her "with a piece of bric-a-brac of their own forging which falls to the pavement on [the] way out of the clinic and luckily smashes to bits, and the patient is glad to be rid of their award." She exaggerated, for the reconstructed shell did not always crack so soon. It always broke eventually, though, and each time the task of putting the pieces together became harder. As in most such cases, the survivors wondered whom to blame.

"Please don't write to me about blame," Zelda quite sensibly asked Scott during her stay at Prangins. How could she accept blame now when in the past she had felt none? "Anyway, blame doesn't matter. The thing that counts is to apply the few resources available to turning life into a tenable orderly affair that resembles neither the black hole of Calcutta or Cardinal Ballou's cage." Fitzgerald could not resist the subject, however, and in the Humpty Dumpty letter to her parents made it a point to quote Dr. Paul Bleuler, the eminent consultant he'd brought in to examine his wife. "Stop blaming yourself," Bleuler told him. "You might have retarded it but you couldn't have prevented it." Fitzgerald needed such reassurance, for he feared that his dissolute life in Paris— often drunk, rarely conjugal—had exacerbated her illness. What he never knew was how much he was to blame for her condition. Zelda's sister Rosalind held him almost one hundred percent culpable.

They had not liked each other from the time of the Fitzgeralds' wedding in St. Patrick's. Rosalind and Newman Smith had come to the affair—a very small wedding, with only family and a friend or two—to represent the Sayres, along with Zelda's other sisters, Marjorie and Clothilde. When Clothilde and husband John Palmer were held up en route to the church, Scott insisted on going ahead without them. After the brief ceremony, he said goodbye, swept Zelda away, and left them standing there, the late-arriving Palmers too, without so much as a glass of champagne. Rosalind, feeling the slight for the family, was furious.

Her opinion of Scott worsened during a February 1928 visit to Ellerslie. Scott returned from a trip to Princeton drunk and on a crying jag. In the course of an argument he threw a favorite vase of Zelda's into the fireplace. When she belittlingly referred to his father as an Irish cop on the beat, he slapped her hard enough to cause a nosebleed. Rosalind, who had witnessed this display with outrage, left the next morning and urged Zelda to do the same. Zelda told her sister, in effect, to mind her own business.

With this scene fixed in her memory, Rosalind became convinced that Scott was badly mistreating Zelda and wrote him a bitterly nasty letter after Zelda's collapse. "I would almost rather she die now," Rosalind declared, "than escape only to go back to the mad world you and she have created for yourselves." Things were bad enough without such correspondence, Scott replied. He knew Rosalind disliked him and disapproved of the life they led, but now he had Zelda and Scottie to take care of and could not be "upset and harrowed still further." As time wore on, he came to interpret Rosalind's remark as signifying that he'd driven Zelda crazy, which was very close to what she did in fact believe.

In his fiction and elsewhere, Fitzgerald vented his dislike of Zelda's sister. The most condemning portrait occurs in "Babylon Revisited," Fitzgerald's 1931 story of how Marion Peters (modeled on Rosalind) prevented Charlie Wales from regaining custody of his daughter. The Peterses had taken charge of Honoria after the death of her mother, who was Marion's sister—and after Charlie had engaged in a long, end-of-twenties binge in Paris. Now, although Charlie has reformed, Marion's hostility toward him will not let her release Honoria. At one stage in the story, Mrs. Peters begins to utter the very phrase Rosalind had used in her letter to Scott. "I think if she were my child I'd rather see her—" she begins, and then manages to check herself as her real-life counterpart had not. Still, Marion Peters represents the most unattractive woman in Fitzgerald's fictional gallery: small-minded, ill-tempered, afraid of life, and vindictive.

In letters and notebooks Scott further denigrated his sister-in-law as "a smooth-faced bitch person" who was "always hiding in closets till the battle is over and then coming back to say, 'I told you so'." In two notes he belittled her intelligence as well. "Rosalind talks in several more syllables than she thinks in," one reads, and the other: "Rosalind gave up thinking some time between the Civil war and the depression, and when I want to get anything over to her I tell it to her two dozen times till she begins to parrot it back to me as if it were an idea of her own." Considering their mutual antipathy, Fitzgerald must have been in desperate straits when he asked Newman Smith for a loan to launch Scottie at Vassar in 1938. The loan was refused, with sanctimonious advice. "I think without doubt Newman's instincts were to do the decent thing," Scott angrily wrote Rosalind, "but knowing the very minor quantity of humanity that you pack under that suave exterior of yours I do not doubt that you dissuaded him."

Relations between Scott and Zelda's mother were never as hostile as that, but they were not good either. Mrs. Sayre—"Mama Sayre" to almost everyone—worried about Scott's drinking and his interest in other women and thought he had exposed Zelda to evil influences. Scott resented her having spoiled Zelda so badly and her Pollyanna-like attempts to smooth over the pattern of mental instability in her family. This posture was the one the Sayres presented to the world, and even, as it turned out, to Zelda's doctors. When Zelda first entered Prangins, Rosalind sent Dr. Forel a letter about the simple life at her girlhood home, adding that there was no history of insanity in the family. That information was contrary to fact.

The euphemism of the day was "nervous exhaustion," and since Zelda suffered from that, Mrs. Sayre acknowledged to Scott in July 1930, her recovery would be slow and he would have to fight relapses. She knew because of experience. "Marjorie [Zelda's eldest sister] could not be taxed for two years and...Judge Sayre was out of his office nine months." The mind was always more or less involved, she said, and there was a tendency to melancholia. She wanted to forewarn Scott, but further than this she would not go. She did not tell him about the suicide of her mother and of her sister. Nor was she entirely frank about the death of Zelda's brother Anthony in the summer of 1933. The ultimate cause, she told Scott, was a liver ailment. In fact he had committed suicide after nightmares that he would kill his mother. Furthermore, when she did admit a strain of "nervous prostration" in the family, she traced it to the "Morgan blood" on her husband's side of the family, not her own. Fitzgerald naturally felt deceived as bits of the truth leaked out. "I believed what Zelda believed about her family until the wheels of the bicycle began to run backward," he observed in his notebooks.

In fact Mama Sayre spoke to no one about certain skeletons from the past, and tended to fix the blame elsewhere. While her children were under her care, she argued, they had all prospered. She could not be responsible for what happened after they went off with Yankee writers to study with Russian ballet teachers who were no better than beasts of burden in a country like France, which with its "putrid literature" was "a good place for things to rot." Scott "was a handsome thing," she told a newspaper interviewer late in her life. "But he was not good for my daughter and he gave her things she shouldn't have." Throughout Zelda's long periods in sanitariums and hospitals, Mama Sayre was convinced that if she could have her baby at home all would be well. She even accused Scott of institutionalizing Zelda in 1932 "for ulterior motives," a charge that must have preyed on his mind during 1938 and 1939, when he was living with Sheilah Graham in Hollywood while the Sayres were trying to persuade him to have Zelda released from Highland Hospital in Asheville.

"That Zelda's illness has wrecked our lives is no more important than the fact that it has cast a dark shadow over Mrs. Sayre's mature years," he observed sarcastically in his notebooks. It seemed to him that the family was less interested in Zelda's well-being than in placating the desire of an eighty-year-old woman to have her baby with her at the end. "I've read that people suffering from her malady usually live to be about forty," Mrs. Sayre wrote Scott in June 1939. "If this is true she is almost free from prisons and frustrations and we may cross over hand in hand." In the end she outlived Scott and Zelda both.

Not only did Rosalind and her mother blame Scott for most of Zelda's difficulties, they also thought that *he* was mentally unbalanced. "I'm sure my family secretly thinks that you're the crazy one," Zelda jocularly wrote her husband in 1932. Matters became less amusing as these opinions became more overt and Zelda came to share them herself. Moreover, almost every doctor she consulted tended to regard theirs as really a joint case, since Fitzgerald's excessive drinking pointed to an inner instability. Some of the psychiatrists who treated Zelda at Sheppard-Pratt Hospital in Baltimore felt that Scott profited more from the treatment than she. Zelda would remain stubbornly silent, refusing to reveal her thoughts and emotions. Then Scott would come to call, and talk freely of his problems, including his sense of guilt.

Nonetheless, Scott could function in the world, however uncertainly, while Zelda could not. It was a distinction she did her best to obliterate. In 1932 she called Dr. Dean Clark (not a psychiatrist) who arrived while Scott was delivering a tirade. He could have him committed, Clark declared, but Scott laid the incident to liquor and insisted that the doctor "could as easily have committed Mencken & half the Balt. Hunt on a Sat. night." Zelda had fooled Dr. Squires the same way, he thought, and tried to convince Dr. Meyer and Dr. Rennie as well that they were treating the wrong person. "I will probably be carried off eventually by four strong guards," he wrote Dr. Meyer in April 1933, "shrieking manicly that after all I was right and she was wrong, while Zelda is followed home by an adoring crowd in an automobile banked with flowers, and offered a vaudeville contract."

Zelda did not recover, of course, but she continued to play the game of self-justification. In the spring of 1938 Scott took her and Scottie on a disastrous trip to Virginia Beach. Scott got drunk, and Zelda persuaded everyone in their corridor of the hotel that he "was a madman." That incident showed him he could never again take care of her. Nor could he care for himself when Zelda was around. The following year, in the fall of 1939, he drank himself into a New York hospital during yet another husband-and-wife "vacation." "I wish," Dr. Carroll wrote him afterwards, "we had you tucked into one of our own beds."

Destructively competitive though they had become when together, neither Scott nor Zelda could forget what once they had meant to each other. They had traveled a long road in tandem— even sharing the same toothbrush on the 1920 cruise of the "Rolling Junk"—and in retrospect the disputes hardly seemed to matter.

Do you remember, before keys turned in the locks,
  When life was a closeup, and not an occasional letter,
That I hated to swim naked from the rocks
  While you liked absolutely nothing better?

Do you remember many hotel bureaus that had
  Only three drawers? But the only bother
Was that each of us argued stubbornly, got mad
  Trying to give the third one to the other.

East, west, the little car turned, often wrong
  Up an erroneous Alp, an unmapped Savoy river,
We blamed each other, wild were our words and strong,
  And, in an hour, laughed and called it liver.

And, though the end was desolate and unkind:
  To turn the calendar at June and find December
On the next leaf; still, stupid-got with grief, I find
  These are the only quarrels that I can remember.

This poem of Scott's, published in March 1935, was moving enough. But for a truly poignant tour of the journey to deprivation, nothing can compete with the letters Zelda wrote her husband from confinement. Only rarely did these letters become assertive: for every time she expressed defiance, there were ten when she rather pitifully thanked him. Forty-six of the more than 300 letters she wrote him began with "Thanks" or "Thank you." Often the thanks were for money. She was the supplicant, he the provider. And she genuinely regretted the things she'd done to hurt them both. "You have never believed me when I said I was sorry—but I am."

Reading through the letters chronologically uncovers an excruciating pattern. In the beginning, Zelda contemplated a full reconciliation, and offered herself up to Scott in tender disguises. The kisses splattering his balcony, she reminded him in one 1930 letter, came "from a lady who was once, in three separate letters, a princess in a high white tower and who has never forgotten her elevated station in life and who is waiting once more for her royal darling." When he came to claim her he would find her changed but still loving:

> We have here a kind of a maniac who seems to have been inspired with erotic aberrations on your behalf. Apart from that she is a person of excellent character, willing to work, would accept a nominal salary while learning, fair complexion, green

eyes would like correspondance with refined young man of your
description with intent to marry. Previous experience unnecessary. Very fond of family life and a wonderful pet to have in
the home. Marked behind the left ear with a slight tendency to
schizophrenia.

These letters were sent from Prangins. Then, while Scott was in
Hollywood and she in Montgomery late in 1931, Zelda took on a
still more abjectly dehumanized persona. "There once upon a time
lived a very lonesome old peasant woman, or maybe it was a faithful
St. Bernard," she wrote him.

> Anyway something very lonesome... had great difficulties
> pushing its thoughts out swiftly enough so they would arrive
> fresh in California. These thoughts were just silly little things
> with practically no sense to them. They were mostly "I love
> you," so one day on the thirteenth of November they went
> walking in the woods and there they met a great big strong
> postman who gave them a letter from El Paso and they all went
> home and married Dudo and loved very happily in the pocket
> of the King of the Roses for ever and ever and ever afterwards.

After her relapse early in 1932, she began to identify her plight
with that of the "crazy people" she saw in Phipps: "a woman's
brother came to pay a visit, I thought how awful and poignant—
that boney casket full of nothing that the man had ever loved and
he was saying that he wanted her to come home again. It made
me feel very sorry. I presume he was addressing his past." That
woman, she came to realize after a series of releases and re-insti-
tutionalizations, was very like herself. "I don't need anything at all
except hope, which I can't find by looking backwards or forwards,"
she wrote Scott at the beginning of one such confinement, "so I
suppose the thing is to shut my eyes."

With eyes shut, she could at least liberate her imagination. From
Highland Hospital near Asheville she wrote Scott a series of "I
wish" letters. Mostly she wished for one of two apparently dissimilar
things: a trip to faraway places or a home of her own. Often she
would write after reading the travel pages of the Sunday newspapers, and plead for journeys—to Cuba or Guatemala or Mexico

City, to France or Greece or Italy—that were somehow mingled
with memories of the past:

> I wish we could spend today by the sea, browning ourselves
> and feeling water-weighted hair flow behind us from a dive. I
> wish our gravest troubles were the summer gnats. I wish we
> were hungry for hot dogs and dopes and it would be nice to
> smell the starch of summer linens and the faint odors of talc in
> blistering bath-houses. . . . We could lie in long citroneuse beams
> of the five o'clock sun on the plage at Juan-les-Pins and hear the
> sound of the drum and piano being scooped out to sea by the
> waves. Dust and alfalfa in Alabama, pines and salt in Antibes,
> the lethal smells of city streets in summer, buttered popcorn
> and axle grease at Coney Island and Virginia Beach—and the
> sick sweet smells of old gardens at night, verbena and phlox or
> night blooming stock—we could see if those are still there.

If they couldn't take trips that would recover their nomadic past,
Zelda implored him, couldn't they have a home of their own? In
all his life Scott Fitzgerald never owned a house or settled in one
spot for longer than a year or two. He even devised a form letter
explaining that his "long delay in answering" correspondence was
because "a pile of letters [was] sidetracked into an answered file
just before I moved from one house to another." The excuse rang
false, but the part about moving was true more often than not. It
was the way he'd been brought up by migratory parents who shifted
frequently between apartments and rented houses. Zelda, on the
contrary, had grown up with a strong sense of place, and was less
well suited to the nomadic life.

At first, to be sure, she had not wanted "rugs and wicker furniture
and a home," since they'd get in the way. "I hate a room without
an open suitcase in it," she commented. "It seems so permanent."
But in 1927, as she watched her husband develop his infatuation
with Lois Moran, she was "*crazy* to own a house" with a "lovely
little Japanese room with pink cherry blossoms" for Scottie and a
garden with lilac trees "like people have in France." However, she
told her daughter with dampened enthusiasm, "Daddy says we
must rent a house first... to see if we are going to like America."
The house they rented was the antebellum mansion Ellerslie, near

Wilmington, Delaware, which functioned more as a site for week-end parties than as a family home.

No roots were sunk at Ellerslie, but Zelda had not given up hoping. The prospect of acquiring a home even cast a silver lining over her 1930 collapse. The "whole disgraceful mess" would be worth it, she wrote, if they stopped drinking because then Scott could finish his novel and they could "have a house with a room to paint and write" in "with friends for Scottie" and "Mondays that were different from Sundays." In 1931, when Scott wrote from Hollywood that he might make as much as $75,000 if his screenplay were produced, Zelda immediately responded, "75,000! Goofo— I would do anything for that! We could build a house with the surplus." She even knew the kind of house: "a great denuded square" painted "all over yellow" with "directoire wall lights with stars."

As prospects for her recovery waned, this rather sophisticated picture-of-a-house became increasingly sentimentalized. "I wish you had a little house with hollyhocks and a sycamore tree and the afternoon sun imbedding itself in a silver tea-pot," she wrote Scott in June 1935. "Scottie would be running about somewhere in white, in Renoir, and you will be writing books in dozens of volumes. And there will be honey still for tea, though the house should not be in Grantchester—" But the way the house or grounds looked did not really matter. "There are so many houses I'd like to live in with you," she added. Couldn't they manage to buy one some-how? "I don't know how you get one but I think if we saved a great many things—stamps and cigar bands, soap wrappers and box-tops we could have it some way."

She was no more willing to give up this dream than the woman in Fitzgerald's story "The Long Way Out," who waits each day for a visit from her husband that can never come. Zelda shared that fancy, too. In one of the many letters from Highland that describe the world outside to signify the one within, she wrote of a rainy afternoon with "abnegatory skies mirrored in the roads" and the houses etched against a silver background. Then the rain turned to snow "and lightly laden branches and a puffed protected world for Sunday. Snow domesticates horizons; the world is a fine white boudoir; the world is cared-for and expensive. I hope always that you'll show up in it soon." With its falling, the snow brought to mind all the things she longed for and did not have: home, boudoir, loving care, money, husband. But all that was fantasy. They could not live together without tearing each other apart, as she knew in times of absolute lucidity. "I want you to be happy," she wrote Scott. If there was any justice he would be happy. Then she signed off:

> Oh, Do-Do
> Do-Do—
> I love you anyway—
> even if there isn't any me or any love or even any life
> I love you

6

The Glittering Things

LOVE PROVIDED Fitzgerald with the emotional crises of his life and the raw material of his fiction. It was not a subject close to the mainstream of American literature. Among his rare antecedents, two very different writers stand out. Theodore Dreiser in his stumbling genius had—especially in *An American Tragedy*—ventured onto the ground Fitzgerald was to explore more thoroughly. This was ground that Henry James, master of awareness and nuance, had already staked out. Fitzgerald recognized the kinship with James. Both of them, he wrote Van Wyck Brooks in 1925, "have to have love as a main concern since our interest lies outside the economic struggle or the life of violence, as conditioned to some extent by our lives from 16–21." What he did not add was that James and himself and Dreiser too were all interested in romantic love as it was complicated and compromised by a given social and financial context. In this respect, the three writers shared an unlikely forerunner in Jane Austen. "I write about Love and Money. What else is there to write about?" Austen had observed. "Everything is either love or money," Fitzgerald remarked. "There is nothing else that counts."

Most authors continually repeat themselves, Fitzgerald knew. "We have two or three great and moving experiences in our lives," he observed, and on the basis of these experiences "we tell our two or three stories—each time in a new disguise—maybe ten times, maybe a hundred, as long as people will listen." One of the two or three stories Fitzgerald told was about the struggle of the poor young man to win the hand of the rich girl. That had always been his own situation. He'd grown up "a poor boy in a rich town; a poor boy in a rich boy's school; a poor boy in a rich man's club at Princeton"—above all, a poor boy in love with a rich girl. "The theme comes up again and again," he said, "because I lived it."

Rudolph Miller in "Absolution" suffers a "furious" attack of shame when he has no money for the church collection box, since Jeanne Brady, in the pew behind him, might notice. As with Rudolph, so with Scott Fitzgerald as a boy: "In church one little girl made him frightfully embarrassed when he didn't have a penny to put in the collection box." And Dick Diver of *Tender Is the Night* suffered through a similar incident in his childhood, long before his marriage to the fabulously rich Nicole. What could happen if you had no money and the girl noticed? At worst: no money, no love. "If you haven't got any money," Philip Dean instructs the hapless Gorden Sterrett in "May Day," "you've got to work and stay away from women."

Sterrett is a weakling who commits suicide after waking from a sodden drunk to find himself rejected by the society girl who used to love him and married to a Jewel of the lower classes. Though he is the only Fitzgerald protagonist driven to this extremity, in many other stories the poor young man engages in unequal combat with a wealthy competitor. "Remember," a precociously cynical Fitzgerald wrote at nineteen, "in all society nine girls out of ten marry for money and nine men out of ten are fools." It did not matter that he himself was not poor in any absolute sense. In competing for the favor of the beautiful rich girl, he thought of himself as very poor indeed.

> Those wealthy goats
> In raccoon coats
>   can wolfe you away from me

as he complained in one jingle. Such levity was rare. He had been badly hurt. "It was one of those tragic loves doomed for lack of money. . . . In the years since then I have never been able to stop wondering where my friends' money came from, nor to stop thinking that at one time a sort of *droit de seigneur* might have been exercised to give one of them my girl."

Fitzgerald rang variations on this theme in his three best novels and in dozens of short stories. These were based, sometimes loosely, sometimes with almost photographic fidelity to the facts, on his pursuit of Ginevra King and Zelda Sayre. Time and again his fiction explored these related yet different relationships: the poor boy spurned by the rich girl, the poor boy put off by the not-so-rich girl until he demonstrates his financial capacities.

The stories he wrote to make the money to win the girl — stories *The Saturday Evening Post* published in 1919 and 1920 — almost always dealt with young love in high society. As early as New Year's Eve 1920, he was complaining to Perkins that he'd "go mad if I have to do another debutante, which is what they want." Readers started a Fitzgerald story not always sure of a happy ending, but confident that he would provide a glimpse of a glamorous social world few of them had ever inhabited. So stereotyped was the social setting that illustrators usually presented his characters as handsome wraithlike creatures in full evening dress, though there might be no reason whatever, on the basis of the story itself, for them to be so togged out. In "The Bowl," the male protagonist is described as customarily wearing tan or soft gray suits with black ties. In the illustrations he's wearing a tuxedo.

The musk of money hung heavy around these early love stories, which usually fell into one of two classifications. One group depicted the success, or seeming success, of the poor young man in wooing the rich girl. In the other group the young man was rejected in his quest or subsequently disappointed.

The trouble with the stories of the first kind is that they are not persuasive. At least subconsciously, Fitzgerald must have realized this, for he often tricked out such tales with fantasy or with outrageous challenges to reader disbelief. "The Offshore Pirate" provides one example. It is — as the first sentence declares — the "unlikely story" of the winning of Ardita Farnam, a yellow-haired embodiment of the golden girl. Ardita is bored by the predictable round of her social life, and eager, so she says, to cast her lot with anyone who will show some imagination. That someone turns out to be Toby Moreland, a rich boy playing at poverty. He attracts her interest by pretending to be a musician who has risen to wealth first by way of his talent, then by stealing the jewels of society matrons. He commandeers Ardita's yacht, but though fascinated she withholds her hand. "What sort of life can you offer me? I don't mean that unkindly, but seriously; what would become of me if the people who want that twenty-thousand dollar reward ever catch up with you?"

It would be different if she were "a little poor girl dreaming over a fence in a warm cow country" and he, newly rich with ill-gotten gains, had come along to astonish her with his munificence. Then she'd stare into the windows of the jewelry store and want the "big oblong watch that's platinum and has diamonds all round the edge" but would decide "it was too expensive and choose one of white gold for a hundred dollars." And he'd say, "Expensive? I should say not!" and "pretty soon the platinum one would be gleaming" on her wrist. She wishes it were that way but it isn't, and so Ardita turns her suitor down—until his identity is revealed at the end, and she finds to her relief that he is both imaginative *and* respectable.

A rich boy might charm his girl by pretending to have been poor, like Toby Moreland and like George Van Tyne in "The Unspeakable Egg," who wins his Fifi by playing the role of a bearded and disheveled roustabout. It did not, of course, work the other way around.

Fitzgerald's tales of rejection and disappointment are more deeply felt, more true to life than those where true love presumably conquers all. The stories of rejection also serve to demonstrate the author's developing maturity of outlook, his disturbing sense that pursuit and/or capture of the golden girl wasn't really worth all the trouble and heartache. He felt anything but philosophical about the matter when he wrote *This Side of Paradise,* however. The section of that novel called "The Debutante"—really a short story in the form of a playlet, with dialogue and stage directions—painfully relives Fitzgerald's rejection by Ginevra King.

When Amory Blaine first meets Rosalind Connage, she describes herself as a commodity: "'Rosalind, Unlimited.' Fifty-one shares, name, good-will, and everything goes at $25,000 a year." Even *before* they meet, she's inquired about his financial status. Nonetheless, though Amory is making a paltry $35 a week, they fall in love and she agrees to marry him.

> "Amory," she whispered, "when you're ready for me I'll marry you."
> "We won't have much at first."
> "Don't!" she cried. "It hurts when you reproach yourself for what you can't give me. I've got your precious self—and that's enough for me."

Mrs. Connage puts a stop to the match. "You've already wasted over two months on a theoretical genius who hasn't a penny to his name," she tells Rosalind sarcastically, "but go ahead, waste your life on him. *I* won't interfere." Both mother and daughter know that Rosalind is extravagant, that Amory's income wouldn't even buy her clothes, and so the rich girl breaks her promise. "I can't, Amory. I can't be shut away from the trees and flowers, cooped up in a little flat, waiting for you." And again, "I don't want to think about pots and kitchens and brooms. I want to worry whether my legs will get slick and brown when I swim in the summer." She marries the rich Dawson Ryder, instead. Her selfishness may seem appalling, but Fitzgerald does not condemn her. In the concluding stage direction, in fact, he assigns her a romantic capacity for feeling akin to his own: "(And deep under the aching sadness that will pass in time, Rosalind feels that she has lost something, she knows not what, she knows not why.)"

In Fitzgerald's fiction of the 1920s, he gradually deromanticized the golden girl and de-emphasized the glory of the quest. At the beginning, Fitzgerald's poor young men concentrated all their drive and ambition on but one goal. Like Dexter Green in "Winter Dreams" (1922), these young men were driven to possess not merely the beautiful rich girl but all she represented. Dexter "wanted not association with glittering things and glittering people—he wanted the glittering things themselves."

To prove himself worthy the young man had to go out and make a financial success. Dexter's money-making ability dramatically transforms his relationship with Judy Jones. On their first dinner date, she confesses that she's had "a terrible afternoon. There was a man I cared about, but this afternoon he told me out of a clear sky that he was poor as a church-mouse." Her interest in him had not been strong enough to stand the shock. Then this dialogue ensues:

> "Let's start right," she interrupted herself suddenly. "Who are you, anyhow?"
>
> For a moment Dexter hesitated. Then:
>
> "I'm nobody," he announced. "My career is largely a matter of futures."
>
> "Are you poor?"
>
> "No," he said frankly. "I'm probably making more money than any man my age in the Northwest. I know that's an obnoxious remark, but you advised me to start right."
>
> There was a pause. Then she smiled and the corners of her mouth drooped and an almost imperceptible sway brought her closer to him, looking up into his eyes.

And then they kiss, her kisses "like charity, creating want by holding back nothing." But Dexter does not win the girl after all. Some years later, when he hears Judy spoken of as "faded" and "a little too old" for her husband, he knows he has lost something precious. "Even the grief he could have borne was left behind in the country of illusion, of youth, of the richness of life, where his winter dreams had flourished."

The loss of romantic illusions provides a central motif in other stories of this period. Jonquil Cary, in "'The Sensible Thing'" (1924), fends off the proposal of George O'Kelly until he is "ready" for her. By this code word—also used by Rosalind Connage to Amory Blaine and Zelda Sayre to Scott Fitzgerald—Jonquil meant that her suitor must first establish himself financially. Until he did, she would remain "nervous" (another code word uttered by both the real Zelda and the fictional Jonquil) about the prospect of marriage. The ambitious O'Kelly strikes out for South America, makes his pile, and returns to claim the girl. But the essential magic has gone. "As he kissed her he knew that though he search through eternity he could never recapture those lost April hours. . . . There are all kinds of love in the world, but never the same love twice."

These ingredients—the unsuccessful quest, the loss of illusions—Fitzgerald blended into his greatest novel. "The whole idea of Gatsby," as he put it, "is the unfairness of a poor young man not being able to marry a girl with money." Gatsby really *is* a poor boy. As a child of poverty Jimmy Gatz grew up with Horatio Alger visions of attaining wealth and happiness and, therefore, the golden girl that Nick Carraway, the voice of Fitzgerald's rational self, can only scoff at. He also is gullible enough to believe that the possession of wealth will enable him to vault over the middle class into a position of social eminence. He does not see—he never sees—that he does not belong in Tom and Daisy Buchanan's world. Fitzgerald sees, all right. He's in the middle class with Nick, looking down at Gatsby and up at the Buchanans with mingled disapproval and admiration, both ways.

Perspective makes all the difference here. As Henry Dan Piper has noted, Fitzgerald invariably wrote about the rich from a middle class point of view. If his work seemed preoccupied with money, that was because money was a preoccupation of the middle class. There stands Fitzgerald outside the ballroom, nose pressed to the window while the dancers swirl about inside. But this is no Stella Dallas, washerwoman, watching her daughter married to the rich boy. For Fitzgerald has been inside the ballroom and hopes to be there again; this is only a dance to which he has not been invited. Then he walks downtown to sneer at the lower classes, who smell bad and talk funny and put on airs when they come into a bit of money. This rather sniffy attitude toward the poor emerges most powerfully in Fitzgerald's first two novels, and survives in *The Great Gatsby* through Nick's snobbery.

What *Gatsby* does, magnificently well, is to show the way love is affected by social class in the United States. One early reviewer complained about Fitzgerald's attributing Gatsby's passion for Daisy to her superior social status. That was nonsense, the reviewer objected: "Daisy might have been a cash girl or a mill hand and made as deep a mark—it is Carmen and Don Jose over again."

But this is not opera, and one lesson of Fitzgerald's book is that love becomes degrading when it roams too far across class lines. Let the fences down and God knows who will start rutting with whom. Tom Buchanan's brutality to Myrtle, together with her pitiful attempt at imitating upper class speech and behavior, make their party and their affair almost entirely sordid. On the surface it seems like the same situation in reverse with Daisy Buchanan and Gatsby. On the day of their reunion after nearly five years, Gatsby shows Daisy his garish house and produces resident pianist Klipspringer for a little afternoon music. Leaping to the conclusion that a casual copulation is imminent, Klipspringer first plays "The Love Nest," then "Ain't We Got Fun?" But he misunderstands. The difference between the two affairs derives from the strength of Gatsby's imagination. He is a parvenu, certainly, and it may be as Nick says that he had no real right to take Daisy since he lets her think he comes from "much the same stratum as herself," but in the meantime he has so idealized her as to make their relationship seem almost chaste.

Daisy Fay she was, and fay she is. She and her friend Jordan Baker do not even observe the laws of gravity. They first appear atop an enormous couch in the Buchanans' living room, "buoyed up as though upon an anchored balloon." Dressed in white, they seem to ripple and flutter in the breeze until the door is shut, the wind is caught, and the balloon and its passengers settle to earth. Money levitates.

Daisy is described: "Her face was sad and lovely with bright things in it, bright eyes and a bright passionate mouth, but there was an excitement in her voice that men who had cared for her found difficult to forget." Over and over Nick Carraway tries to catch the essence of her "low, thrilling voice," the voice that "with its fluctuating, feverish warmth" held Gatsby all through the years, "because it couldn't be overdreamed." Finally Gatsby instructs him:

> "She's got an indiscreet voice," I remarked. "It's full of—" I hesitated.
> "Her voice is full of money," he said suddenly.
> That was it. I'd never understood before. It was full of money—that was the inexhaustible charm that rose and fell in it, the jingle of it, the cymbals's song of it. . . . High in a white palace the king's daughter, the golden girl. . . .

What does Daisy do with the "warm human magic" of her voice? She talks nonsense, she strikes poses, above all she flirts—even with cousin Nick. "I love to see you at my table, Nick. You remind me of a—of a rose, an absolute rose." As the somewhat literal-minded Nick objects, he is not even faintly like a rose. Daisy "was only extemporizing, but a stirring warmth flowed from her, as if her heart was trying to come out to you concealed in one of those breathless, thrilling words."

When Nick calls to invite her to tea, she decides to treat it as an assignation with him.

"Don't bring Tom," I warned her.
"What?"
"Don't bring Tom."
"Who is 'Tom'?" she asked innocently.

On arrival she inquires with an "exhilarating ripple" in her voice, "Is this absolutely where you live, my dearest one?" And then, low into his ear, "Are you in love with me, or why did I have to come alone?" Later, at Gatsby's party, she tells Nick in a voice that's "playing murmurous tricks in her throat" that if he'd like to kiss her any time during the evening, she'd be glad to arrange it. "Just mention my name," she proposes. "Or present a green card. I'm giving out green—"

Daisy feels nothing particularly for Nick. It's just that flirting has become second nature. While Gatsby gazes worshipfully at the green light across Long Island Sound, she gives out green cards, or pretends to. Nick had sensed Daisy's basic insincerity that first evening at the Buchanans when she stagily proclaimed, "Sophisticated—God, I'm sophisticated!" Generally, Daisy stays cool and pretends her emotions. She is offended at Gatsby's party when the moving-picture director very slowly bends toward his Star and kisses her on the cheek—offended "because it wasn't a gesture but an emotion." It is a measure of Gatsby's own powerful love that he can persuade her to contemplate leaving Tom. But when that prospect threatens to touch reality, to become more than a gesture, she slips back into her cocoon of wealth and position. As Tom elaborates on the sources of Gatsby's fortune in the terrible heat of that day at the Plaza, Daisy gives up all heart and substance. Only "that lost voice across the room" remains, begging Tom to stop and for the scene to end.

While Daisy was obviously modeled on Ginevra King, Fitzgerald originally based the figure of Gatsby on a stock manipulator he'd encountered in Great Neck and then let the character gradually change into himself. "Gatsby was never quite real to me," he admitted. "His original served for a good enough exterior until about the middle of the book he grew thin and I began to fill him with my emotional life."

Fitzgerald did not really *know* the model for the early Gatsby, actually or imaginatively, and kept him off center stage until page 47, more than one-fourth of the novel's length. Before his appearance this Gatsby is propped up with rumors. He's the nephew of the Kaiser, it's thought, or he'd been a German spy in the war. One girl has heard that Gatsby went to Oxford, but doubts it. Another has heard that he's killed a man, and believes it. There's a natural letdown when this mystery man turns out to be—so it seems at first—only another *nouveau riche* who drives a too-ornate cream-colored "circus wagon," wears pink suits, and takes unseemly pride in the number and variety of his shirts. He also recites for Nick's benefit a highly improbable tale about his distinguished origins and colorful past, which included—so he says—living "like a young rajah in all the capitals of Europe" while collecting rubies, "hunting big game, painting a little... and trying to forget something very sad that had happened to me long ago." It's all Nick can do to keep from laughing, but the story continues. Gatsby had gone off to war, where he'd tried "very hard" to die but had instead fought so valiantly that "every Allied government" had decorated him.

This Gatsby is almost totally inept in dealing with social situations. His lavish parties are monuments to bad taste and conspicuous display; he thinks them splendid gatherings of the best and brightest. Moreover, he does not know when he is not wanted. Tom Buchanan, Mr. Sloane, and a lady friend stop off at his house during a horseback ride one day, and the lady invites Gatsby and Nick to come to dinner that evening. Nick at once realized that Mr. Sloane opposes this plan and politely declines, but Gatsby, eager to mingle with the plutocrats, accepts. While he's upstairs changing, they ride off.

This Gatsby "represented everything," Nick says, for which he feels "an unaffected scorn." Even when he tells Gatsby, on their last meeting, that he's "worth the whole damn bunch put together," Nick continues to disapprove of him on a social level. So does Fitzgerald. Gatsby has redeeming qualities, however. (If he did not, the novel would amount to nothing more than the most obvious satire.) Parts of his fantastic story turn out to be true. He *had* been a war hero, and has the medal from Montenegro to prove it. He *had* actually attended Oxford—for five months, as a postwar reward for military service, and produces a photograph in evidence. Above all, there was nothing phony or insincere about his dream of Daisy.

The power of Gatsby's imagination made him great. Parvenu though he was, he possessed "an extraordinary gift for hope, a romantic readiness" such as Nick had never found in anyone else. He even brought part of his dream to life. "The truth was that Jay Gatsby of West Egg, Long Island, sprang from his Platonic conception of himself." The seventeen-year-old James Gatz invented just the kind of Jay Gatsby that a poor boy from the cold shores of Lake Superior was likely to invent: a man of fabulous wealth, like the Dan Cody who lifted him from the lake and installed him on his dazzling yacht. In the service of Cody and Mammon and by whatever devious means, Gatsby had won through to wealth. To fulfill his dream it remained only to capture the golden girl, the king's daughter (the *Kings'* daughter) he had idealized in his mind. He had come close during the war, but Daisy had married Tom (and produced a little girl in whose existence Gatsby can barely bring himself to believe, until he is confronted with her in reality) and so sullied the purity of the dream.

To restore his ideal, Gatsby attempts to obliterate time and return to that moment in Louisville when as they kissed "Daisy blossomed for him like a flower and the incarnation was complete." Nick warns Gatsby that he cannot repeat the past, but he cries incredulously, "Why of course you can!" All that's required is for Daisy to tell Tom that she had never for one moment loved him, that she had never loved anyone but Gatsby. Then the impurity would be scrubbed away, and they could "go back to Louisville

and be married from her house—just as if it were five years ago."
But Daisy fails him. In the confrontation scene at the Plaza, she
cannot bring herself to repudiate Tom entirely.

> "Oh, you want too much!" she cried to Gatsby. "I love you
> now—isn't that enough? I can't help what's past." She began to
> sob helplessly. "I did love him once—but I loved you too."
> Gatsby's eyes opened and closed.
> "You loved me *too?*" he repeated.

Even then, Gatsby refuses to give up his dream. "I don't think she
ever loved him," he tells Nick the next morning. Tom had bullied
her into saying that she had. Or perhaps, he concedes, she'd "loved
him for a minute, when they were first married—and loved me
more even then, do you see?" In any case, Gatsby adds, "It was
just personal."

For Gatsby, the dream itself mattered far more than the person
in whom the dream found expression. Toward the end Nick keeps
insisting that Gatsby must have given up his dream, but there is
no evidence that he did. He was still waiting for Daisy's phone call
when the man from the ashheaps came calling instead.

Fitzgerald transferred to Gatsby both a situation from his own
emotional life—the unsuccessful pursuit of the golden girl—and
an attitude toward that quest. Like Gatsby and the sad young men
of his best love stories, Fitzgerald was remarkable for the "colossal
vitality" of his capacity for illusion. "I am always searching for the
perfect love," he told Laura Guthrie in 1935. Was that because
he'd had it as a young man? "No, I never had it," he answered. "I
was searching then too." Such a search worked to prevent him from
committing himself fully to any one person, for, as common sense
dictated and his fiction illustrated, there could be no such thing as
the perfect love, up close.

Only at a distance could Fitzgerald idealize the girl of his dreams.
Anthony Patch, in *The Beautiful and Damned*, looks out his window
at a girl in a red negligee, drying her hair on a nearby roof. He
feels sure the girl must be beautiful, but she rises and he has a
better view of her: "fat, full thirty-five, utterly undistinguished."
The attraction derived from "her distance, not a rare and precious

distance of soul but still distance, if only in terrestrial yards." The worst disillusionment of all awaited Fitzgerald's fictional *alter egos* who actually win the girl and then discover, as in stories like "Gretchen's Forty Winks" and "The Adjuster," that they have married creatures of exquisite irresponsibility and selfishness. For Fitzgerald as for Emily Dickinson, "It was the Distance—/Was Savory—"

It is easy enough to find flaws in Rosalind Connage or Daisy Buchanan or any other fictional embodiment of the golden girl, but clearly Fitzgerald's attitude placed them in an untenable position. His young men either live in an eternal romantic dream, nursing the sorrow of their unrequited love for the magical girl in the distance, or they actually capture her and are inevitably disillusioned. It's a no-win situation for the girl, either way. For the young men, however, the sorrow-dream is preferable. Dexter Green covets his "winter dreams" because they cannot be realized, while the summer variety might come true. He does not regret losing Judy Jones nearly so much as he regrets losing his dream of her.

As John Berryman, one of Fitzgerald's first and best critics, realized, what Fitzgerald most valued was "a beauty and intensity of attachment, which his imagination required should be attachment to something inaccessible." Anthony Patch laments that "you can't have *any*thing, you can't have anything at *all*." Desire was "like a sunbeam skipping here and there about a room. It stops and gilds some inconsequential object, and we poor fools try to grasp it—but when we do the sunbeam moves on to something else, and you've got the inconsequential part, but the glitter that made you want it is gone—." Whether gilded by the sun or the glow of riches, the girl did not really matter. Her glitter did.

For all the futility and evanescence of their quest, at least Fitzgerald's poor young men could dream. His one rich boy—"The Rich Boy" of the story he wrote immediately after *The Great Gatsby*—is deprived of even that consolation. Anson Hunter's money confers on him a fatal incapacity for illusion. Understanding too soon and too well why people pay him deference, he suspects everyone's motives and resolves to stand aloof. Like the Buchanans, Anson feels no compunction about behaving badly. Breaking Dolly Karger's heart bothers him no more than getting drunk at a dinner party. He will not apologize in either case. Anson pays for these privileges, though. Not only is he incapable of idealizing any woman, he is also incapable of love. He cannot give, only receive. But how he receives!

What Anson Hunter seems to require of women, the story's narrator speculates at the end, is that they "spend their brightest, freshest, rarest hours to nurse and protect that superiority he cherished in his heart." From these women he takes whatever contribution of emotion he can elicit. He becomes an emotional cannibal, a hunter in fact as in name. Fitzgerald underscores the point by emphasizing Anson's increasing girth. He is tall and thick-set to begin with, next a little heavy without being definitely stout, and then—progressively—Anson's shirt damps "upon his portly body in the deep heat" as he is about to accept Dolly's love; he is "rather stout" in the Plaza bar where he can find no companions; his "increasing bulk" is obvious under a fairly tight cutaway coat on his last meeting with Paula Legendre and her husband.

In "The Rich Boy" (1926), money militates against true love, since those who possess too much of it "lose the capacity to feel for others." Later stories like "The Swimmers" (1929), "The Bridal Party" (1930), and "Babylon Revisited" (1931) demonstrate the impotence of money to purchase either happiness or love. What money did do, in Fitzgerald's mature view of the issue, was to facilitate corruption. The poor, overestimating its value, would cheat or steal or (like Dick Diver) compromise their integrity to acquire it. The rich, like the Buchanans, "smashed up things and creatures and then retreated back into their money or their vast carelessness, or whatever it was that kept them together, and let other people clean up the mess they had made." Fitzgerald never portrayed the rich sympathetically in his fiction.

Yet this was the writer Hemingway took to task for romanticizing the rich as "a special glamorous race." To illustrate this point, which Hemingway introduced into the opening paragraphs of "The Snows of Kilimanjaro," he told a now-famous anecdote about how Scott Fitzgerald had once said, "The very rich are different from you and me," and someone had replied, "Yes, they have more money." Writing with remarkable self-control to his former friend, Fitzgerald objected that riches had never fascinated him, "unless combined with the greatest charm or distinction." But he did not deny that he thought the very rich different from the rest of us. He knew they were. (Hemingway knew it too, and built *A Moveable Feast* around the difference.) They were different in character, since they were brought up spoiled, selfish, soft, egotistical, and irresponsible. If Jimmy Worthington had the bad luck to run over someone while drunk, he knew his father would "buy off the family and keep him out of jail."

The rich were also different in having been granted the leisure to accomplish good and worthwhile things in politics, or art, or simply living well. The trouble was that the American rich did not realize that leisure was a privilege, not a right, "and that a privilege always implies a responsibility." In England, the rich ran the government; in America, they dissipated their time away. Fitzgerald knew very few rich people who, he thought, had managed to use the gift of leisure well. His total list of rich friends ran to only three names, he wrote Edmund Wilson in the mid-1930s: Tommy Hitchcock and Gerald and Sara Murphy. The Murphys and Fitzgerald became close friends on the Riviera during the mid-1920s. In doggerel Fitzgerald joshed the Murphys about their interest in art, but he always liked and respected them.

> Dopey Sal and Penthouse Jerry
> Pixilated and contrary
> Took the money that the boss
> Wrang from toilers in Mark Cross
> Spent it—oh that wealthy set!—
> On the galleries Lafayette
>
> Still and all I call you "Pal"
> Penthouse Jerry, Dopey Sal

Nonetheless, Fitzgerald felt uncomfortable around the Murphys and often acted outrageously at their parties. Their easy social self-assurance may have disturbed Fitzgerald, who invariably thought himself on trial. When he needed a small loan to pay for Scottie's tuition at Miss Walker's school in 1939, he hesitated before asking the Murphys. It was not that he feared they'd turn him down, for he knew they wouldn't. He simply did not want to confess his poverty to them. Sara Murphy had once seen him chew up hundred-franc notes in a Paris taxicab.

Fitzgerald's attitude toward his own money betrayed more Gatsbyism than Murphyism. "It is the custom now," he wrote during the Depression, "to look back [on] the boom days with a disapproval that approaches horror. But it had its virtues, that old boom. . . . These eyes have been hallowed by watching a man order champagne for his two thousand guests, by listening while a woman ordered a whole staircase from the greatest sculptor in the world, by seeing a man tear up a good check for eight hundred thousand dollars." The Murphys spent their inherited money tastefully, and Fitzgerald admired them for it. But he spent his own income, earned by writing stories and novels, as recklessly and ostentatiously as possible.

"Money and alcohol," Scottie Fitzgerald Smith observed, "were the two great adversaries" her father battled all his days. As if to make his actual earnings seem the more impressive—and impressive they were—Fitzgerald exaggerated the extent of his initial poverty. In the opening paragraph of "Early Success" (later cut out of the 1939 essay), he insisted that he had been "both richly poor, which means a crazy state of large earnings, large expenditures and larger debts, and poorly poor which means that you know which shoe has the cardboard in it but hope nobody else does." For a brief time at the start of his writing career in 1919, Fitzgerald may have walked about New York with cardboard in his shoes, but mostly he was "richly poor."

According to his ledger, he made over $400,000 from 1919 to 1936. At the peak of his popularity as a writer of fiction for mass market magazines, Fitzgerald received $4,000 per story from *The Saturday Evening Post*. He also earned as much as $1,250 a week during his last years in Hollywood. In 1938 MGM paid him a total of $58,750. Fitzgerald made a fortune from writing. He also spent it all.

Where did the money go? If Fitzgerald were to go over his expenses "with some kind of a celestial bookkeeper," Fitzgerald's agent Harold Ober believed, he'd discover that much of the money had been spent on things that brought him no return at all. Or no

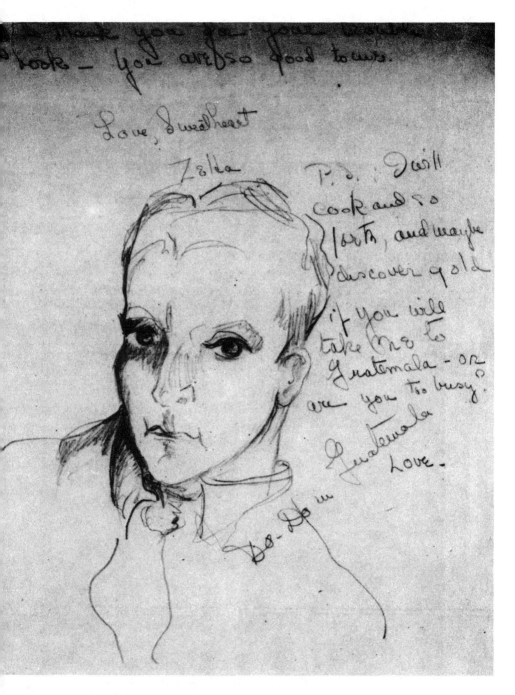

Zelda's sketch of Scott, with a poignant appeal

Sara Murphy at 19: she liked—and scolded—Fitzgerald.

tangible return, anyway. Unlike Gatsby, he did not buy an imitation Hotel de Ville on Long Island. Nor did he ever own a car to compare with Gatsby's cream-colored monstrosity. Fitzgerald did not display the things money can buy. He displayed the money itself. In the first flush of financial success, he sallied forth onto the streets of New York with $20, $50, $100 bills poking out of his vest and coat pockets. For the benefit of grateful bellhops, he kept a plate of money on a table in his hotel room. At restaurants, he sometimes tipped more than the bill. In France, his pockets were always full of "damp little wads of hundred-franc notes that he dribbled out behind him...the way some women do Kleenex." If anything, Zelda was even more extravagant. Money went through her fingers like water. They were headed for catastrophe, Alex McKaig warned them as early as 1920. He was right.

7

War Between the Sexes

THE COURSE of true love does not run smooth in Fitzgerald's fiction. In all his work he created no lovers whose emotional attachment was honest, mutual, and permanent, no unions in which partners equally shared burdens and blessings. Instead, they engage in competition. During courtship his young men and women vie for dominance; once they are married, their struggle becomes fiercer. This pattern closely followed that of his own experience, and there is no blinking the fact that Fitzgerald was among the most autobiographical of authors. The situations and characters sometimes take on disguises, but in his best fiction he wrote about himself, and above all about his own feelings. As Wilfred Sheed has observed, Fitzgerald was one of those writers "who like the opposite sex but don't trust it an inch." His fiction portrayed sexual relationships as potentially incendiary, and uncovered some of his own burns.

In stories of childhood and adolescence, Fitzgerald treated the conflict between the sexes more as a game than a dangerous encounter. *This Side of Paradise* illustrates the point. In a pre-puberty confrontation, Amory Blaine manages to kiss Myra St. Claire and then, seized with revulsion, humiliates her by refusing to do it again. Several years later, Amory as a Princeton sophomore pits his skills against those of Isabelle Borgé, an accomplished flirt visiting Minnesota for the Christmas holidays. In this scene, modeled on Fitzgerald's first meeting with Ginevra King, Amory takes

116

the initiative at once by remarking, "You're my dinner partner, you know. We're all coached for each other." At this stage Isabelle begins to "lose the leadership," and she suffers another setback when Amory piques her curiosity with his old gambit, "I've got an adjective that just fits you." Then Isabelle begins to assert herself. If he has an adjective for her, it is she who encourages the after-dinner rendezvous where she may hear it in private. Others burst in just before the moment of consummation—consummation by kiss, for Fitzgerald's teen-age lovers—and so nothing happens. Neither of them is defeated, and both imagine themselves in love.

When they next meet for a weekend of parties at Princeton and her parents' house, matters proceed swimmingly until, during an embrace, one of Amory's shirt studs makes a telltale mark—"a little blue spot about the size of a pea"—on her neck. Isabelle is frantic, and when Amory does not sympathize properly, she refuses to kiss him. Though he hasn't "an ounce of real affection" for her, Amory wants to kiss Isabelle, "kiss her a lot, because then he knew he could leave in the morning and not care." Not kissing her "would interfere vaguely with his idea of himself as a conqueror. It wasn't dignified to come off second best, *pleading*, with a doughty warrior like Isabelle." Predictably, they argue, with Isabelle, who's annoyed by Amory's insisting on analyzing every little emotion, holding firm. To save face, the unkissed Amory cuts the weekend short and leaves early the next morning.

It was a heady game these young competitors were playing, Fitzgerald realized while watching Scottie grow up. Life promises so much "to a pretty girl between the ages of sixteen and twenty-five," he wrote in 1938, "that she never quite recovers from it." Unless sobered by a flock of children, she was "liable to go on seeking the intensity of that game of playing with men. None of our colleges have succeeded in inventing anything to compete with the kind of love that doesn't have to be paid for with responsibility." But as in all games someone had to lose, someone had to pay. If they played too long even the Isabelles and Rosalinds of yesteryear were sure to be defeated. Recently, Fitzgerald had run into two such belles of his time "now ravaged by dope."

Once women stopped playing games and settled down, however, Fitzgerald usually depicted them as ruling the roost. Married women did not have to be beautiful to dominate their men. "Women with receding chins and shapeless noses go about in broad daylight saying 'Do this!' and 'Do that!' and all the men, even those of great wealth, obey implicitly." America was a woman's country, Fitzgerald thought. "No Englishman would endure one-eighth of what an American takes from his wife." To Anthony Patch, it seemed as if "all the distress he had ever known, the sorrow and the pain" had been caused by women. He determines not to marry, and in support of his resolution tells the parable of the Chevalier O'Keefe, an Irishman exiled to France in the last days of chivalry. O'Keefe has a debilitating weakness for the opposite sex. For twenty years women have "hated him, used him, bored him, aggravated him, sickened him, spent his money, made a fool of him—in brief, as the world has it, loved him." To escape his obsession, O'Keefe becomes a monk. Mounting his tower of Chastity, he takes one last look at the world he is renouncing. At just that moment a peasant girl below lifts her skirt to adjust a garter, O'Keefe leans out too far to get a better view, and so falls to "hard earth and eternal damnation." The poor Chevalier could not help himself. Neither could Anthony, who rapidly gives up his bachelorhood when he meets the bewitching Gloria Gilbert.

There were two methods men might adopt to wrest dominance from their wives. If they were strong enough, they could assert their wills so powerfully as to brook no objection. Hamilton Rutherford in "The Bridal Party" makes it clear in advance who will run his marriage. So does Tommy Barban in *Tender Is the Night* and Philippe in the "Count of Darkness" stories Fitzgerald wrote after completing that novel. But these men were modeled on Ernest Hemingway or Tommy Hitchcock, not on himself. Fitzgerald's own way of resistance involved a more subtle procedure, as an entry in his notebooks indicates. "One advantage of politeness," according to his note, "is to be able to deal with women on their own grounds, to please or to torture the enemy, as it may prove necessary. And not to fire random shots and flowers from the pure male camp many miles away."

The references to the enemy and to gunfire are not accidental. What had begun as a fairly harmless game had become, for the

Fitzgerald of the late 1920s and early 1930s, a deadly serious battle. In his most complicated and interesting novel, this battle between the sexes escalates to full-scale warfare.

The central character in *Tender Is the Night* (1934) is Dick Diver, a young man of middle-class origins who attends Yale and Oxford, rapidly becomes a leading psychologist, and, while practicing his profession in Zurich, meets and marries one of his patients, the lovely, troubled, and immensely rich Nicole Warren. As a girl Nicole had been seduced by her father, and Diver, a combination doctor and husband, works to restore her to full mental health. In the process of making her whole, he loses most of his own vitality. Early in the novel Diver is attracted to a young movie actress, Rosemary Hoyt, and the progress of their affair also traces Diver's decline. At the end Nicole determines to divorce Dick and marry soldier-of-fortune Tommy Barban. Now that he has transferred his strength to her, Diver accepts her decision and simply fades away.

The novel is rife with military references. On several occasions Diver is compared to General Grant, another man who came out of obscurity and retreated back into it. He is sentimental about past wars. On a trip to Thiepval, Diver characterizes the World War I battle there as "a love battle... the last love battle." Seeing a group of gold-star mothers in Paris, come to mourn for their dead, Diver is carried back in memory to his father's knee and his story (Edward Fitzgerald's story, too) of riding with Mosby's cavalry in the Civil War. He is even saddened by a parade of German World War I veterans in Munich.

Men had once expended their energies and their lives on grander causes. Dick, however, confines his strategic efforts to the social front, brilliantly organizing parties "as dependent on supplies of attention as an infantry battalion is dependent on rations," bestowing on others "carnivals of affection" he later looks back on "as a general might gaze upon a massacre he had ordered to satisfy an impersonal blood lust."

Dick is armed with intelligence and charm for the struggle between the sexes. It is not enough. Rosemary is virtually impervious to defeat, "protected by a double sheath of her mother's armor and her own." Economically, she is reminded by her mother, a woman who has outlasted two soldier-husbands, Rosemary is "a boy, not a girl." Nicole is similarly powerful. Her principal weapon—besides her beauty—is wealth, and she uses it.

At one stage of their marriage the Divers had presented such a facade of harmony ("Dicole," they called themselves to signify the union) as to drive the militaristic Tommy Barban back to actual warfare. "When I'm in a rut," he tells Rosemary, "I come to see the Divers, because then I know that in a few weeks I'll want to go to war." Yet under the surface tensions were building from the start, when Nicole virtually forced Dick to kiss her on the mountain slopes of Switzerland, so dissolving the doctor-patient barrier, and then thought, "Oh, wasn't it wonderful! I've got him, he's mine" while cannons boomed across the lake to break up hail-bearing clouds and to symbolize, as they do on other occasions, a crucial incident in the novel. By the time Rosemary comes into their lives, Nicole is steeled for combat and Dick has sensed this happening. "Though he thought she [Nicole] was the most attractive human creature he had ever seen, though he got from her everything he needed, he scented battle from afar, and subconsciously he had been hardening and arming himself, hour by hour." He is not hard enough, however, to resist the combined lure of beauty and wealth. He drinks, he lets his work slide, he becomes increasingly self-indulgent, while Nicole, "wanting to own him, wanting him to stand still forever, encouraged any slackness on his part." Diver had somehow "permitted his arsenal," the narrator comments, "to be locked up in the Warren safety-deposit vaults."

Only with an understanding that the war between the sexes constitutes the pervasive theme of *Tender Is the Night* does the extraordinary violence of the book make sense. Here among wealthy expatriates in the fashionable resorts of Europe, where one would least expect them, occur the shootings, stabbings, beatings, duels, and brawls that function symbolically to underscore the theme. Similarly, the device of indicating turning points in the plot by gunfire takes on an added significance.

In the war of the novel Nicole wins through in the end, while Dick Diver struggles and eventually succumbs. Things have always come too easily to him. As "Lucky Dick" he coasted through college and medical school, established himself quickly as a psychologist, and married a rich and beautiful wife. But along the way he has acquired a debilitating weakness: he cannot do without love.

He wants, so he tells Franz Gregorovius during their early days together at Dr. Dohmler's clinic in Zurich, "to be a good psychologist—maybe to be the greatest one that ever lived." He also wants to be good and kind and brave and wise. But above all he wants to be loved. To that end, he has developed the power of "arousing a fascinating and uncritical love" among all save the "tough-minded and perennially suspicious." So, when he senses Rosemary becoming "critical" and Nicole "tough-minded" enough to fall out of love with him, he is driven to seek the adoration of others. Soon he finds himself "in love with every pretty woman" he sees, but his own power of attraction is waning and fewer and fewer of them respond. Finally, he is reduced to attracting young girls.

Actually, Diver's conquests are almost always of those much younger than himself. Nicole could hardly avoid falling in love with him, a combination doctor and father-replacement figure ten years her senior. Rosemary succumbs to his charm with the dew still on her, not quite eighteen to Dick's thirty-four. And there are others.

The Divers go to Gstaad for the skiing, where Nicole suggests to Dick, who has turned an ankle and is loafing away the days, that he "meet some of these ickle durls and dance with them in the afternoon." Dick insists that he doesn't like "ickle durls" who smell of "castile soap and peppermint." It's a "dangerous subject," Doctor Diver realizes: he is careful to "stare far over the heads of young maidens."

The subject is dangerous because Nicole knows—from her own experience and from that of Rosemary (who played the lead in "Daddy's Girl")—of Dick's appeal for young girls, and she is prepared to become, quite literally, insanely jealous. Besides, Dick has in fact been contemplating a flirtation with one of the peppermint girls. Even as he, Franz, and Baby Warren, Nicole's sister, are exploring the possibility of opening a clinic, Dick looks and speaks with half his attention on the "special girl" who may be listening, who is picking up something from the floor, who is tying her sled to a sleigh outside.

This seemingly inconsequential scene foretells Nicole's subsequent attempt, in the throes of jealous rage, to kill herself, Dick, and the children. Her jealousy is aroused by a letter from a former patient who accuses Doctor Diver of having seduced her young daughter (Dick is old enough to be the girl's father). The letter, Dick tells Nicole, is "deranged," but he is not entirely blameless in the matter, for on one occasion "he had let the girl, a flirtatious little brunette, ride into Zurich with him, at her request," and had that evening kissed her in "an idle, almost indulgent way." When the girl tried to carry things further, Dick "was not interested," perhaps because he had already made the conquest. Nicole, however, had seen the way "that little dark girl" looked at her husband and was prepared to believe the worst. She has, after all, learned a bitter lesson of her own about young girls and older men. Dick has provoked her jealousy very indulgently indeed.

Dick Diver decides, after Nicole's attempt to drive their car off a cliff, that he requires "a leave of abstinence" (so Franz puts it). The subsequent trip becomes a journey of deterioration. He travels alone, dreaming on the train to Munich of "the peasant girl near Savona with a face as green and rose as the color of an illuminated missal," attracted despite himself in Innsbruck to a girl stopping at his hotel ("God," he thinks, "I might as well go back to the Riviera and sleep with Janice Caricamento or the Wilburhazy girl"), and suffering at the hands of women in Rome a series of humiliations.

It is in Rome that Dick and Rosemary finally consummate "what had begun with a childish infatuation on a beach," but there is not much pleasure in the consummation, since Rosemary is now in command. Dick cannot stop asking about her adventures with men during the past four years, and she is repelled by his unjustified jealousy ("I've slept with six hundred and forty men—if that's the answer you want"). She determines when and how they will make love. She takes Dick along to the movie set one day, and buys him lunch the next. Finally, she breaks off the affair with the news that she is half-engaged to the Italian actor Nicotera, whom Dick calls a "spic." She saves her last evening in Rome for Diver, but by then he is disillusioned and angry, hating Rome as the place where his dream of Rosemary died, and he goes on to abject drunkenness, an unsuccessful attempt to pick up a young English girl, a disgraceful brawl with taxi drivers, and jail.

When Baby Warren finally secures his release from the Roman jail, Doctor Diver has lost his dignity and, she believes, any moral superiority that he, as guardian of the skeleton in the family closet, had formerly possessed. A crowd of Italians boos and hisses as he walks toward freedom. They think Dick has "raped and slain a five-year-old child." It is a case of mistaken identity, but the incident is suggestive symbolically. After Nicole dismisses Dick, he practices general medicine in one small town after another in upstate New York. He is, Nicole hears, "much admired by the ladies," but is forced to leave at least one town when he becomes "entangled with a girl who worked in a grocery store." Fitzgerald does not reveal how old she is, and he does not have to.

Despite what happens to Dick Diver, Fitzgerald still believed that it was a man's world and that women could not directly usurp their position of leadership. The point is driven home forcefully in the most obviously autobiographical section of the novel. An exceptionally pretty American painter, thirty years old, comes to Diver's clinic in Switzerland and is there transformed by eczema into "a living, agonizing sore." The situation exactly parallels that of Zelda, trying to establish herself as a ballet dancer and then undergoing terrible attacks of eczema. After some preliminary sparring, the distressed artist locates the cause of her troubles.

> "I'm sharing the fate of the women of my time who challenged men to battle."
> "To your vast surprise it was just like all battles," he answered, adopting her formal diction.
> "Just like all battles." She thought this over. "You pick a set-up, or else win a Pyrrhic victory, or you're wrecked and ruined— you're a ghostly echo from a broken wall."
> "You are neither wrecked nor ruined," he told her. "Are you quite sure you've been in a real battle?"
> "Look at me!" she cried furiously.
> "You've suffered, but many women suffered before they mistook themselves for men."

The patient is suffering for having challenged men to battle. Doctor Diver attempts to minimize the gravity of his patient's struggle: Is she sure she's been in a real battle? But he knows she's right. In the course of three nights' vigil by her bed, Diver comes to love "the scabbed anonymous woman-artist," for he recognizes in her someone like himself, marked for defeat in the war between the sexes. The artist was doomed because she openly issued a declaration of hostilities. His lover-enemies were different. They worked from within, covertly.

Nicole Warren, Rosemary Hoyt, Mary North: In background they represented "the enormous flux of American life," yet shared common ground in their attitude toward men. "Their point of resemblance to each other and their difference from so many American women, lay in the fact that they were all happy to exist in a man's world—they preserved their individuality through men and not by opposition to them." They were marvelously adaptable creatures, more dangerous to men because not officially recognized as opponents.

Regarded autobiographically, *Tender Is the Night* represents the dark side of what might have been. In Fitzgerald's depiction of the war between the sexes, what was more or less innocent fun in 1920 became the most deadly of intramarital conflicts by 1934. The change reflected his own experience, with significant variations. Fitzgerald did not marry into money and become swallowed up like a gigolo by wealth. Nor did he crack under the strain of combat with the unstable woman he did marry. Yet in at least two important respects—the loss of vitality, the compulsion to attract women—Dick Diver's ills were also Fitzgerald's. He was the survivor, but in such wars no one emerged unscathed. Even the winners were losers.

8

Running Amuck

"As to women," Father Sigourney Webster Fay warned Fitzgerald at Princeton, "it is not a convention that holds you back as you think, but an instinct that if you once begin you will run amuck." That prospect may have amused the undergraduate, but Father Fay was right. Like Gatsby, like Diver, like the young Terrence of "That Kind of Party," Fitzgerald became a fool for love. Twenty years later he very nearly did run amuck.

In signing letters or inscribing books to women, Fitzgerald used to call himself "Your Chattel," a curious and seemingly inappropriate phrase that conveyed no less than the truth: that he was a virtual slave to his need to attract nearly every woman he met.

> Scott Fitzgerald so they say
>   Goes a-courting night and day

So reads a notebook entry and so he did, especially after the Fitzgeralds' estrangement and Zelda's illness kept husband and wife apart.

In Baltimore he made sexual overtures to Fluff Beckwith MacKie and to Margaret Turnbull. During 1934 the relationship between Dorothy Parker and himself reached its climax. In late June of that year he went to New York, where he spent a wild night on the town with John O'Hara and a "crazy week" at the Plaza with a woman who was touring with "the four Yale acrobats." When drinking, apparently, he could not stop pursuing women. In the summer of 1935 this propensity got completely out of hand. "Women and liquor take up so much time and get you into so much trouble," he wrote Arnold Gingrich in May. "I have always been woman crazy," he wrote H.L. Mencken in August. The intervening months were spent demonstrating the truth of these observations.

There were good reasons for Fitzgerald to go through a period of reckless womanizing at that time. His drinking was out of control. *Tender Is the Night,* his too-long-in-progress novel, had come out the previous year without achieving the financial or critical success he had counted on. And by the end of 1934 it had become clear that Zelda could not live permanently outside the boundaries of one institution or another. Scott required reassurance about himself as a writer and a man, and now was liberated from one source of restraint. "What I gave up for Zelda was women," he'd written Dr. Oscar Forel, the head psychiatrist at Prangins Clinic in Switzerland, in 1930, "and it wasn't easy in the position my success gave me."

For whatever reason, women were attracted to Scott Fitzgerald, though not so many as he liked to claim when drinking. "There are no good women," he once said. "When better women are made," he declared in his notebooks, "I will make them." He boasted about the number of his conquests (20, he told a woman friend in 1935; 100, he told a male acquaintance the same year). Some of these were clearly imaginary. In the late 1930s he suggested that John O'Hara invite two movie stars to a party the O'Haras were having for him in Hollywood, with the strong implication that he had made love to both of them. That, according to O'Hara, was an exaggeration. "Well, he had laid one of them, but not the other, and the one he laid he had laid in her dressing-room but not at home. He did not have a real affair with her." To Laura Guthrie—his amanuensis and (at first) worshipful admirer during the summer of 1935 in Asheville—he related a series of tales that challenged credulity. He had slept with one girl from Montgomery two nights before her marriage, and she winked at him walking down the aisle. Dorothy Gish had tried to seduce him, without success, a year ago. Hamilton Basso's wife had made a pass at him last night at dinner. He could see the headlines now, he told Laura: "Old Roué Taken in Love Nest!" Mrs. Guthrie did not believe all his yarns. She thought the idea of women chasing men and trying to "make them perform" ran contrary to nature. Yet she could not doubt the evidence of her own feelings, or of the intrigue swirling around her.

For nearly three months in the summer of 1935, Laura Guthrie listened to everything Scott Fitzgerald had to say. Then she went home and wrote it down, and because she did and because she served as his confidante and co-conspirator, it is possible to reconstruct that dangerous time more fully than any other in Fitzgerald's life. In September, he collapsed, and not only from drink. "My life has a cycle," he told her, "work, drink, love." If he had enough money, it would be drink and love all the time.

From the evidence of his ledger, with its notes on each month's activities, it is clear that Fitzgerald devoted much of 1935 to the pursuit of women. The ledger notes little significant work prior to "The Crack-Up" articles written in October and December. Instead, the entries speak of women sought and sometimes won, including—to list them chronologically—Elizabeth (Lemmon), Nora (Flynn), Atlanta Girl (a mystery), Beatrice (Dance), Bert (Barr), and Margaret Case (Harriman). Together with the drinking, it made for a full programme.

The beautiful, cultivated, and well-bred Elizabeth Lemmon was the platonic love of Maxwell Perkins's life. Fitzgerald met her at a dinner party in Perkins' home in March 1934, then in July of that year accompanied Perkins on a weekend visit to Welbourne, Elizabeth's handsome antebellum home in the hunt country of Virginia. Fitzgerald was predictably impressed by the "spacious grace" of the house and by its romantic memento of the War Between the States: a windowpane where the Gallant Pelham, a Confederate hero, had scratched his name and the year (1864) with a diamond ring the morning of the day he died in combat. He put that detail into a story called "Her Last Case," which ran in the November 3, 1934, *Saturday Evening Post*. And he pleased Elizabeth and her Virginia friends by concocting a fantasy about Appomattox in reverse, with Grant surrendering to Lee.

In return, Elizabeth asked him down again, and Fitzgerald—touching base with Perkins—wondered if Max could join him in such a pilgrimage late in August. Max could not, so Fitzgerald went to Virginia alone, more than once in the fall of 1934. Perkins knew about these visits and approved of them, for he thought that Elizabeth's sprightly wit and good sense, to say nothing of her beauty, might have a calming effect on Fitzgerald, if she could persuade him to work instead of to play. That was not easy, for when in Virginia Fitzgerald assumed the role of the gentleman novelist among the gentry and refused even to read galleys. Then, uncomfortable in the part, he drank too much and managed to offend several of Miss Lemmon's friends.

Fitzgerald may have misinterpreted Elizabeth Lemmon's interest in him. Between September 1934 and April 1935 (when the entry reads "Good-bye to Elizabeth") her name appears nine times in his ledger, more often than that of anyone else. After she closed up her Virginia house and moved to Baltimore for the winter, they dined together on several occasions. Scott invited her to meet Gertrude Stein when Stein swept through Baltimore at the turn of the year. He called Elizabeth up to tell her how much he liked John Peale Bishop's novel, *Act of Darkness*. Throughout he seems to have considered her a potential, though not an actual, conquest. "This *used* to be Max Perkins' girl," he said when he introduced her to Archibald MacLeish, implying that she was now *his* girl. "But my God," Miss Lemmon objected, "after knowing Max Perkins, how could anyone be Scott's mistress!" Her interest in Fitzgerald stemmed largely from his being one of Max's authors. She entertained him in Middleburg just as she entertained Thomas Wolfe, another prominent member of the Perkins/Scribner's stable. Wolfe behaved with more dignity than Fitzgerald, Elizabeth thought. "Scott's inferiority complex made him always the showoff," she said, and especially with women. Perkins knew all about that. He had seen Fitzgerald make grandstand passes at his wife and one of his daughters. "Of course," he said with a wry smile, "Scott thinks all women are in love with him." He exaggerated. Fitzgerald only *talked* as if that were true.

Certainly he talked that way about Nora Langhorne Flynn, the second of his romantic attachments in 1935. Fitzgerald made repeated visits to Tryon, North Carolina, where Nora and her husband Maurice (Lefty) lived, during that year: in February, at mid-summer, in October, in December. He also saw Nora in New York in March. Nora Flynn was an attractive, vivacious woman, part of whose appeal for Fitzgerald came from her background and her unconventional life. She was the youngest of the famous Langhorne sisters of Virginia. Her oldest sister was Lady Nancy Astor; another sister had married Charles Dana Gibson, creator of the "Gibson girl." Nora herself had fled from her first marriage in order to run off with Lefty Flynn, a former football player at Yale and—like Nora herself—a gifted musician. Fitzgerald enjoyed her wit, envied her happiness, and admired her fearlessness. "I never look behind," she told Scott. "Tighten up your belt, baby," she'd announce, "let's get going. To any Pole."

It was to Nora that he turned as he sank into depression during 1935 and 1936. He'd call her on the phone, in tears, and she'd try to cheer him up. She also tried to get him to quit drinking and, in Tryon, provided him by her example with a gaiety that did not depend on liquor. "He loved her, I think," Zelda told Henry Dan Piper in 1947, "not clandestinely, but she was one of several women he always needed around him to stimulate him and to turn to when he got low and needed a lift." But talking about Nora disconcerted Zelda. Probably, Piper thought, Zelda was wondering whether she'd known the whole truth about the relationship.

What was there to know? The answer depends on the source. According to Scott himself, as he spun out the story to the eminently shockable ears of Laura Guthrie, Nora Flynn was deeply in love with him and wanted to go away with him just as she once had with Lefty. But he would not go, Fitzgerald said, because he did not want to hurt Lefty. Besides, she was a few years older than Scott, and he did not want—as he put it—to be the last bus that Nora took. Scott did not claim they had been lovers, however. "Nora's passion lingers so long, because nothing happened," he said.

To the Flynns' friends in Tryon, it did not seem that way at all. It looked to them as if Scott had been crazy about Nora, and she had led him on. According to Nora Flynn's own account, Scott "always said he was terribly in love with me, and it was so foolish. I cared so much for Lefty, and he did too. And it was such an obvious relief to Scott when I finally told him off, and we could forget the sex and be just friends. He was so charming and such fun to talk with."

Whatever the nature of their relationship may have been, it is clear that Scott Fitzgerald did not want it to end. He called Nora the same day his actual lover Beatrice Dance left Asheville in August 1935, and phoned her the following day as well. "Who's your girl now, Scott?" she asked him. "No one," he lied. In October of the following year, after he'd returned to Asheville, there was a fashion show at the Grove Park Inn where Fitzgerald was staying. When Nora, who was to do some modeling, called Scott from the lobby to come down, he ran his nurse ragged helping him get dressed presentably. Fitzgerald never felt sure of his clothes with Nora. Once in New York, he picked her up "in a strange get-out: top hat, white gloves, black opera cape lined in white silk—like a stage magician." At other times he'd ask her: "Is this tweed suit all right?" "Does this jacket fit properly?" He probably had an inferiority complex, she thought. Gentlemen did not worry about the way they were dressed, or if they did they didn't talk about it. Another thing they didn't do was to reproduce as fiction the semi-scandalous details of their friends' lives, as Fitzgerald did in "The Intimate Strangers," a June 1935 story in *McCall's* based very clearly on the affair between Nora and Lefty Flynn. The Flynns did not say they were offended by the story; the lovers were portrayed sympathetically, after all. But Nora's son by her first marriage pointedly snubbed Fitzgerald six months later.

Laura Millar Guthrie first met Scott Fitzgerald on June 6, 1935, the night after the plumbers' convention dance at the Grove Park Inn in Asheville. Fitzgerald had come to the mountains to arrest a mild attack of tuberculosis. (Zelda was in Sheppard-Pratt Hospital in Baltimore and Scottie farmed out to friends.) He was in financial difficulties at the time, but characteristically decided to stay at a large, expensive hotel that served the carriage trade as well as the plumbing contractors. Laura Guthrie did not belong to either group. She read palms for guests of the Inn, evenings. On June 6, she read Fitzgerald's. It was shaky and somewhat damp, but Fitzgerald's soulful gray-green eyes grew deeper and deeper as she told—wonderfully well, he said—of his past and future accomplishments.

A week later, the handsome author called her at 6 P.M. one

evening. Wouldn't she like to read a story about a gypsy he'd just finished (based in part on her fortune telling)? She would, and cancelled a date to do so. But she was still fixing her hair when he arrived and so nervous that she knocked over a lamp. Fitzgerald was all compliments. He liked her garage apartment, he said. "You have put your spirit in it." He admired her royal blue evening dress. It showed off her figure beautifully, he said. They decided to have dinner in his room at the Inn, where she finished fixing her hair and then discovered she hadn't brought any lipstick.

"We can get some downstairs," Fitzgerald said.

"It doesn't matter," Laura replied, and he came over, looked at her mouth, and bent down to kiss her very gently. To the reader of palms, "it seemed quite inevitable and foreordained." She was smitten, and became more so as Scott kept looking at her lovingly and saying how her voice had first attracted him, and how he felt something queer when they met and knew they were going to love each other. "I knew you were one of us," he said, "whatever one of us means."

Dinner arrived but Scott ate practically nothing. Instead, he kept drinking beer and ale and smoking Sanos. Laura was surprised that he carried no watch or ring or fountain pen. She was more surprised when he leaned toward her and said, "I love you, Laura." It was nice that he had a sense of humor, she answered, for she did too. But Fitzgerald repeated the declaration. "I do love you, Laura, and I have only said that to three women in my life." Oh, was she infatuated then!

Mrs. Guthrie was in several ways particularly vulnerable to Fitzgerald's overtures. She was going through a divorce at the time. She did some writing herself (Fitzgerald polished a story she wrote and sent it off to *Esquire,* which sent it back), and envied Fitzgerald's talent. She was, like Nora Flynn, a few years older than Scott. And he *had* told her he loved her. For five days after their dinner together she suffered terribly. "I was nearly crazy some of the time with thoughts of him," she confessed to her diary. "He reaches women through their minds and yet he wants their bodies. He makes a woman who must keep her body to herself a wreck, either mental or physical—whichever part is weakest goes." In her case it was the mind that nearly snapped, and then, on June

17, the siege abated. She wished they had never met and loved, she proclaimed in a poem to Fitzgerald. Her life was "placid sunshine" a week ago, and now she could think of no one else. But she resolved to become free once more.

Fitzgerald's behavior helped make it easier for Laura to escape from her "wayward passion." For one thing, he demanded absolute and immediate obedience. Be ready, he'd say, and then pick her up five minutes later to go to the movies or sit in a nightclub until all hours while he spoke of other women he'd known. He also expected her to perform certain services for him as a matter of course—to take dictation, write letters, and help him relax by rubbing his head "hard, right in the back." Laura did everything he asked—told—her to do from early June until the middle of September, but she did not like being bossed around. She was not his mother.

Fitzgerald's drinking posed another problem. He began the summer on a beer and ale regimen, and, though Laura liked a glass of beer herself, she was not prepared for his level of consumption. One day he downed thirty-seven cans. "Beer ran down his throat like a waterfall runs down a rock, but with more disastrous results." Fitzgerald was bloated with the stuff. His mind wandered and he couldn't finish telling stories aloud, much less get them down on paper. Then it got worse when he switched back to gin early in September and Laura discovered that "being tied to an alcoholic whether as secretary, nurse, or wife" constituted the hardest work in the world. She put him in the hospital on Friday the 13th of September and counted it a lucky day. "I never felt less in love with a man in my life," she wrote in her diary.

Yet she could not entirely shake off his effect on her. When he moved back to Baltimore in October, she was his "Sweet Laura" by mail, helping him with trunks and books and things left behind in Asheville. She sent him a tie that fall along with a poem that admitted, "Your magic is with me yet." She sent him flowers the next summer when he broke his shoulder. He sent her nothing except letters asking for favors. Two of the checks he gave her to pay for her secretarial help bounced. She got $27 for the summer's work.

Laura was understandably annoyed about Fitzgerald's lack of

generosity. After all, she had seen him overtip waiters and bellhops all summer. A deeper resentment lay beneath this one, however, for one of the tasks that she performed for Fitzgerald was to act as a go-between and occasional cover-up during his affair with Beatrice Dance. In time, Laura Guthrie came to like Beatrice. In the abstract she understood that Scott "lived on women's love and if it ever stopped he would die." But she could hardly forgive him for preferring another woman.

"I've simply got to arrange something for this summer that will bring me to life again," Fitzgerald wrote Max Perkins in mid-April 1935, "but what it should be is by no means apparent." He found out in Asheville, early in June, with the arrival of Beatrice Dance and her sister Eleanor from San Antonio. By mid-June Scott and Beatrice had become lovers. Their affair lasted only seven weeks before ending, painfully and abruptly, but it was no casual summer romance. In fact, it was the *only* important extramarital relationship he discussed with Sheilah Graham during their years together in Hollywood. He'd been in love with Beatrice Dance, he told Sheilah. She was the first woman to make him forget Zelda.

Six years younger than Fitzgerald, Beatrice had pretty golden hair, large but well-formed hands and feet, and—most noticeably—an oddly appealing stutter. He wrote a tribute to Mark Twain that summer, and one evening asked her to read it aloud. When she got stuck on the "H" in Huckleberry Finn and said despairingly, "I'm so excited I can't do my 'h's' tonight," Fitzgerald was enchanted. "All I know," he was to write at the end of their affair, "is I'd like to sit for a thousand years and look at you and hear your voice with the lovely pathetic little *'peep'* at the crescendo of the stutter." The word that most often came to mind when he thought of her, he said, was "lovely."

Beatrice's father, who had made a great deal of money, was "*somebody*" in Texas, and she acted like a queen, expecting the best and getting it. It was not accidental that Fitzgerald was more attracted to women of social position—Elizabeth Lemmon, Nora Flynn, Beatrice Dance—than to others. Though Beatrice was married and the mother of a young daughter, she decided that she loved Scott Fitzgerald almost on sight and set out to do something about it. He was agreeable, but at first did not expect the affair to amount to anything. What swept him away was the strength of her passion, which simultaneously frightened him and stimulated an unexpected response. Beatrice held nothing back. She gave him praise and adoration. She told him the most intimate details about herself and her marriage. She proposed that they go off together to some remote corner of the world and live on her income. She wanted to have his child. She made him feel alive, certainly.

Mrs. Dance and her sister, who was in ill health, had come to Asheville in hopes that the mountain air might provide a respite from the heat and humidity of San Antonio summers. Recognizing Fitzgerald at the Grove Park Inn, she attracted his notice by reading *The Great Gatsby* in the writing room. There followed dinners for three with Scott, Beatrice, and Eleanor, long evening talks on the Inn's veranda, nights at the Castle (Asheville's closest approach to a nightclub), and finally rendezvous in Fitzgerald's room. The help at the summer hotel soon discovered what was going on, and so did Laura Guthrie, although Fitzgerald delayed before telling her. Even when he did acknowledge the affair, he denigrated Beatrice as spoiled and not particularly intelligent. Nothing would have happened, he said, if Laura had given herself instead. Since she hadn't, she was given another role to play.

On July 15 Beatrice's husband Hop came for a two-week stay in Asheville. To avoid a confrontation, the Dances stayed at the nearby resort of Highlands, where Beatrice let Fitzgerald know when her husband was leaving. By this time, Laura had been enlisted as go-between, and duly relayed a message to Beatrice that Scott would return and meet her at 11:15 A.M. Saturday, August 3, at the "little rathskellar place" where they'd had "the bad caviarre." Beatrice would know what he meant. He intended to break things off, Fitzgerald told Laura. Instead, the lovers took a room at the George Vanderbilt hotel downtown, Beatrice having told her sister that they'd gone for a ride in the mountains. Laura was left to alert them to trouble.

It came almost immediately, for Hop had left Asheville aware that something was wrong and determined to keep in touch. That same night, Laura had to help act out a charade by telephone. Hop called the Inn from Memphis, Tennessee, looking for Beatrice. She was not in her room. The telephone operator at the Inn called

Laura at home, wondering if she knew where Beatrice was. Laura called Beatrice at the Vanderbilt. Beatrice called Hop: she'd been to a movie with Laura, she told him. An hour later an operator in Memphis called Laura asking for Beatrice. Would Mrs. Dance call this operator number when she returned? Laura called the Vanderbilt. Again Beatrice called Memphis and tried to reassure Hop.

The lovers were obviously courting danger, a process that seemed to exhilarate Fitzgerald. He worked hard on his correspondence the next day and that evening regaled both Beatrice and Laura with a deadpan rendering of the humorous song about dogs he and Edmund Wilson had concocted:

> Dog, dog—I like a good dog!
> Towser or Bowser or Star—
> Clean sort of pleasure—
> A four-footed treasure—
> And faithful as few humans are!
> Here, Pup: put your paw up—
> Roll over dead like a log!
> Larger than a rat!
> More Faithful than a cat!
>   Dog! Dog! Dog!

Both Beatrice and Laura urged Fitzgerald to leave the George Vanderbilt and return to the Grove Park Inn, where it would be relatively simple to avoid telephone mixups. But Fitzgerald stayed put, Beatrice stayed with him, and when Hop phoned at midnight once more his wife was not in her room.

Eleanor thought her sister was foolish to get entangled with Fitzgerald. He was very weak, Eleanor thought, a drowning man grasping for a straw to hold him up. Left too much to herself, Eleanor's own health had deteriorated; she began to succumb to depression. On August 5 Fitzgerald undertook to right matters. He saw Eleanor alone and either tried to comfort her (as he told Beatrice) or to seduce her (as Eleanor believed). In any event, Eleanor became disturbed and Beatrice called San Antonio to summon Dr. Cade, the family doctor. He arrived on August 7. So did Hop.

Fitzgerald had long been fantasizing about a confrontation with Beatrice's husband. He would throw his dressing gown over Hop's head and knock him down and attack him before he could do anything, Scott told Laura. He'd arrange beer bottles so he could grab one and swing at anyone who tried to get into the room. He'd use a sharp beer-can opener as a weapon. The actual meeting was less melodramatic. On the evening of August 7, Fitzgerald had dinner with Laura Guthrie. As usual, he consumed a great deal of beer but little food. Then they went to a Shirley Temple movie that he couldn't stand. On leaving, he called the room where Beatrice and Hop were staying and wangled an invitation to come over. The four of them chatted two by two, first Scott with Beatrice and Hop with Laura, then the men and the women. At 11:30 the visitors got up to go.

Scott came over to Beatrice's bed and asked, his voice throaty, "May I kiss you good night?"

"Of course," she said, and gazed up radiantly as he kissed her cheek.

Laura saw a murderous look come over Hop's face and hustled Scott out of the room. Hop banged the door shut and noisily turned the key in the lock. On the way home, Scott told Laura that he really did love Beatrice. But the affair was over. He never saw her again.

The next morning, the family doctor—who had decided that Beatrice and not Eleanor was most in need of his services—held an interview with Fitzgerald. As a man of the world, Dr. Cade said, he understood what had happened. He'd had mistresses himself. But Scott must not try to see Beatrice again. Her marriage was in jeopardy. Trouble might ensue. These things ran their course. Fitzgerald agreed and made polite conversation. By afternoon the doctor and the Dances were gone, though Beatrice sent a stream of phone calls and wires and letters for days. In San Antonio she broke down and had to be hospitalized twice. Laura Guthrie recorded Fitzgerald's reaction in her diary.

> Scott was awfully upset. "I always have my way. I wanted it to end this way, but though I win, I lose." He walked up and down and threw himself on his bed with his head in his arms

and cried. Then he got control again and paced up and down. "I am glad I kissed her last night in her bed," he declared. "Love dies of course, but it is awful to have it torn apart when it is strongest. This is leaving an awful wound. But it doesn't matter—nothing matters." And he sobbed aloud and went in the next room and threw himself upon the bed there.

As the philosophical "Love dies of course" hints, Scott was presenting something of a performance. In the same spirit he berated himself for being a marriage wrecker. "I break everybody I touch," he sobbed. "I'm no good any more." Directly to Beatrice, he sent a message of farewell.

> The writ of *habeas corpus* that extradited you was not a surprise but it was a shock. Of *course* you were right to go—anything less than a complete separation would have been a perfectly futile temporizing.
>
> But you have become the only being with whom I have a desire to communicate any more and when you were gone there was the awful stillness of a desert.
>
> Love seems to be like that, unexpected, often tragic, always terribly mortal and fragile.
>
> When this reaches you a little of the past, our past, will have already died, so I'm trying to write without the emotion I feel. For the moment we are both life-tired, utterly weary—and unreconciled. The old dizziness has come back (don't worry—it'll probably leave in a day or so) & I simply lie & think. Except that I hate to think of you in the heat of Tennessee I am glad I didn't have to go again. And to stay here with Hop and Doctor Cade between us was impossible. I didn't even mind much when they ganged up on us & could have faced fifty more of them with you at my side—but that was not to be.
>
> This is letter number 4, the others having been destroyed, each one antiquated by the changing conditions. Some day darling Beatrice I will write something about you "that the world will not willingly let die", but that time isn't yet and I cannot get much in the form of a letter....
>
> ...I am too sick & miserable to think today. There doesn't seem to be anything in the world but you & me. You are the lovliest human being I have ever known.

Oh darlin I cant write any more. There is lots more to say &
if you'll send me some safe adress I'll write you there. I love
you—you are chrystal clear, blown glass with the sun cutting
always very suddenly across it.

Thank you for the Sanos. I am sending you some books

Your loving

Scott

Goodbye, goodbye, you are part of me forever.

Despite his protestations, Fitzgerald seems almost entirely rec-
onciled to the separation in this letter, written but three days after
Beatrice left. He generalizes about the ephemerality of love, promises to immortalize Beatrice in fictional form, spins a phrase about
her loveliness, and bids adieu. Fitzgerald had another matter on
his mind, anyway. He thought he might have contracted syphilis,
though not—he assured Laura Guthrie—from Beatrice. Not until
the tests came back negative did he achieve a state of equanimity.
Then, hearing of Beatrice's hospitalization in San Antonio, he sent
her a blunt telegram: TAKE YOUR MEDICINE AND GO ON STOP THE
WORLD WASN'T BUILT FOR A PARLOR CAR BUT THE BRAVE INHERIT THE
RAILROAD SYSTEM STOP COURAGE OUGHT TO MEAN SOMETHING TO US
NOW. Early in September, when she suffered a relapse, he wrote
a harsh letter instructing her in her obligations. "There are emotions just as important as ours running concurrently with them—
and there is literally no standard in life other than a sense of
duty.... We can't just let our worlds crash around us like a lot of
dropped trays." Beatrice had to "be good," he insisted.

Fitzgerald obviously found it easier to break off the affair than
did Beatrice. When he went to the hospital himself a month later,
he wanted it understood that it was not for love. "Don't let Beatrice
think I broke because of her," he told Laura. In the same spirit of
overt masculinity, perhaps, he had said something to Dr. Cade
that made Beatrice feel he'd betrayed her. "FIND OUT WHY S. DID
WHAT HE DID TO ME," she wired Laura Guthrie on the day of her
departure. Fitzgerald professed not to know what she was talking
about. As long as seven months later, he still couldn't imagine what

he might have said to the doctor that so troubled Beatrice. He and Dr. Cade had discussed the doctor's medical career in Texas, Beatrice and Hop's marriage, Fitzgerald's "instinctive liking" for Hop, the futility of fortune hunting in this case, the possible problem of custody for Beatrice's daughter, and Eleanor's illness. Nothing more that he could recall. But Fitzgerald left out the man-to-man talk about women, in which it would have been entirely within his pattern to speak indiscreetly about Beatrice's feral passion. Finally she let him know by letter what was bothering her. "Our medical tycoon was single-minded, to put it mildly," he replied on May 15, 1936. "I was amused at the 'gorilla' *motif* as I hadn't credited him with such powers of invention."

Beatrice, like Scott's mother, was prepared to forgive him anything. Often she sent him presents: a sweater, a kimono, handkerchiefs, books, flowers, annual subscriptions to *Life* and *Fortune*. Fitzgerald responded with newsy letters in which he painted his world rather brighter than it was and referred occasionally to a happy moment they had shared. "A lot must have happened to you too in these five years," he wrote her the month before he died. "Write me if you should ever feel like it and tell me." Fitzgerald did not want the thread to snap entirely, and it did not. In 1964, the year after Hop's death, an old friend of Hop's tried to kiss Beatrice while his wife was waiting in the car. She'd have none of that, she wrote her old confidante Laura Guthrie. She'd had her life. No other man would ever interest her.

Scott Fitzgerald was a desperately lonely man, Laura Guthrie concluded. Wherever he went, that summer of 1935, he felt compelled to win the admiration of a woman. In Asheville, the woman was Beatrice Dance. But once in June and again in July, Scott left the Grove Park Inn long enough to visit Baltimore, where Zelda was confined to Sheppard-Pratt Hospital. On each occasion he worked in a brief visit to New York to see a woman; and on each occasion, if his account is to be believed, the encounter was intimate. In June he spent a day with Bert Barr, in July with Margaret Case Harriman.

Fitzgerald had first met the blonde and beautiful Bert Barr in February 1931, while sailing back to the United States for his father's funeral. In mid-ocean all the passengers rushed on deck to watch the brand new *Bremen* pass in the night with all her lights ablaze. "Papa, buy me that!" Bert exclaimed to the Texas oilman in whose party she was traveling. Still clutching her hand from an interrupted bridge game, Bert whispered to Fitzgerald that she was a card shark. He was charmed, and wooed her with a succession of humorous notes. "I put in a new razor blade for you & the texture of my skin is like duveteen or Gloria Morgan 'Pond's Extract' Vanderbilt—it would not shame the greatest fairy that ever knitted a boudoir cap—and still no word. Are you recieving? Do you ever recieve?" Was she just going to sleep and sleep? Hadn't she any feeling of public responsibility, any invitations to fine country houses? Did she know what she might face on awakening? "I am in terror you will wake up with an open trunk in front of you & confuse it with the trunk you last saw early this morning tottering, I might say weaving from your palatial suite—what I mean is I am sober, de-alcoholized, de-nicotinized, de-onionized and I still adore you."

Bert Barr's real name, Fitzgerald soon discovered, was Mrs. Bertha Weinberg Goldstein, sister to financier Sidney J. Weinberg and wife of a prominent Brooklyn judge. He called her Mickey Mouse instead, for no good reason except that she liked it. They had fun together, for she possessed a verbal wit like his own and was a gifted mimic as well. At least two assignations followed the shipboard romance. One occurred in Paris in June 1931, but everything possible went wrong and the evening ended "with a hotel keeper's wife shrieking curses through the telephone." The other, a 1935 meeting in New York, may have been their last. "I had 24 hrs with nothing to do," Fitzgerald wrote Max Perkins, "and went to N.Y. to see a woman I'm very fond of—its a long peculiar story (...—one of the curious series of relationships that run thru a man's life)." He would have called Perkins, Scott added, but she'd given up her weekend at the last minute and "it was impossible to leave her to see you." Fitzgerald cared enough about Bert to send her all his books, autographed, and she cared enough about his work to accumulate and keep typescripts and galley proofs of articles and stories he wrote for *Esquire* during the last five years of his life.

Margaret Case Harriman liked Fitzgerald's work too, and since she was a writer herself, author of numerous profiles for *The New Yorker* and eventually of several books—including *The Vicious Circle*, an account of the famous round table at the Algonquin hotel where her father was manager and she herself grew up—Scott coveted her good opinion. According to Fitzgerald's ledger, the two of them foregathered in New York twice, in late July 1935 and in December 1936. The 1935 meeting concluded with Fitzgerald badly hungover and nursing a wounded ego from Margaret's remark that novelist Joseph Hergesheimer was "more established" than he. They were simply different kinds of writers, Fitzgerald insisted. Margaret was quick to agree, and used "Babylon Revisited" as a point of comparison. "I bet if Joe had written a story about a man who wanted his child to come and live with him and who couldn't have her, after all, I bet he would have put in a few lines beautifully phrased, about what the man did or what he thought, or—which is worse—*why* that had to happen to him. . . . The way you wrote it, of course, the man didn't think anything or do anything, because there wasn't, simply, anything to think or anything at all to do. And when you read it you know, without being told, that it would have to happen to him—That's why you can't bear it when it does." She'd read everything Scott had written, Margaret told him, and remembered everything too. Scott needed to be told these things just as he needed to be loved.

Fitzgerald considered using Margaret in *The Last Tycoon*. "Put in Margaret Case episode after his wife's death," one of his working notes reads. And he did depict the liveliness and charm of Bert Barr in "On Your Own," a story he wrote in 1931 which did not appear in published form until 1979. Like many Fitzgerald stories, "On Your Own" deals with love, but the principals are properly unmarried and there is no question of adultery or unfaithfulness. Fitzgerald approached these subjects rather gingerly. "I am writing a picture for Joan Crawford called 'Infidelity,'" he wrote Beatrice Dance in 1938. "I feel they should not have given me a subject that I know so little about."

Fitzgerald and Beatrice may have enjoyed the irony in that remark, but he did not do what he had planned: write about her in a way that wouldn't hurt anyone, and only the two of them would understand. He made notes toward telling that tale twice, the first in the form of a chronology of "Tragic July," the second listing a series of scenes for a play to be called "It Was Just Too Bad." As he'd told fellow novelist James Boyd shortly after he and Beatrice parted, "I have just emerged not totally unscathed, I'm afraid, from a short violent love affair. . . . It's no one I ever mentioned to you . . . and I had done much better to let it alone because this was scarcely a time in my life for one more emotion. Still it's done now and tied up in cellophane and—maybe someday I'll get a chapter out of it. God, what a hell of a profession to be a writer. One is one simply because one can't help it." That story, or play, or chapter never got written.

Neither did the other tales of adultery he proposed in his notebooks. "How about a *girl's* point of view about me," for example. "That is Beatrice or the North Carolinas [nurses in Asheville] or Nora or Marice [Hamilton]. Their point of view on a philanderer. . . . He thinks he's getting away with so much—takes it for granted. And really they are." Other notes suggested anecdotes rather than stories. "For Esquire: Jealous husband meet wife's lover on train. The bluff that convinces all, including the reader that the wife has 'boasted.'" And "Idea of husband who had on convention badge and lover on tram who pretends he doesn't know husband and convinces indirectly of innocence. When he's gone husband remembers badge." And

"Time Lapse"

(1) Man, girl, friend. Former thinks may happen but
    won't—it is happening.
(2) Later—thinks it is now. Has happened and is over.

Two good reasons kept Fitzgerald from writing more about adultery. First, he understood the fiction marketplace well enough to understand that few mass-market magazines would publish stories that cast adulterous behavior in a favorable or amusing light. *The Saturday Evening Post* wanted what it had always wanted: stories of young love, boy getting girl after surmounting obstacles. *McCall's* had printed "The Intimate Strangers" in June 1935, and that story had depicted an adulterous affair without punishing the participants, but it did not—like the plots Fitzgerald envisioned in his notes—celebrate the gulling of the cuckolded spouse. Besides, Fitzgerald was writing about the Flynns in that story, and not about himself. Very few of his stories portray the male protagonist in the role of the seducer, and when they do—as in "Indecision"—the Casanova is converted to monogamous love before the story ends.

In his novels, Fitzgerald was free to deal with the issue of adultery more openly. But even there, he rarely wrote about a love affair outside the bounds of marriage without making it seem degrading. Anthony Patch's affair with Dorothy Raycroft in _The Beautiful and Damned_ was "an inevitable result," the author-narrator declared, "of his increasing carelessness about himself." Late in the novel, Anthony suffers the consequences of this carelessness; he goes over the edge into insanity when Dorothy appears in New York and threatens to make trouble. In _The Great Gatsby_, Fitzgerald invests the brutal physical love affair of Tom Buchanan and Myrtle Wilson with no redeeming overtones, and obviously disapproves of the casual couplings precipitated by Gatsby's parties. Gatsby and Daisy's affair remains different because Fitzgerald keeps it on an ethereal plane. But Gatsby pays a staggering price for his error. When he is shot by George Wilson, it is for the wrong woman, but the right offense. _Tender Is the Night_ conveys a similar bias against adultery. By the time Dick and Rosemary make love in Rome, their romance has died away, and their consummation has no more appeal than that of Nicole and Tommy Barban, or the French _poules_ and the American sailors.

Fitzgerald's novels portray adultery as ugly, wrong, or both. He wrote about the subject this way because public _mores_ demanded it and because he shared those _mores_. Privately, he thrilled no one with his tales of sexual conquest more than himself. Each one brought a tremor of guilt.

During the summer of 1935, letters from Zelda served to remind Scott of his marital bond. She'd love to go to Antibes again, Zelda wrote, or back to the pine woods of Alabama where they'd fallen in love on "a radiant night... of soft conspiracy" and she'd called him "Darling" for the first time. "Of course," she added, "if you invited me to North Carolina it would be very nice too." When he did visit her in Baltimore, the days turned to gold. "I play the radio and moon about... and dream of utopias where its always July the

24th 1935 [her birthday], in the middle of summer forever," she wrote him. By then he had gone back to Asheville and the summer faded away and why, she wanted to know, couldn't they spend the fall together and take care of each other?

In response, Scott wrote a story. It was not about Beatrice and himself, or about any other actual or imaginary love affair of 1935. Instead it was about Zelda's involvement with a young French aviator in the summer of 1924, while Scott was writing *The Great Gatsby*. In "Image on the Heart" Fitzgerald disguised the principal characters, but in any guise the story functioned to absolve him of guilt and to delay the painful introspection that lay just ahead. He wrote "Image on the Heart" in September 1935. A month later he faced himself more openly in the first of the three "Crack-Up" essays.

9

Cracking Up

WHEN LAURA Guthrie walked into Scott Fitzgerald's room at the Grove Park Inn on the morning of Friday, September 13, 1935, she found empty glasses and cigarette butts everywhere and Fitzgerald himself on the bed, with bloodshot eyes, drawn lips, skin raw from eczema, twitching leg muscles, and a distorted look about the eyes. "My nerves are going," he told her. "I'm about to break." He couldn't do any work at all, he said. He wept, as he often had that summer. He pretended he was having a heart attack. Then he demanded one more favor of the woman who had served as his "secretary" (that is, his always-to-be-available companion, good listener, potential conquest, and occasional typist) all summer in Asheville. She'd have to get him dressed and packed and deliver him to the hospital, but only after marching through the lobby and checking out as if on his way to the train. He might be at death's door, but appearances mattered.

Though she knew it wasn't fair that she should have to do the job, Mrs. Guthrie helped her invalid pack up his filthy clothes and ushered him through the lobby to a waiting taxicab. Three months earlier she had thought Fitzgerald "a lost soul, wandering in purgatory—sometimes hell" and had hoped to "save him and help him write steadily and really be his good angel." Now, after lying to cover up his affair with Beatrice Dance and witnessing his daily attempt to achieve oblivion through drink, she only wanted to be quit of her charge. When she'd deposited him at the hospital she "felt like a kid out of school," her responsibility over.

Fitzgerald's collapse in Asheville was his fourth breakdown in two years, he told Mrs. Guthrie. Liquor was the immediate cause of the problem, though Fitzgerald was also distressed about Zelda's illness and about his dwindling capacity to do the kind of work expected of him. The previous spring when Arnold Gingrich had come calling on him in Baltimore, Fitzgerald—clad in a "ratty old bathrobe"—moaned about having to write a story of young love for the *Saturday Evening Post*. He could no longer write such stories with conviction, he said, and the idea of producing one brought up his "cold gorge." "Well, why not write about that?" Gingrich had suggested.

Still other difficulties contributed to Fitzgerald's periodic breakdowns, chief among them his constitutional tendency toward sadness. "Please don't be depressed," Zelda had written him in 1931, eighteen months after her own collapse. "Nothing is sad about you except your sadness and the frayed places in your pink kimono and that you care so much about everything." Her husband was temperamentally unsuited to happiness, however. Hemingway's "instinct [was] toward megalomania," Fitzgerald later commented, "and mine toward melancholy." What psychic kink lay behind that disposition to melancholy? What was it, as his three "gloom articles" in "The Crack-Up" put it, that cut off the sun and caused him to crack like a plate?

Fitzgerald's three articles, which ran in *Esquire* for February, March, and April 1936, precipitated an extraordinary response from the magazine's readers. "I get letters from all over," Fitzgerald wrote Gingrich on March 20. These letters came from old friends who wanted to cheer him up, from total strangers who recognized something of their own plight in Fitzgerald's account of emotional exhaustion, and most of all from other writers, among them James Boyd, John Dos Passos, Ernest Hemingway, Nancy Hoyt, John O'Hara, Marjorie Kinnan Rawlings, G. B. Stern, Julian Street, and Alexander Woollcott.

As O'Hara remarked in an April letter, "I suppose you get comparatively little mail these days that does not dwell at greater or less length on your *Esquire* pieces, and I guess few of the writers resist, as I am resisting, the temptation to go into their own troubles for purposes of contrast." (O'Hara then revealed that he had recently been jilted by his girl and had picked up a dose of clap on the rebound.)

The very nature of "The Crack-Up" articles called for *some* response. Here a well-known writer was admitting in print that he had cracked like a plate and lost much of the vitality that made him successful. Furthermore, at the end of the second article, Fitzgerald openly appealed for reader reaction.

The correspondence that found its way back to Fitzgerald varied enormously in tone. Much of it sympathetically proposed solutions to his dilemma. Some letter-writers suggested God, some Alcoholics Anonymous, some a rendezvous. Others recounted their own troubles, delivered pep talks, tried to jolly him up. The worst were those who could not resist the opportunity to preach at Fitzgerald. "Please write me," he asked Max Perkins in February 1937. "You are about the only friend who does not see fit to incorporate a moral lesson, especially since the *Crack-Up* stuff. Actually I hear from people in Sing Sing & Joliet all comforting & advising me."

The media reaction was mixed. The *New Yorker*'s "Talk of the Town" dismissed the essays with an air of superiority. "F. Scott Fitzgerald has been telling, in *Esquire*, how sad he feels in middle life," the item began, and went on to refer to his "picturesque despondency." *The San Francisco Chronicle* observed in similar vein that the "gentleman in question is being a little too sorry for himself," but acknowledged that one could "hardly help being interested in what he has to say," the more so since he seemed to strike a common chord, and his essays went far "to explain the spiritual troubles of many another member of the almost-lost generation."

Such friends as Margaret Turnbull and Marie Hamm agreed. "Your story is a mental snapshot of a rather universal experience," Mrs. Turnbull wrote after reading his first article. All of us end up "more or less defeated," but since so many shared this experience, Fitzgerald would discover "a chain of people, stretching around the world, to catch hold of [his] hands." One hand that reached out was that of Scott's first girl in St. Paul, Marie Hersey Hamm. "Cheer up, darling, life begins at forty!" she wrote early in October, responding both to the *Esquire* articles and to the account, in *Time*,

of Fitzgerald's disastrous fortieth birthday interview with Michel
Mok for the *New York Post*. Mrs. Hamm granted that Fitzgerald
had probably gone "on a more prolonged binge than the rest of
us," and that therefore his "hang-over, awakening, or what have
you" was that much more oppressive. But life, she insisted, was
pretty swell, especially when you considered the alternative. Among
their mutual friends, Joe Ordway was in a sanitarium and Theodore
Schultze had died the week before. "When you're dead, you're
dead, my pet, so why not enjoy it while you're here." It was nice
of Marie to write, Fitzgerald acknowledged. "However, child," he
told her, "life is more complicated than that."

Not all of his female friends were so sympathetic. Nora Flynn,
who'd seen the shabby hotel room in Hendersonville, North Carolina, where Fitzgerald began the articles, imagined him lying
prone, "thinking about himself. He never was interested in anyone
or anything but himself." And to Sara Murphy too, Fitzgerald
seemed so wrapped up in himself as to be unable to sympathize
with others. Did Scott really, honestly think that "life was something you dominated if you were any good"? That kind of arrogance
brought an incident to mind:

> I remember once your saying to me—in Montana at Harry's
> Bar, you & Dotty [Parker] were talking about your disappoint-
> ments, & you turned to me and said: I don't suppose you have
> ever known despair? I remember it so well as I was furious, &
> thought my god the man thinks no one knows despair who isn't
> a writer & can describe it. This is my feeling about your articles.

John Dos Passos also proposed that Fitzgerald stop regarding
his own navel. "Christ, man, how do you find time in the middle
of the general conflagration to worry about all that stuff?... We're
living in one of the damnedest tragic moments in history—if you
want to go to pieces I think it's absolutely O.K. But I think you
ought to write a first-rate novel about it (and you probably will)
instead of spilling it in little pieces for Arnold Gingrich—"

The important thing, to Dos Passos and other writer-friends, was
that Fitzgerald should continue to do his work. "Katy & I...wish
like hell you could find some happy way of getting that magnificent

working apparatus of yours to work darkening paper, which is its business," as Dos Passos put it in another letter. Even if he remained unhappy, Fitzgerald ought to turn that sorrow to literary account. "I suppose you know that nothing is wasted," Marjorie Kinnan Rawlings asserted. "The hell you've been through isn't wasted. All you have to do, ever, is to forget everything and turn that terrible, clear white light you possess, on the minds and emotions of the people it stirs you to write about." Ernest Hemingway had offered much the same advice after reading *Tender Is the Night* and detecting traces of self-pity in the portrayal of Dick Diver. Forget your personal tragedy, he told Fitzgerald. "But when you get the damned hurt use it—don't cheat with it." Neither of them were tragic characters. They were only writers, and what they should do was write.

Hemingway did not intend, however, that Fitzgerald should bleed all over the page. "The Crack-Up" articles struck him as a despicable whining in public. His old friend Scott had become the "Maxie Baer" of writers, he wrote Max Perkins, sunk to the canvas in the "shamelessness of defeat." In "The Snows of Kilimanjaro," which appeared in the August 1936 *Esquire*, Hemingway dismissed Fitzgerald openly. "Poor Scott Fitzgerald" had been "wrecked," Ernest wrote, by his worship of the rich. When Fitzgerald objected, Hemingway explained that since Scott had written himself off in "The Crack-Up" he figured it was open season on him. (It must have been something of the same savage distaste for public confession that inspired syndicated columnist Westbrook Pegler's ill-spirited obituary of Fitzgerald: his death recalled to Pegler "memories of a queer band of undisciplined and self-indulgent brats who were determined not to pull their weight in the boat and wanted the world to drop everything and sit down and bawl with them.")

Though he did not share the vehemence of Hemingway, the gentlemanly Perkins was also embarrassed by "The Crack-Up" articles. Parading one's troubles in public simply wasn't done. A man of reticence himself, Perkins was one of those—Fitzgerald so described them in his second "Crack-Up" article—"to whom all self-revelation is contemptible, unless it ends with a noble thanks to the gods for the Unconquerable Soul." He regarded Fitzgerald's articles as an "indecent invasion of his own privacy," and thus faced a delicate problem when Fitzgerald proposed on March 25, 1936, that his autobiographical magazine writing might be stitched together into a good and saleable book. Perkins had already discouraged this idea once, but since "the interest in this *Esquire* series has been so big," Fitzgerald pointed out, "I thought you might reconsider the subject." Perkins replied tactfully that he'd much prefer "a reminiscent book—not autobiographical but reminiscent. . . . I do not think the *Esquire* pieces ought to be published alone. But as for an autobiographical book which would comprehend what is in them, I would be very much for it." It would need integration, however, and should not be a mere collection of articles.

By the fall of 1936, Fitzgerald had abandoned any idea of collecting "The Crack-Up" articles. Both Perkins and agent Harold Ober had by then indicated that the articles were doing real damage to his reputation as a writer. "My Hollywood deal," he wrote Beatrice Dance in September, "was seriously compromised by their general tone. It seems to have implied to some that I was a complete moral and artistic bankrupt." As a consequence he began disavowing "those indiscreet *Esquire* articles." They were not to be taken too seriously, he told Hamilton Basso. Later he withheld the articles from Sheilah Graham for some time before showing her the tearsheets with the admonition, "I shouldn't have written these."

When Edmund Wilson began assembling the volume of Fitzgerald's nonfiction and critical praise that emerged in 1945 as *The Crack-Up*, he encountered some opposition from both Perkins and Ober. As early as February 1941 Wilson had suggested to Perkins that "The Crack-Up" should be brought out in book form. "I hated it when it came out, just as you did," Wilson remarked, "but I have found several intelligent people that think highly of it. There was more truth and sincerity in it, I suppose, than we realized at the time. He wanted it published in a book himself, and after all I dare say it is a part of the real Fitzgerald record." These were excellent reasons for Scribner's to publish such a book, but Perkins remained adamant. Eventually Wilson took his project to New Directions, but not before he'd lobbied on its behalf with Fitzgerald's financial executor John Biggs. He intended to call his book

The Crack-Up, editor Wilson explained, not because he was enamored of the title, but because

> Glenway Wescott's appreciation is largely based on *The Crack-
> Up,* and . . . if you read *The Crack-Up* through, you realize that
> is not a discreditable confession but an account of a kind of crisis
> that many men of Scott's generation have gone through, and
> that in the end he sees a way to live by application to his work.

What was that crisis? The words of "The Crack-Up" tend to blur
the issue. Only by reading between the lines do the dimensions
of Fitzgerald's crack-up begin, fuzzily, to take shape.

When *The Crack-Up* emerged as a book in 1945, Lionel Trilling
hailed Fitzgerald's "heroic self-awareness," Glenway Wescott
praised his candor, and Andrews Wanning detected "a desperate
effort at self-disclosure." Yet Fitzgerald was far from totally forth-
coming in his articles for *Esquire*. As Alfred Kazin realized, "The
author is somehow offering us certain facts in exchange for the right
to keep others to himself." The thing most conspicuously left out
was, naturally, Fitzgerald's alcoholism—"naturally" because as both
Wescott and Malcolm Cowley have observed, denying that one
has a drinking problem constitutes one of the symptoms of the
disease. Fitzgerald disingenuously attempted to dispose of the issue
in his first "Crack-Up" articles. There he referred to William Seabrook's book about alcoholism that "tells, with some pride and a
movie ending, of how he became a public charge." Seabrook's
nervous system had collapsed, and so, admitted Fitzgerald, had
his own, but not because of drink: "The present writer was not so
entangled," he lied, "—having at the time not tasted so much as
a glass of beer for six months."

Such denials did not convince everyone. John V. A. Weaver,
another writer associated with the Jazz Age, found the first two
Esquire articles disturbing, since they described so exactly what
had happened to him. "I can't drink a *drop*," he wrote Fitzgerald.
"I can only sit impotent, day by day, and see a strange world careen
by—a world in which I have no place." Weaver mailed his letter
early in 1936, while George Martin (who did not know Fitzgerald)

waited until after the publication of "An Alcoholic Case" in February 1937 to offer his assurance that he'd been in the same boat. "From the stuff you write in *Esquire* you seem to be having one hell of a time," Martin began. "If it's true...please know that I've lived all through it—will to die, dts, friends gone, money gone, job gone, self respect gone, guts gone...everything." He then suggested that Fitzgerald get hold of Peabody's *Common Sense of Drinking*.

This letter struck a nerve, for Fitzgerald answered by proposing external reasons for his malady. Martin gently chided him in reply: "Certainly, as you say, the cause precedes the curse, but it is also true that the old ego breeds rationalizations like guinea pigs." Indeed, much of "The Crack-Up" reads like a rationalization of Fitzgerald's breakdown, and the three articles represent more an apologia than a confession. (He does not mention his womanizing at all.) The blame for his breakdown, Fitzgerald implies, lies not within himself but elsewhere: the deficient genes he was bequeathed, the contemporary climate of materialism and insincerity, the growth of motion pictures that threatened to put fiction writers out of business. There was more to it than that.

The dramatic logic of "The Crack-Up" demanded that some *immediate* cause be located, and so in the first of his essays Fitzgerald indicated that it was a piece of unexpected good news from his doctor—a reprieve from an earlier death sentence—that led him to crack like an old plate. Such an event may have happened, but no biographer has documented it. In the remaining "Crack-Up" essays, significantly, he dropped all reference to this medical reprieve. Instead, in "Pasting It Together," he cited three specific blows that led to his breakdown: dropping out of Princeton because of ill health (he does not mention his academic difficulties), temporarily losing Zelda because of lack of money, and suffering an unspecified, more violent third blow that "cut off the sun last spring."

Obviously and understandably, Fitzgerald was telling less than the whole truth about himself and his family. Similarly, though he acknowledged Edmund Wilson as his "intellectual conscience," he eliminated almost all names of real people from his articles. To populate his prose he referred instead to the Bible, to William Ernest Henley, to Wordsworth and Keats, to Lenin and Dickens and Tolstoy, to Spinoza, to Descartes, to the Euganean Hills. This wealth of references suggests not only a kind of evasion, but some authorial confusion. Working in a genre new to him, Fitzgerald was searching for a form but had not quite found it.

He had not settled on a consistent tone, either. The language varied from the tough wise-guyism of "All rather inhuman and undernourished, isn't it? Well, that, children, is the true sign of cracking up" in the first essay to the ornate prosiness of "The dullest platitude monger or the most unscrupulous Rasputin who can influence the destinies of many people must have some individuality so the question became one of finding why and where I had changed, where was the leak through which, unknown to myself, my enthusiasm and my vitality had been steadily and prematurely trickling away" in the third. Re-reading "The Crack-Up," one is inclined to share the ambivalent reaction of the woman who wrote Fitzgerald that she found it hard to believe his articles really touched the depths of tragedy, yet they were "so convincing as to leave little room for doubt that the author had at some time *lived* those bitternesses and depressions."

Clearly, Fitzgerald was suffering from nervous exhaustion, or from—in his phrase—"emotional bankruptcy." But that is not what "The Crack-Up" is about. The subject of these essays is Fitzgerald's misanthropy, and the self-hatred behind it. All three articles, but especially the first and last, deal with the author's attempted escape from people—more particularly his escape from that large group of people to whom he felt obliged to give something of himself. He had given too much in the past. He would give no more.

When the writing touches on this subject, it achieves a vividness missing elsewhere. On hearing the "grave sentence" of his doctor, Fitzgerald writes in the first article, he "wanted to be absolutely alone" and so cut himself off "from ordinary cares." Instead, he sat around making lists. "It was not," he reveals, "an unhappy time." Then came the crack-up and with it the realization that "for a long time I had not liked people and things, but only followed the rickety old pretense of liking." In his casual relations—"with an editor, a tobacco seller, the child of a friend"—he had merely done what was expected. Even with love, he had been going through the motions. He had, in short, been guilty of emotional insincerity for some time. Instead of blaming himself, he transferred his self-disgust into distaste for most other human beings.

He still admired the looks of Midwestern Scandinavian blondes. He liked "doctors and girl children up to the age of about thirteen and well-brought-up boy children from about eight years old on." He liked old men and Katharine Hepburn's face on the screen, and Miriam Hopkins' face, and old friends if he only had to see them once a year. But there was a large category of people he had come to detest:

> I couldn't stand the sight of Celts, English, Politicians, Strangers, Virginians, Negroes (light or dark), Hunting People, all retail clerks, and middlemen in general, all writers (I avoided writers very carefully because they can perpetuate trouble as no one else can)—and all the classes as classes and most of them as members of their class. . . .

Under the pressure of his crack-up Fitzgerald withdrew from contact with the real world into a period of "vacuous quiet" during which he was forced to think for himself. He then discovered, according to the second article, that he had never done this before. All his ideas had been borrowed from Edmund Wilson and from four other unnamed men, one of whom, his "artistic conscience," was surely Ernest Hemingway. Not only had he given too freely of himself to people he didn't care about, but he had submerged his mental development by passively adopting the ideas of others. There was no "I" anymore, Fitzgerald concluded, no basis on which he could organize his self-respect.

The third article, "Handle with Care," picks up this theme. Unlike Descartes, Fitzgerald's motto had been, "I felt—therefore I was." He had, in fact, felt too much, and so he decided that if he wished to survive he must cease "any attempts to be a person—to be kind, just or generous." In this mood he cynically resolved to develop a false smile to win the favor of those who might be of use to him, and otherwise to cultivate the habit of saying no in a voice that would make "people feel that far from being welcome they are not even tolerated."

In a series of metaphors of degradation, Fitzgerald revealed the self-disgust that he would not openly articulate. He compared himself to a cracked plate good enough to hold leftovers but not to be brought out for company, to a beggar carrying the "tin cup of self-pity," to a bankrupt who has overdrawn his account, to a lecturer about to lose his audience, to an empty shell, to a conjurer fresh out of tricks, to a Negro woman cutting out a rival. Then, in the last paragraph of the last article, he made two more telling comparisons that fix the source of his malady. He had concentrated on pleasing others too long, and not without cost:

> ...And just as the laughing stoicism which has enabled the American negro to endure the intolerable conditions of his existence has cost him his sense of the truth—so in my case there is a price to pay.

Now that he had determined to change, Fitzgerald concluded, life would no longer be as pleasant as it once was. He was a different sort of dog now, one who no longer liked "the postman, nor the grocer, nor the editor, nor the cousin's husband...and the sign *Cave Canem* is hung permanently just above my door." He would not lick your hand now, Fitzgerald says, if you threw him a bone. In repudiating a past in which he had too often played the fawning servant or the lovable lap dog, Fitzgerald was implicitly condemning himself.

Joan Didion has uncannily echoed the theme of "The Crack-Up" in her essay on "Self-Respect":

> To have that sense of one's intrinsic worth which constitutes self-respect is potentially to have everything: the ability to discriminate, to love and to remain indifferent. To lack it is to be locked within oneself, paradoxically incapable of either love or indifference. If we do not respect ourselves, we are on the one hand forced to despise those who have so few resources as to consort with us, so little perception as to remain blind to our fatal weaknesses. On the other, we are peculiarly in thrall to everyone we see, curiously determined to live out—since our self-image is untenable—their false notions of us. We flatter ourselves by thinking this compulsion to please others an attractive trait....At the mercy of those we cannot but hold in

contempt, we play roles doomed to failure before they are begun, each defeat generating fresh despair at the urgency of di-
vining and meeting the next demand made upon us.

It is the phenomenon sometimes called "Alienation from
self.". . . Every encounter demands too much, tears the nerves,
drains the will.

This "alienation from self" lies behind Fitzgerald's breakdown, and
behind his announced misanthropy. The very process of putting
"The Crack-Up" on paper may have helped free him from that
alienation, but the therapy did not work immediately.

Certain of Fitzgerald's readers were sure that his gloom articles
would have a purgative effect. He'd be willing to bet, critic Burton
Rascoe observed after seeing the first two essays, that Fitzgerald
was "already feeling immensely better. . . self-confident and creative again." "You've been finding out a lot of things that have hurt
like hell," Julian Street told Fitzgerald, "and at the end of it you'll
be grown up. . . a bigger and better man and a bigger and better
writer for it." His long spell of despondency was far from over,
however. Fitzgerald wrote the "Crack-Up" articles in the fall of
1935, *Esquire* published them early in 1936, and in the summer
and fall of that year he was back in Asheville where he broke his
shoulder attempting a fancy dive, struck up a romantic liaison with
one or more of his nurses, drank continually, and wrote virtually
nothing. In September the *New York Post* printed an interview on
Fitzgerald that depicted the one-time chronicler of the Jazz Age
as drunken, cynical, and washed-up.

"My life looked like a hopeless mess there for a while," he later
confided to his notebooks, "and the point was I didn't *want* it to
be better. I had completely ceased to give a good god-damn."
Twice, perhaps half-heartedly, Fitzgerald tried to kill himself. After
those attempts failed, he started to rebuild his life.

Significantly, he referred to "The Crack-Up" in his ledger as
"biography," not "autobiography." This apparent slip of the pen,
as critic Robert Sklar has observed, revealed the "essential truth"
that the Scott Fitzgerald described in the essays was not the same
as the man who wrote about him. "I don't know whether those
articles of mine in *Esquire*—the 'Crack-Up' series—represented

a real nervous breakdown," Fitzgerald remarked in July 1939. "In retrospect it seems more of a spiritual 'change of life'—and a most unwilling one." "Transformation" might be an even better term, for in "The Crack-Up" Fitzgerald sloughed off the skin of the old Irish charmer and declared his determination to let work instead of play dominate the time left to him. He would henceforth be "a writer only," he announced in his last gloom article. The following year, in Hollywood, Fitzgerald set out to realize that goal. He also continued to wage his long battle with the demon of drink.

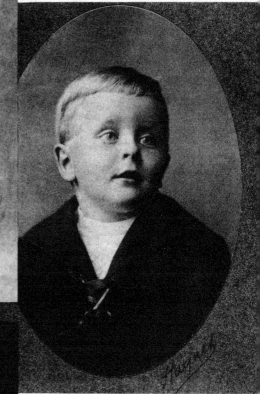

F. SCOTT FITZGERALD

THROUGH THE YEARS

10

Demon Drink

SCOTT FITZGERALD would have flunked all the tests in the Sunday supplements. He could not quit drinking—or rather, like Mark Twain with cigars, he quit a hundred times. He could not drink without getting drunk. He did terrible things while in his cups, then tried to apologize or rationalize his behavior away the next day.

His daughter Scottie, who saw him during some of the worst times, once proposed two tests for alcoholism. (1) Does liquor have a strongly deleterious effect on one's life? (2) Does one undergo a change of personality when drinking? Her father qualified on both counts, she believes. "He was a totally different person when drunk: not just gay or tiddly, but *mean*." After a few drinks, Fitzgerald fastidiously blew his breath into his hands to see if it was offensive. After a few more, he went out of his way to offend.

Fitzgerald had plenty of company in his addiction to alcohol. During the 1920s a revolution in morals was in the air, and it became almost obligatory for members of the younger generation to defy prohibition. Fitzgerald signed a petition against the eighteenth amendment, along with hundreds of other artists. Liquor obviously had its appeal for many of them, especially for the writers. In the twentieth century, as Alfred Kazin has observed, booze "has come to seem a natural accompaniment of the literary life. . . . The list of American literary drunks is very long." Dr. Donald Goodwin, who has made a study of the matter, suggests several reasons why:

Writing is a form of exhibitionism; alcohol lowers inhibitions and brings out exhibitionism in many people. Writing requires an interest in people; alcohol increases sociability and makes people more interesting. Writing involves fantasy; alcohol promotes fantasy. Writing requires self-confidence; alcohol bolsters confidence. Writing is lonely work; alcohol assuages loneliness. Writing requires intense concentration; alcohol relaxes.

Still, this does not explain the extraordinarily high incidence of alcoholism among *American* writers. Of the seven American Nobel prize winners, Sinclair Lewis, Eugene O'Neill, and William Faulkner were alcoholics, and two others, John Steinbeck and Ernest Hemingway, drank a great deal more than was good for them.

Kazin thinks the American writer carries a special burden in "the drive for success of every kind, the hunger for prestige, fame, and money." It has not been enough, in a culture that measures achievement with dollar signs, simply to fulfill one's artistic promise. Fitzgerald himself provides a classic example, caught as he was between a naive ambition to become "the greatest writer who ever lived" and a practical and often contradictory goal of making as much money as possible. Then, too, American culture has usually regarded writers as different and therefore suspect, and as if in resentment at the difference, has come to expect their self-destruction. Drink provides one of the most convenient ways to destroy oneself, and one of the most public. College campuses around the country anticipate the annual visit of the drunken poet who brags like Dylan Thomas of downing eighteen whiskeys before collapsing into a coma or who blacks out at his reading as John Berryman did. Nor is this a new phenomenon. Charles H. Foster was given the task, as a promising Amherst undergraduate in the late 1930s, of introducing Edna St. Vincent Millay. At reading time she had disappeared, but Foster found the obviously inebriated Millay in the men's room and escorted her on stage, where she announced, weaving perceptibly, that "some poems are standing-up poems, and some are sitting-down poems. Tonight I shall read some of the sitting-down ones." And settled unsteadily into a chair for the balance of the reading. Almost everyone who has attended poetry readings could tell a similar story. Perhaps, as writer Lewis Hyde suggested in his article on Berryman's alcoholism, "it would be nice if it were a little harder for the poet to come to town drunk and have everyone think it's great fun."

Donald Hall, writing in the same vein, acknowledges that writers like all human beings must suffer, but argues that they need not commit fast or slow suicide to prove it. "In our culture," he points out, "an artist's self-destructiveness is counted admirable, praiseworthy, a guarantee of sincerity. There seems to be an assumption, widely held and all but declared, that it is *natural* to want to destroy yourself... that if we did what we really wanted... we would be drunk all the time or addicted to heroin or at least suicidal." Such ideas are actively pernicious, encouraging young writers to drink themselves into insensibility or cirrhosis in imitation of the Thomases and Berrymans and O'Neills and Fitzgeralds while the "consumers of vicarious death" in the audience sit on the sidelines and applaud. This is all wrong, Hall insists. "The poet who survives is the poet to celebrate."

Whatever the public's expectations, not all American writers become drunks. If Fitzgerald did, like Miniver Cheevy he had his reasons—too many reasons. Alcoholism seems to run in families, and his father drank. He was Irish, and the Irish drink. He was romantic, and liquor provided a glow that satisfied his yearnings. "There was a kindliness about intoxication—there was that indescribable gloss and glamor it gave, like the memories of ephemeral and faded evenings." When life was drab, the rhythm of the weekend, with its "planned gaieties," offered a welcome substitute. He was beset with guilt—guilt at misuse of his talent, guilt at possible complicity in Zelda's illness, guilt about other women, guilt about the drinking itself—and drank to assuage it. He felt insecure about the worth of his work, and drinking brought relief from his doubts. Evil luck dogged his path, and he drank to put the bad breaks out of his mind. When sober he repressed hostile feelings that drinking allowed him to release. Besides, he could almost literally escape himself by ingesting enough alcohol. In his notebooks Fitzgerald copied out this fragment from Karl Billinger's *The Human Mind:*

> Seeking desperately for some personality to replace his own, which he has temporarily lost, he [the alcoholic] may adopt a

field of reference totally foreign to his own persona—the mild-tempered fellow who imagines himself a gangster, etc.—and support this role with such factual lying and ready invention that the layman is more than half ready to believe him.

Drunk, Fitzgerald was a terror. Yet always just below the surface lay an accusing voice that said "Christ, how can you stand me?" or "I'm really no good" to anyone who would listen. Like almost all alcoholics, Fitzgerald was suffused with self-hatred. Unlike most of them, he did not usually project that hatred onto other people. "When drunk," he once said, "I make them all pay and pay and pay." But the one who paid most of all was himself.

There was nothing particularly remarkable about Fitzgerald's youthful experiments with liquor, aside from his meticulous recording of them. After some fairly innocent tippling on drugstore sherry in September 1911, when he was not quite fifteen, he went off to school and further drinking adventures. He took his first whiskey in March 1913 and in April got drunk on "four defiant Canadian Club whiskeys at the Susquehana in Hackensack." As a Princeton freshman that fall he drank Great Western champagne at the Trent House in Trenton and groggily returned to campus. From there through the 1920s he went on to sample practically every form of alcoholic beverage from absinthe to home brew, from Canadian ale with Ring Lardner to Gerald Murphy's grenadine cocktails, "the one flaw to make everything perfect in the world's most perfect house." All of this he recalled in surprising and telling detail for "A Short Autobiography (with Acknowledgments to Nathan)," a *New Yorker* piece in the May 25, 1929 issue, which ended with his ironic remark that it seemed "all liquor has been drunk and all it can do for one has been experienced, and yet—'Garçon, un Chablis-Mouton 1902, et pour commencer, une petite carafe de vin rose. C'est ça—merci.'" Never again would Fitzgerald admit his involvement with liquor so publicly or treat the issue so lightly.

In the beginning booze was something to boast about. Reeling about on the streetcar amused his boyhood companions and provided him with an acceptable way of showing off. "Pardon me if my hand is shaky," he wrote a girl friend from Princeton, "but I just had a quart of sauterne and 3 Bronxes." With Max Perkins, he struck a world-weary pose. "I should like to sit down with ½ dozen chosen companions and drink myself to death but I am sick alike of life, liquor and literature," he wrote Perkins in August 1921. With Ring Lardner, another alcoholic, he kidded around. "Looked up Capri in the encyclopedia and learned the water supply for drinking was unsatisfactory," Lardner wrote the touring Fitzgerald from Great Neck. "Hope to God this is not ruining your stay." With strangers, Fitzgerald adopted shock tactics. "Don't you know I am one of the most notorious drinkers of the younger generation?" he'd ask, or introduce himself as "F. Scott Fitzgerald, the well-known alcoholic."

Brag though he might, Fitzgerald did not want anyone else commenting on his drinking in print. When Edmund Wilson proposed to do so in his March 1922 *Bookman* article, Scott asked him to omit his comments on "the liquor thing." The legend about his liquoring was "terribly widespread," he objected, and Wilson's comments would hurt him with "relatives and respectable friends," with moralistic critics, "and, what is much more important, financially." Wilson complied, but eventually Fitzgerald's drinking— the liquor itself and the debilitating effect it had—took its toll, and not solely on his earnings as a writer.

During his early drinking days, Fitzgerald had a very low tolerance for alcohol. In the mid-1920s he "would pass out cold at the number of drinks that would just make you feel good," Ernest Hemingway recalled, adding that "he enjoyed passing out because it made him the center of attention." Hemingway's comments were uncharitable, but others confirm his view of Fitzgerald's capacity during those days. He "simply couldn't drink," Louis Bromfield commented. "One cocktail and he was off. It seemed to affect him as much as five or six drinks affected Hemingway or myself." Then he would become "very disagreeable and rude and quarrelsome, as if all his resentments were released at once." Carl Van Vechten also agreed. "He was a very bad drinker, and he used to get drunk on very little, and then be almost impossible."

There are those who believe, Edmund Wilson and John Dos Passos among them, that Fitzgerald was by no means always so drunk as he seemed, and that he used liquor as an excuse for behaving outrageously. In any event, his tolerance had vastly increased by the mid-1930s, when he regularly consumed thirty bottles of beer and/or a quart of gin a day. John Biggs remembers meeting Fitzgerald after his doctor had told him he'd die if he didn't stop drinking. The doctor allowed him a gill of gin a day. Sitting on the lawn under the trees at Biggs's house, Fitzgerald drank a whole bottle, carefully measuring it out a gill at a time. Still later, he took pains to conceal the evidence of his alcoholism. One of the first duties assigned to Frances Kroll, his secretary in Los Angeles in 1939 and 1940, was to gather empty gin bottles in a gunny sack and drop them over the side of a canyon.

The furtive drinker of the Hollywood years had come a long way from the first year of his marriage, when he and Zelda exhibited themselves for the applause or head-shaking of the New York public. From the start there was something almost desperate in their antics. As James Thurber has observed, they "did not know how to invite gaiety. They twisted its arm, got it down, and sat on its chest." Nor did the Fitzgeralds invariably enjoy themselves. Max Eastman, who knew them on the Riviera in 1925, detected no trace of conviviality in their drinking. They drank automatically, it seemed to him. Liquor took them out of themselves and the dull quotidian round into a more colorful if more destructive world. Drinking made things happen. And for a long while it did not seem to matter what those things cost.

The principal cost was in fractured relationships. As time wore on, their alcoholic playfulness turned destructive. "If you want to get your furniture antiqued up," a friend remarked, "you want to get the Fitzgeralds in—they'll antique it up in a single night." Scott did most of the antiquing. Zelda's tendency when drinking was toward suicide—threatening to drive the car off a cliff, parking on the railroad tracks—while Scott indulged in various forms of outrageous behavior. In July 1923, feeling like it, he drove his car into a lake. He also developed the habit of throwing things when drunk. Anita Loos recalls one evening in Great Neck when he bombarded her and Zelda at close range with "two enormous candelabras with lighted candles, a water carafe, a metal wine cooler and a silver platter." The two women took refuge under the oak table.

This sort of mad drunkenness reached its nadir during the time the Fitzgeralds spent in France during the middle and late 1920s. Significantly, the major victims were the elegant and socially confident Gerald and Sara Murphy. One evening at Juan-les-Pins, Dos Passos remembered, Scott crawled under the doormat at the entrance to the Casino and stayed there until Sara coaxed him out like a cat from under a bed. On another occasion he deliberately kicked over a tray of nuts and candies offered for sale by a female street vendor, then offered her a roll of bills to pay for the damage. He also continued to throw things. During a caviar and champagne party given by the Murphys, he started lobbing ashtrays at adjacent tables. At one of their dinner parties he threw a fig and hit the Princesse de Caraman-Chinay between her shoulder blades. She ignored it, but when Archibald MacLeish remonstrated with Fitzgerald, Scott slugged him. Later he began tossing exquisite gold-flecked Venetian wineglasses over the wall, smashing three before the Murphys exiled him for three weeks.

This destructive pattern was often accompanied, when Fitzgerald was drinking, by a series of insistent and intimate questions. The gambit, as Dos Passos commented, "was to put you in the wrong. You were backward in your ideas. You were inhibited about sex." These things might have been true, but Dos Passos was damned if he thought they were anyone's business but his own. Fitzgerald would ask whether couples had slept together before marriage and seek details of their current sex life. Few friendships survived this sort of interrogation. The Murphys, who knew how charming Fitzgerald could be sober and who genuinely admired his work, were more tolerant than most, but eventually Sara sent Scott a scathing letter. "We consider ourselves your friends," she wrote, but Fitzgerald had been treating them instead "as objects for observation" and could hardly expect them to accept "a *Continual* feeling of analysis & sub-analysis, & criticism—on the whole unfriendly." Scott ought to know that he couldn't have *"Theories about friends."* He'd have to change if they were to remain friends, Sara implied. He didn't.

Following his drunken excesses, Fitzgerald would usually be overcome with remorse. On the morning after, he was perfectly capable of being shocked by his own behavior the night before.

"Did I say that?" he'd ask. "Did I do that? My God!" There would follow a torrent of apologies, and a gentle reminder that he could, sometimes, be almost human. This tack did not satisfy everyone. "Between being dangerous when drunk and eating humble pie when sober," Anita Loos remarked, "I preferred Scott dangerous."

By the late 1920s Zelda had stopped drinking with him. Her immersion in the world of ballet had something to do with this, but even before she began to dance seriously—homeward bound from Europe in December 1926—she warned Ludlow Fowler (who'd been best man at the Fitzgeralds' wedding) not to drink like Scott if he wanted his own marriage to be any good. When they returned to Europe again, first in the summer of 1928 and again in 1929, the drinking and the marriage slipped out of control.

Fitzgerald's private ledger provides a shorthand guide to that time. "Carried home from Ritz," notes the ledger entry for June 1928, and then, later that summer, "Drinking and general unpleasantness...first trip jail...dive in Lido...second trip jail." In 1929 the story was much the same: "Being drunk and snubbed...Fairies, breakdown...Rows and indifference...The Murphy yatch [sic] and a last row." Zelda fleshed out this sparse account in a long letter written after her collapse. In 1928: "You didn't work and were dragged home at night by taxi-drivers when you came home at all," she told her husband. "You got up for lunch. You made no advances toward me and complained that I was unresponsive. You were literally eternally drunk the whole summer." In 1929: "You disgraced yourself at the [Philip] Barrys' party, on the yacht at Monte Carlo, at the casino with Gerald and Dotty. Many nights you didn't come home. You came into my room once the whole summer."

Not only did Fitzgerald's marriage fall into disrepair with his drinking, he also "wrecked" himself "with dozens of people." One reason was his propensity to get into quarrels or actual fights when drinking. On one well-documented occasion, in Rome in 1924, he took a swing at a policeman in the course of an argument over taxi fare (the incident, thinly disguised, is described in *Tender Is the Night*) and was severely beaten and jailed. Despite that humiliation Fitzgerald went on to a series of brawls. To the end of his life he became belligerent when drinking, a man "In the dark time of drink who raged,/Who struck to hurt," as a poem of his phrased it. According to Hemingway, when the two of them went out together Scott would insult someone and Ernest "would have to square it to keep him from being beaten up." Scott "could never fight a lick on the best day he ever lived" yet "he got so he liked to hit people" and he would have to take over, Ernest said. Hemingway decided that Fitzgerald liked being humiliated. Surely he invited punishment.

He especially liked baiting Southerners. In June 1923 Fitzgerald got into a fight with a Texan visiting in Great Neck who insisted, as Ring Lardner put it, "that there weren't no real decent fellas nowheres but in the south." In the early 1930s he walked up to a stranger in the Norfolk, Virginia, railway station and made derogatory remarks about the size of his stomach. During the summer of 1935 in Asheville, he conducted a mock court case in which he, as prosecutor, tried half a dozen men for the crime of being Southerners. That time bravado carried the day and no one beat him up, despite his insulting remarks. But there were other times when he managed to provoke fights, extending well into his last years in Hollywood, and usually he lost. Sheilah Graham reports one memorable incident when Scott began making audibly flattering remarks about the girl sitting in front of him in an airport limousine. "Such lovely hair, such poise," he said, and so forth. The girl self-consciously glanced at her escort at first, then as the flattery continued turned to smile at Scott. At this he said, "You silly bitch." The man with her "turned to face Scott, white with anger," but the limousine reached the airport and nothing further ensued.

All the warning signs of alcoholism loomed in Fitzgerald's path: a ruined marriage, broken friendships, fistfights, brushes with the law. But like other alcoholics he refused to recognize these signs for what they were and made excuses for himself instead. To conceal his addiction from others, he drank water-white gin by the tumblerful. To conceal it from himself, he rationalized his actions away.

When Zelda was first hospitalized in 1930, the issue of her husband's drinking came to a head. In his letter "written with Zelda gone to the Clinique," Fitzgerald acknowledged his "insane indulgence in drink" but linked that indulgence to her "almost me-galomaniacal selfishness" and suggested that the heavy drinking had begun when Zelda was ill during 1925 and 1926. "I had to get drunk before I could leave you sick and not care," he explained. To Dr. Oscar L. Forel, Zelda's psychiatrist, he also claimed that Zelda had led him to drink, but not because of her illness. "During the first seven years of our marriage," he wrote Dr. Forel, "it was she who wanted to drink" while he worked. When they went to Europe in 1924, it was "upon her urging" that he began to look forward to wine at dinner. (She drank it at lunch, he didn't, he said.) He'd inaugurated "the ballet idea" in 1927 "to stop her idle drinking," Fitzgerald went on. But now he'd found that a moderate amount of wine at each meal "made all the difference" in how he felt. The dark circles under his eyes disappeared, the coffee didn't beat in his head at night, he looked forward to dinner instead of dreading his wife's "long monologues about ballet steps, alternating with a glazed eye toward any civilized conversation whatsoever." Forel would understand why he could not promise to stop drinking entirely. The fact that he had abused liquor was "something to be paid for with suffering and death but not renunciation . . . [He could not] consider one pint of wine at the day's end as anything but one of the rights of man." Besides, wouldn't giving up alcohol prove to Zelda's relatives and friends that his drinking had caused her "calamity"? Any human value he possessed would disappear if he condemned himself to a lifelong asceticism to which he was "not adapted either by habit, temperament or the circumstances of my metier."

This letter to Forel, a classic litany of rationalizations, minimized Fitzgerald's drinking problems and made a number of contradictory assertions. Zelda was the drinker, not him, or at least she had been at first. He drank very little himself, only a pint of wine with dinner. But he wasn't about to give that up, because it would make him unhealthy, constitute an admission of complicity in Zelda's illness, and even deprive him of any value he possessed as a human being.

Forel undoubtedly diagnosed Fitzgerald's self-justification, just as Dr. Adolf Meyer did when in the course of treating Zelda in Baltimore two years later he referred to Scott as "a potential but

unwilling patient" also. Fitzgerald immediately bridled at the suggestion. He was not to be confused with the local Hunt-Club alcoholic, since he had his drinking well in hand. Besides, Dr. Meyer
ought to be able to discriminate "between an overextended, imaginative, functioning man using alcohol as a stimulus or a temporary *aisment* and a schizophrene." The doctor shouldn't believe
everything Zelda told him.

From his editor and agent, who knew that Fitzgerald was *not*
functioning as well as he once had, Scott asked for mercy. "The
assumption that all my troubles are due to drink is a little too easy,"
he wrote Ober in a December 1934 "apologia pro sua vita." As
alternate causes he mentioned "all the horrors in Montgomery" in
the winter of 1930 and 1931, particularly the recurrence of Zelda's
illness, and his own submersion in *Tender Is the Night* following
a realization that his "literary reputation, except with the *Post*
readers, was at its very lowest ebb." He'd struggled to finish the
book, but the effort left him totally exhausted with "no time or
space for recuperation." His holiday in Bermuda was ruined when
he came down with pleurisy. Zelda had collapsed again shortly
thereafter. Finally he shifted his tone in an incomplete sentence
that broke off the letter: "Of course any *apologia* is necessarily a
whine to some extent, a man digs his own grave and should, presumably, lie on it and I know that the fault for this goes back to
those years, which were really years of self-in-. . ."

Self-indulgence, yes, but as he'd appealed to Perkins the previous month, "without drink I do not know whether I could have
survived this time." Liquor offered him surcease from sorrow, helped
him put Zelda's tragedy out of his mind, kept up his morale: so he
wrote in correspondence during 1935 and 1936, while his own
drinking drove him to degradation and drying-out trips to hospitals.

James Thurber, another drinking writer, probably understood
Fitzgerald's problem as well as anyone. He recognized the process
of self-justification that provided Scott with multiple reasons for
drinking: "Zelda's tragedy, his constant financial worries, his conviction that he was a failure, his disillusionment about the Kingdom
of the Very Rich, and his sorrow over the swift passing of youth
and romantic love." But all these excuses put together, Thurber

concluded, did not commit Fitzgerald to alcoholism so powerfully as the idea that "his creative vitality demanded stimulation"—that he had to drink in order to write.

To begin with, Fitzgerald disputed this notion. Told that Bret Harte had written a 6,000-word story between midnight and 5 A.M. while fueled by whiskey, the twenty-five-year-old author of _This Side of Paradise_ couldn't imagine how. "To me," he said, "narcotics are deadening to work." Coffee might help, but not whiskey. He'd written _Paradise_ on Coca-Cola. But by 1928, when he and Zelda were living at Ellerslie, Scott had begun relying on liquor as an aid to work. Then he conveniently began finding lots of forerunners, in addition to Harte. "Can you name a single American artist except James & Whistler (who lived in England) who didn't die of drink?" he challenged a correspondent. Alcohol, he decided, was the writer's vice, and like the others he needed it to do his work. "Drink heightens feeling," he told Laura Guthrie. "When I drink, it heightens my emotions and I put it in a story. . . . My stories written when sober are stupid . . . all reasoned out, not felt." In this vein he liked to compare himself to General Grant and recall Lincoln's famous remark about finding out what kind of whiskey Grant drank so he could send some of it to his less successful generals. At the same time he realized that liquor did not always contribute to art, that while drinking might heighten the emotions, it also befuddled one's powers of organization and interfered with revision. "A short story can be written on a bottle, but for a novel you need the mental speed that enables you to keep the whole pattern in your head." He would give anything, he said, if he "hadn't had to write Part III of _Tender Is the Night_ entirely on stimulant."

Realizing this, and knowing with part of his mind that booze was ruining him as a man as well as an artist, Fitzgerald was constantly going on the wagon and telling people about it. In time it may have come to seem to him that making the declaration was equivalent to actually quitting. He was "on the absolute wagon and working on the novel, the whole novel and nothing but the novel," he wrote Perkins from Paris in July 1928, a few days after being carried home from the Ritz and a few days prior to his first trip to jail that summer. More than anyone else Perkins heard Fitzgerald's claims:

"I haven't had a drink for almost six weeks and haven't had the faintest temptation as yet." "Except for a three day break last week (Xmas) I have been on the absolute wagon since the end of October. Feel simply grand." Like Ring Lardner before him, he began setting specific dates for abstinence. "Am going on the water wagon from the first of February to the first of April," he wrote Perkins early in 1933. In May 1935 he told Arnold Gingrich that he'd noticed his prose getting "rather watery" and decided to "quit drinking for a few years." But he did not resolve to stop drinking altogether. Always at the end of a rainbow period of sobriety lay the crock of liquor. And with that golden end in sight, he could hardly be expected to stick to a specific time schedule. He could always stop drinking when there was something to be done, he insisted, and took another drink.

One theory holds that the alcoholic cannot successfully stop drinking until brought to the very brink of self-destruction. Fitzgerald reached this point at the end of 1936. He was doing less and less writing, and what he produced wasn't selling to the *Saturday Evening Post* or anyone else. He'd worn out his welcome with most of the people he knew in Baltimore. ("Paul and I stopped at his house to take him to Pimlico [one day]," Fluff Beckwith MacKie reported, "and he fell the length of the steps to the bottom—drunk.") He'd been hospitalized several times to dry out. At home he had to hire nurses to keep him from the bottle. He'd made at least two attempts at suicide. But the final degradation came at the tea dance he gave for Scottie in December 1936.

Fitzgerald's letters to his daughter are peppered with reminders that she was not herself a rich girl. At times Scottie probably needed such reminders, since her father saw to it that she was surrounded, in school and college, by the daughters of extremely wealthy families. He was proud of Scottie—of her charm and wit and popularity—and obviously wanted her to have the kind of social success he'd been denied as a boy. Thus he was delighted to send her, with the help of a partial scholarship, to Ethel Walker's school in Connecticut. During his first fall visit there he promised to give her a party at Christmastime in Baltimore. After consultation with Margaret Turnbull and others, he decided that a tea dance would be more appropriate and less expensive than an evening affair.

Zelda, institutionalized at Highland Hospital near Asheville, would not attend. It was to be a father-and-daughter venture. The cards, he wrote Scottie, should read something like

Miss Frances Scott Fitzgerald
F. Scott Fitzgerald

December 22nd
Four to six
Hotel Belvedere   Dancing

To amuse his fifteen-year-old, he told her he was "determined to have a hurdy-gurdy for the orchestra—you know, an Italian with a monkey." That would be good enough for the children, while the adults would dance to a swing band in an adjoining room. Jesting aside, he obviously wanted to do the right thing for Scottie.

When the day of the dance arrived, he did the worst thing imaginable. He became conspicuously tipsy and insisted on weaving around the dance floor with some of Scottie's young friends, to their general amusement and her acute embarrassment. She had seen him drunk often enough. Once he had slapped her for supposedly interrupting his writing. Another time he sailed an inkwell past her ear. But never before had he so publicly and socially disgraced himself and his daughter. To her credit Scottie carried on bravely, attending another party that evening as if nothing had happened. Both father and daughter knew better. At the new year Fitzgerald once more resolved to stop drinking. This time he did not schedule an end for his trip on the wagon.

Through the winter and spring of 1937, he stuck to his new regimen, aided by the friendship and understanding of Nora and Lefty Flynn in Tryon, North Carolina. Then Ober secured him a contract with MGM in Hollywood, and at mid-summer Fitzgerald reported that "everyone is very nice to me, surprised and rather relieved that I don't drink. I am happier than I've been for several years." In October he wrote the Finneys in Baltimore (who had supplied Scottie with "eggs and consolation" after the tea dance debacle) that he thought he was through drinking for good. He wasn't, quite, and suffered some horrendous relapses during the next two years. But he stayed dry for all of 1940, the last year left to him, drinking gallons of Coke and taking sedatives to calm his nerves and enable him to sleep.

It was characteristic of Fitzgerald that even while rationalizing the disasters of drink, he simultaneously realized the toll that alcohol was exacting. As he told St. Paulite Clifton Read in the winter of 1926, he and Zelda had gone to the Pyrenees to cut back on their drinking, but it hadn't worked. "Wherever you go, you take yourselves and your faults with you. In the mountains or in the city, you make the same things happen." Those things, he knew, were ruining him socially:

> Just when somebody's taken him up and is making a big fuss over him he pours the soup down his hostess' back, kisses the serving maid and passes out in the dog kennel. But he's done it too often. He's run through about everybody, until there's no one left.

He wrote in his notebooks with cynical self-awareness that when sober he wouldn't be able to stand the people he'd like when drunk, and that when "anyone announces to you how little they drink, you can be sure it's a regime they just started."

As her doctors made clear, the reckless round of parties had a devastating effect on Zelda. In a 1932 letter, Fitzgerald chided a friend for trying to restore the alcoholic haze of the past:

> You annoyed me ... by insisting on a world which we will willingly let die, in which Zelda can't live, which damn near ruined us both, which neither you nor any of our more gifted friends are yet sure of surviving; you insisted on its value, as if you were in some way holding a battle front and challenged us to join you. If you could have seen Zelda, as the most typical end-product of that battle during any day from the spring of '31 to the spring of '32 you would have felt about as much enthusiasm for the battle as a doctor at the end of the day in a dressing station behind a blood battle.

Perhaps in another year Zelda would be well; in the meantime, "she must live in a state of teutonic morality."

Liquor could not only wound but kill. The prognosis was particularly dark for those who started drinking early. "Drunk at 20, wrecked at 30, dead at 40," a notebook entry reads. "Drunk at 21, human at 31, mellow at 41, dead at 51." He and Zelda both thought that people should start at the North Pole and gradually work south and that they should first "drink at 35 and progress to a champagne-pink three score and ten." Parties, he once remarked, were "a form of suicide." By the 1930s he was carrying around with him a collection of photographs showing the grisly effects of liquor on various human organs. He knew that booze would eventually kill him and with black humor joked about the idea of drinking himself to death. "Then I was drunk for many years," he wrote in his notebooks, "and then I died."

Even more than in his notebook entries, Fitzgerald revealed his attitudes toward drinking in his fiction. From the beginning it was a subject he liked to write about. There are drunks or drinking bouts in all his novels, just as there had been one in *A Regular Fix*, the first of the Elizabethan dramatic club plays he wrote and participated in as a St. Paul teen-ager. Amory Blaine of *This Side of Paradise* goes on a binge after Rosalind Connage throws him over. Anthony Patch of *The Beautiful and Damned* is "wrecked on the shoals of dissipation." *The Great Gatsby* (1925) displays a curious ambivalence about drinking. Gatsby's parties attract some of Long Island and New York City's more conspicuous and unsavory freeloaders. Rather shockingly—or at least Fitzgerald seems to have found it shocking—women get so tight at these parties that they have to be dunked to sober up or to be "lifted, kicking, into the night" by their escorts. Yet the tone remains more humorous than judgmental in the wonderfully comic scene where Owl Eyes and the "pale dangling individual" manage to sever a wheel from their new coupé.

By the end of the decade, however, liquor was no longer a laughing matter in Fitzgerald's fiction. Whatever he might say in private conversation or correspondence, he confronted his demon openly in his stories and novels, with all the rationalizations stripped away. Several of the stories trace the downfall of potentially likable and worthwhile characters, defeated by the bottle. Producer Bill McChesney loses wife and career to liquor and social pretentiousness in "Two Wrongs" (1930). It becomes clear to Michael Curly, in "The Bridal Party" (1930), that expatriates in Paris were "too weary to be exhilarated by any ordinary stimulant," even though they downed cocktails like Americans, wine like Frenchmen, beer like Germans, and whiskey-and-soda like the English. The liquor produced no gaiety, merely a temporary amnesia.

One of the points made by "Babylon Revisited" (1931), the best of Fitzgerald's drinking stories, is that such amnesia does not last. No matter how he squandered time and money in order not to remember, Charlie Wales cannot forget what his drinking has caused: "his child taken from his control, his wife escaped to a grave in Vermont." He has apparently solved his drinking problem, but Wales is not permitted to recover his daughter Honoria—not until he has paid a still longer and more bitter penance for the wild days and nights of the boom in Paris. The story is obviously autobiographical. Scottie was not taken from him after Zelda's breakdown, but there were those—Zelda's sister Rosalind, for example—who thought that she should have been.

Similar autobiographical patterns emerge in the depiction of such characters as Joel Coles, the screenwriter in "Crazy Sunday" (1932) who disgraces himself at a producer's party, and Dr. Forrest Janney in "Family in the Wind" (1932), whose hands shake so badly that he cannot operate safely. And nothing struck so close to home as the case of Doctor Richard Diver in *Tender Is the Night* (1934).

Just as "Absolution" and "Winter Dreams" served as preliminary studies for *The Great Gatsby*, such stories as "One Trip Abroad" (1930) and "A New Leaf" (1931) prepared for *Tender Is the Night*. Nelson and Nicole Kelly of "One Trip Abroad" do not begin as excessive drinkers. But life in Europe makes them restless, neither has a strong commitment to a profession, and the evenings are long, so they drink a lot of wine at dinner. Eventually, they start spending their time at "several famous bars, all the night clubs except one or two that were highly decorous, all the early-morning clubs of every description, and all summer resorts that made whoopee for its own sake—whoopee triumphant and unrestrained—the main attraction of the season." They try to slow down, unsuccessfully. Finally, like handsome Dick Ragland of "A New Leaf," Nelson finds he cannot face people socially without the stimulus of liquor. "I found that with a few drinks," Ragland explains, "I got expansive and somehow had the ability to please people, and the idea turned my head. Then I began to take a whole lot of drinks to keep going and have everybody think I was wonderful." Then he would get plastered and quarrel with his friends and insult the new bunch of drinking companions that replaced them.

Ragland's situation parallels that of Dick Diver. Both are successful with women. Both possess a charm that liquor seems to heighten. Both become victims of alcohol. Dick Diver loses his ambition and his energy and his wife in his slow downward journey. Dick Ragland's death is more immediate. He drowns himself at sea, realizing that he can never change. "What makes you think that people change their courses?" the narrator asks.

Actually, Ragland's sudden demise resembles Abe North's more than Dick Diver's. North, a prominent figure in the first section of *Tender Is the Night*, has quit tryng to fight his addiction. While "walking in a slow dream," he inspires "a curious respect... rather like the respect of simple races for the insane. Respect rather than fear. There is something awe-inspring in one who has lost all inhibitions, who will do anything." But no one wants him around in his terrifying stupor, not even his friend Diver. When Dick sends him away, Abe reproaches him with a garbled version of one of Fitzgerald's own justifications: "remember what George the third said, that if Grant was drunk he wished he would bite those other generals." Then he takes ship for New York, where he's beaten to death in a speakeasy and crawls home to the Racquet Club to die.

In the novel Abe North's grisly end foreshadows Diver's more gradual deterioration. What both were courting, what Bill McChesney and Dick Ragland were courting, what the drunks in "An Alcoholic Case" (1937) and "A Lost Decade" (1939) were courting, what Fitzgerald himself was courting, was self-destruction. "Now

you are drunk at last," John Peale Bishop wrote in his memorial
poem for his old Princeton friend,

> And that disgrace
> You sought in oblivious dives you have
> At last, in the dissolution of the grave.

11

The Worst Thing

Egyptian Proverb: The worst things:
To be in bed and sleep not,
To want for one who comes not,
To try to please and please not.

—FITZGERALD'S NOTEBOOKS

SCOTT FITZGERALD did not think highly of himself. As a child he read a nursery book about a battle between the small animals, like the fox, and the large ones, like the elephant. The book was no David-and-Goliath story: The big animals wore down the smaller ones and won. Nonetheless, Fitzgerald identified with the fox and many years later could still be moved by remembering its plight. In adolescence he conceived an admiration for various lost causes; like Amory Blaine in *This Side of Paradise*, he was for Bonnie Prince Charlie and Hannibal and the Southern Confederacy. Rather romantically he thought of himself as condemned to lose, despite a valiant effort. Each actual or imagined defeat could move him to tears, but they were tears of sorrow and not of indignation. Losing, he believed, was no more than he deserved.

Looking back on himself during his adolescence, Fitzgerald set down a self-assessment that is remarkable for its judgmental tone:

... Physically—I marked myself handsome; of great athletic *possibilities*, and an extremely good dancer.... Socially... I was convinced that I had personality, charm, magnetism, poise, and the ability to dominate others. Also I was sure that I exercised a subtle fascination over women. Mentally... I was vain of having so much of being talented, ingenious and quick to learn. To balance this, I had several things on the other side: Morally— I thought I was rather worse than most boys, due to a latent unscrupulousness and the desire to influence people in some way, even for evil... lacked a sense of honor, and was mordantly selfish. Psychologically... I was by no means the "Captain of my fate"... I was liable to be swept off my poise into a timid stupidity. I knew I was "fresh" and not popular with older boys... Generally—I knew that at bottom I lacked the essentials. At the last crisis, I knew I had no real courage, perserverance or self respect.

In this devastating catalogue, committed to paper for the first draft of *This Side of Paradise*, Fitzgerald allowed himself certain *talents* but no important *virtues*. Like Amory Blaine he "despised his own personality": his lack of courage, his selfishness, his weakness.

During a football game at Newman, second-stringer Fitzgerald once shied away from a tackle so obviously as to provoke his teammates to call him "yellow." He never forgot the incident, and as an adult sometimes went to extremes to demonstrate his courage, even though basically he considered himself a coward. By the time he'd reached his late thirties, Fitzgerald was deathly afraid of cars. He was frightened crossing streets on foot, and liked to have a woman take his arm as if *she* wanted protection. He was also terrified when riding in cars, and used to cry out "like a nervous woman" as they put on speed. Yet when he was at the wheel, he sometimes drove fast and recklessly. He would arm himself with Dutch courage before sallying forth, and a wild ride would ensue. "Mr. Fitzgerald was one real bad driver," Aquila Keating, his Negro chauffeur during the early 1930s, laconically remarked.

Fitzgerald considered himself terribly self-indulgent. If he'd inherited enough money, he told Laura Guthrie in 1935, he would have killed himself with dissipation years earlier. He longed for physical power and "hardness." "If it wasn't for Zelda," he wrote Max Perkins in 1921, he'd like to disappear for three years. "Ship as a sailor or something and get hard." That would have required a discipline—and a scorn for conventionality—he did not possess. The knowledge of psychology he acquired as a consequence of Zelda's illness made Fitzgerald feel somewhat better about his failings. The "salient points of character," he observed in an April 1932 letter to the *Princeton Alumni Weekly,* were "fixed before the age of twelve." In college a young man might be subjected to broadening or narrowing influences, "but the deeper matters of whether he's weak or strong, strict or easy with himself, brave or timid—these things are arranged in the home, almost in the nursery." His parents, especially his mother, had made him what he was.

They had also provided him with a physical appearance he did not find entirely satisfactory. In particular, he felt ashamed of his feet (which seemed perfectly normal, though his *legs* were rather short for his torso). At six, a neighbor boy "went barefoot in his yard and peeled plums," he wrote in his ledger. "Scott's Freudian shame about his feet kept him from joining in." He often refused to go swimming for the same reason, and not just in boyhood. "All the time I knew him," Sheilah Graham commented, "he always refused to take off his shoes and socks on the beach." Phobic though he was about his own feet, he found women's feet particularly erotic. It was one of the categories he graded when revisiting in his mind the women he'd known, along with looks, age, profession, social position, and shape of breasts.

As for the rest of his appearance, Scott was vain of his good looks—sharply chiseled profile, blond hair, and pale complexion—without considering them ideal. "Perfection—black hair, olive skin and tenor voice": He listed all the things he didn't have in a ledger entry, and underlined the point by adding, "My fake tenor." Hemingway concentrated on the weakness of Fitzgerald's mouth in the course of his savage description in *A Moveable Feast.* Fitzgerald shared those reservations. The face of the autobiographical Nelson Kelly, in "One Trip Abroad," he described as "so weak and self-indulgent that it's almost mean—the kind of face that needs half a dozen drinks really to open the eyes and stiffen the mouth up to normal."

Scott wrote and talked about his weakness so much that he seemed not only resigned to it, but almost to revel in it. His uncertain social position troubled him more. Of relatively humble origins herself, Mollie Fitzgerald had ambitions for her children. Scott despised her for these aspirations, and despised himself for sharing them.

He could not help thinking—and acting—with these aspirations in mind; he even joined the Army on that basis. "About the army please lets not have either tragedy or Heroics," he wrote home after receiving his commission. "I went into this perfectly cold bloodedly and purely for social reasons." The urbane Father Fay, the mentor Fitzgerald had met at Newman, did in fact lay plans for his protégé's social success abroad. "The Honorable Mrs. Guinness and Lady Margaret Orr Ewing will take you on in London. Ronald Guinness will put you up at my Club, which is also one of his." With such a giddy prospect in view, the twenty-year-old from the Midwest felt doubly deprived when he did not in fact cross the Atlantic. His only story that deals with the war, the 1936 "'I Didn't Get Over,'" is concerned with social snobbery. Captain Hibbing, who is closely modeled on Fitzgerald, causes Abe Danzer, a fellow officer and former college classmate, to take the blame for a fatal training camp accident. As a consequence, Danzer is incarcerated and commits suicide. The motive for Hibbing's despicable conduct is that when he'd first joined the company, his old classmate Danzer "acted as if he'd never seen me before."

Though he longed for a card of admission to the world of the wealthy and socially secure, Fitzgerald was not blind to the shortcomings of its inhabitants. In articles and notes Fitzgerald consistently made satirical comments on the rich as a group. As the graduate of a little-known Catholic prep school, he singled out more fashionable schools as special targets. "You could tell a St. Mark's boy by his table manners," he noted. "You see they ate with the servants while their parents divorced and remarried." And: "At Groton they have to sleep in gold cubicles and wash at an old platinum pump. This toughens them up so they can refuse to help the poor." In a June 1923 article, Fitzgerald imagined pompous dowagers on a charity mission, advocating to a poverty-stricken

Italian that he spend his evenings playing family charades: "Suppose some night your wife and the girls take the name 'Viscountess Salisbury,' or the words 'initiative and referendum,' and act them out—and you and the boys guess what words they're acting. So much more real fun than the saloon."

Despite such satirical thrusts, he still dreamed of an ideal aristocracy. About the poor he felt no such ambivalence. In his early fiction, especially, he portrayed the lower classes as brutish, dirty, lazy, and unintelligent. "Yet," as critic John Kuehl has pointed out, "he once said that if he were unable to live with the rich, his next choice would be the poor. Anything was better than the unstable middle class." Sprung from the higher levels of that middle class, he could not make the final leap upward.

"A person always of contrasts," Elizabeth Beckwith MacKie wrote of him. "A split social level. Very shy & very bold. Success or failure. Never in-between." Xandra Kalman of St. Paul sensed his inferiority complex. Nora Flynn did too, and traced to it "a certain streak of something queer in him—gaudy, blatant, almost vulgar." After reading Emily Post's *Etiquette* he'd considered writing "a play in which the whole motivation and conflict should arise from the hero's trying to do the right thing." He remembered the socially incorrect things he'd done, like sending the orchestra second-rate champagne, and masochistically recorded them into his notebooks. And he was inordinately sensitive to snubs and putdowns by others. He was never angrier in his life than one evening in Italy, in 1924, when he was removed from his restaurant table to make way for a Roman aristocrat. In his papers at Princeton are at least three lists of snubs, with the longest of them naming a total of sixty-six people who had snubbed him during the 1925–29 period. To have been put down by so many in so short a time suggests (1) that some of the snubs were imaginary rather than real, though it was during these years he and Zelda became *personae non gratae* because of their drinking and quarreling, and (2) that out of masochism or self-hatred he was actually courting the disapproval of others.

When he put on airs himself, the manner almost always rang false. In Paris he gave *Chicago Tribune* correspondent Henry Wales the dubious information that while at Princeton he'd turned down innumerable invitations to New York coming-out parties. In London he concealed how much mingling with the nobility had meant to him by belittling the occasion. He'd gone on some very high-tone parties with the Mountbattens "and all that sort of thing," he wrote Perkins in 1925. "Very impressed, but not very, as I furnished most of the amusement myself." At Ellerslie in 1927 and 1928 he struck a neighbor as rather ridiculous in the role of squire of the manor, strutting about the grounds and asking nearby residents in for drinks. And he was capable, without intentional irony, of writing a story in 1932 that hinged on the mistake of the heroine in marrying beneath her social station. "Aghast, Caroline realized [on meeting her in-laws for the first time] that she had stepped down several floors. These people had no position of any kind." Anyone in American fiction who thinks like that can expect to get her comeuppance, but not Fitzgerald's heroine. In an improbably happy ending she is liberated from her bad marriage and launched toward a new one with a rich beau whose social position is higher than her own.

That was pretty much the future Fitzgerald had in mind for his daughter when he sent her first to Ethel Walker's school in Connecticut and then on to Vassar. There was some trouble getting Scottie into Vassar, since she'd gone off bounds during her last days at Miss Walker's. But Fitzgerald wrote letters and cajoled connections and pulled strings. "He never wanted anything more in his life," writer Margaret Culkin Banning believed, than for his daughter to go to Vassar. He wanted Scottie to have the best, which to him obviously meant contact with the best families, yet he disapproved of them as a group. So, after placing Scottie in intimate proximity to the daughters—and, through the connections of Vassar with the Ivy League schools, to the sons—of the plutocracy, he then inveighed against them, warning Scottie not to have anything to do with the Park Avenue crowd and attacking the exploiters on Wall Street. In this case, as in all his attitudes toward the upper class, he was a man divided.

That division—the two-sidedness that complicated his life and gave his fiction its particular flavor—undoubtedly derived in part from his Irishness. In his 1922 article about Fitzgerald, Edmund

Wilson stressed his Irish background, along with his Midwestern origins, as essential to understanding the man and his work. Like the Irish, Wilson observed, "Fitzgerald is romantic, but also cynical about romance; he is bitter as well as ecstatic; astringent as well as lyrical. He casts himself in the role of playboy, yet at the playboy he incessantly mocks. He is vain, a little malicious, of quick intelligence and wit, and has an Irish gift for turning language into something iridescent and surprising." Sent the article in advance for comment, Scott hastened to point out that he was Irish, common Irish, on his mother's side alone. This was inaccurate: His paternal grandfather was Irish too, but he chose not to acknowledge the fact. Clearly he was sensitive about his Irishness. For that reason he had difficulty reading James Joyce with pleasure. The picture of middle-class Ireland in *Ulysses* gave him "a sort of hollow, cheerless pain," he wrote Wilson a few months after the article appeared. "Half of my ancestors came from just such an Irish strata or perhaps a lower one. The book makes me feel appallingly naked." Not all Irish were afflicted by "intense social self-consciousness," Fitzgerald realized. But he definitely was; it helped to account for many things about him, not least his snobbery.

The most virulent form of snobbery traditionally occurs in the reaches of the middle class where upward mobility becomes an obsessive goal. The already situated upper class can afford to be democratic, while the aspiring need others to look down on. Hence it is not surprising that Fitzgerald's early fiction is full of ethnic slurs. Yet apparently, judging from the treatment of Jews and Negroes in his novels and stories, he was able to shed this ugly and uncharitable snobbery as he grew older.

To begin with, Fitzgerald depicted Jews as grasping and calculating. *The Beautiful and Damned* is full of unflattering vignettes about Jews; one of the major figures is the unpleasantly aggressive Joseph Black (born Bloeckman), theatrical producer. Then, in *The Great Gatsby*'s Meyer Wolfsheim, he created his most memorable and despicable Jewish character. Wolfsheim is personally repulsive. Luxuriant hairs grow out of his "expressive" nose and he sports cufflinks made of "finest specimens of human molars." Interested solely in making money, he defies legal and moral standards at will. He is "the man who fixed the World Series." He refuses to attend the funeral of his supposed close friend Gatsby, since to acknowledge the "gonnegtion" might be bad for business.

In private utterances too, Fitzgerald revealed his dislike of Jews. They ruined the best resorts. All the "marvellous" places like Majorca, he wrote Tom Boyd in March 1923, "turn out to have one enormous disadvantage—bugs, lepers, Jews, consumptives or philistines." They would adopt whatever manners were profitable. "You begin by pretending to be kind (politeness). It pays so well that it becomes second nature. Some people like Jews can't get past the artificiality of the 1st step." They could not be trusted in business. "You know that the merest discussion of [story] ideas among the Yids would mean they were public property," he wrote Harold Ober in February 1936.

During his last three and a half years in Hollywood, this attitude changed. Originally, he had regarded the men who ran Hollywood's studios with scorn. "I am about to sell my soul to a certain wretched Semite named Goldwyn and go to the coast to write one moving picture," he wrote James Branch Cabell in February 1920. "I have a scurvy plot in my mind suitable to his diseased palate and leprous brain." During his subsequent visits in 1927, 1931, and 1937–40, Fitzgerald learned that it required considerable talent to make successful movies. In particular, he came to admire Irving Thalberg, perhaps the greatest of Hollywood producers. It was the legend of Thalberg that inspired him to create the charismatic figure of the last tycoon, Monroe Stahr, by far his most sympathetic Jewish character.

Individually, Fitzgerald managed to rid himself of the ingrained stereotypes he'd been brought up with. Collectively, it was another matter. "Hell, the best friend I have in Hollywood is a Jew [Eddie Mayer]—" one of his notes begins, and

> another of my best dozen friends is a Jew. Two of the half dozen men I admire most in America are Jews and two of my half dozen best men in History are Jews. But why do they have to be so damned conceited. That minority conceit—like fairies. They go ostrich about their faults—magnify their virtues which anyone is willing to grant in the first place. They point at Benny Leonard

[a champion prize-fighter] or this war hero here and say we got
pugnacity. When the nurses in the hospital admit that a Jewish
patient groans at the sight of a needle.

And so on. At the same time he had come to respect their achievement and their power. Taking "whacks at Jews"—as he had done
all his life—was "a moron's game," he cautioned his daughter.

With Negroes, it is easier to establish the growing maturity
of Fitzgerald's outlook. Initially, he regarded blacks as figures of
fun called "coons" or "niggers" or "pickaninnies." They are so
portrayed in much of his fiction, and that is how he treated them
himself to start with. At five, he made friends with a "colored
boy, name forgotten—name Ambrose." At six, after performing
his duties as ringbearer at his cousin Cecilia's wedding in Maryland, he "turned on his two black friends Roscoe and Forrest
and with the help of a bigger boy tried to tied them up with
ropes." Thirty years later, he was still capable of playing pranks
on Negroes. At La Paix—his house near Baltimore—he bewil-
dered a Negro clergyman, who had come to solicit funds for a
local orphanage, by introducing him as a distinguished visitor
from Africa. The clergyman fled in panic.

The case of Aquila, Fitzgerald's chauffeur at La Paix, is more
ambiguous. Aquila suffered from a speech impediment so that he
pronounced *th* as if it were *s*, and Fitzgerald devised a sentence
full of *th*'s, which he made his chauffeur practice over and over.
It may be, as critic Robert Forrey has suggested, that he did so as
a continuing joke at Aquila's expense. Margaret Turnbull saw the
practice, however, as an example of Fitzgerald's desire to help
people. "Aquila...had a bad lisp, and Scott would try to work
with him everyday to correct it."

Whatever one's interpretation of the Aquila incident (there may
be some truth in both versions), it is clear that as a young man
Fitzgerald adopted the conventional, stereotypical Southern view
of Negroes. They had rhythm. One was so talented at teaching
white ladies how to play guitar that after "two lessons, you'd think
some of 'em was colored." They stole chickens. They were casual
about sexual morality. They got drunk on Saturday night and cut
each other up.

Blacks, in short, were happy, amoral children, and yet there was something frightening about them. Running out of gas in a small Virginia town "which bore the sinister name of Niggerfoot," Fitzgerald was at first unable to purchase fuel from the recalcitrant Negroes. The incident is described in detail in "The Cruise of the Rolling Junk" (1924):

> They shook their heads. They mumbled melancholy and ineffectual protests. As I grew more vehement, their stubborn stupidity grew hazy rather than gave way—one of the old men vanished into the darkness to return with a yellow buck of reasonable age. Then there was more arguing until finally one of the little boys went sullenly in search of a pail. When he returned a second boy carried the pail up the road, and fifteen minutes later an absolutely new boy arrived with three quarts of gasoline.
>
> Meanwhile I had gone into the store for cigarettes and found myself enclosed immediately in a miasmatic atmosphere which left on me a vivid and unforgettable impression. I could not say clearly even now what was going on inside that store—a moonshine orgy, a pay-day gambling bout, something more sinister than these or perhaps not sinister at all. Nor could I determine whether the man who waited on me was black or white. But this I know—that the room was simply jammed with negroes and that the moral and physical aura which they cast off was to me oppressive and obscene.

That this aura might have an unacknowledged sexual source (Zelda was traveling with her husband when the car stalled in Niggerfoot) is suggested by an incident in the abortive novel, "The World's Fair," an early version of what became *Tender Is the Night*. The protagonist of the fragment is Francis Melarky, who is a Southerner by origin. Visiting a Paris nightclub, Melarky sees "a huge American negro, with his arms around a lovely French tart," roaring "a song to her in a rich beautiful voice and suddenly Melarky's Tennessee instincts remembered and were aroused." Melarky begins looking at everyone "disagreeably and truculently," and slugs "another colored man" who has the ill luck to brush against him accidentally. After knocking out the innocent black, Melarky is immediately contrite: "God, what a son-of-a-bitch I am. He was a nice-looking fellow." But he had been powerless to stem the tide of anger and antipathy that welled up within him.

During the 1930s Fitzgerald came to regard Negroes as dignified beings whose stoic behavior gave him an example to follow. In "One Hundred False Starts," a 1933 article, he goes to "Uncle Bob," an old Alabama Negro, for advice. "When things get so bad that there isn't any way out," he asks (thinking of his own recent literary and personal problems), "what do you do then?" Half-cynically expecting "a platitudinous answer, a reflection of something remembered from Uncle Remus," Fitzgerald is pleasantly disappointed. "Mr. Fitzgerald," Uncle Bob said, "when things get that-away I wuks." That was good advice, and during his last years in Hollywood, working to pay his debts, he turned for help in his bouts of nervousness to Gay Lloyd Smith, a Negro he had employed. Smith talked to him—and joined him in putting golf balls on a rug—to make the sleepless nights pass.

Still, Uncle Bob and Gay Smith were blacks who could be safely categorized as servants, like the "*very best* negro nurses in the South" who proved an exception, he wrote Helen Hayes in 1936, to his rule that "it is impossible to get a first rate American governess who will not make home a hell." Furthermore, his stories continued to describe Negroes in derogatory terms. Earl W. Wilkins, referring to "No Flowers," a July 1934 *Saturday Evening Post* story, wrote to Fitzgerald in mild protest. "Must all male Negroes in your books and stories be called 'bucks'?" he asked. Why couldn't he treat Negroes with dignity, as Sinclair Lewis had in *Arrowsmith?* Perhaps influenced by this letter, in two late pieces of fiction Fitzgerald went one step further and did portray Negroes as characters deserving of sympathy and respect. In *The Last Tycoon* Stahr meets a Negro intellectual walking along the beach. A serious person who reads Emerson and thinks for himself, the black man tells the producer that he never goes to the movies and never lets his children go because he considers the movies a waste of time. Then he goes away, unaware that he has "rocked an industry." This Negro is not a "poor old Sambo," nor can members of his race be described by any such belittling nicknames: "We don't call them anything especially," Stahr remarks.

The second instance is that of "Dearly Beloved," a story that was first published in 1969. A miniaturized biography in format, "Dearly Beloved" tells in three pages the life history of Beauty Boy and Lilymary, Chicago blacks. Like the Negro on the beach, Beauty Boy is an intellectual whose reading runs to Plato and Thoreau. He is also colored golf champion of Chicago, though he works in a menial capacity as steward of the club car on the railroad. One night, after his long-awaited son is born, Beauty Boy loses a leg to the iron monster, and things are never the same again. Finally both Beauty Boy and Lilymary die in an influenza epidemic and go to heaven where his leg grew whole "and he became golf champion of all heaven, both white and black, and drove the ball powerfully from cloud to cloud through the blue fairway. Lilymary's breasts became young and firm, she was respected among the other angels, and her pride in Beauty Boy became as it had been before." But something is missing, and they cannot quite find what it is. "So," Fitzgerald ends his story in an anticipation of Kurt Vonnegut, "things go."

What they miss in heaven, apparently, is the capacity to dream, the romantic readiness that had given brightness to their youth as it had to Scott and Zelda Fitzgerald's. The loss of this gift of illusion is a persistent theme in Fitzgerald's fiction, and it is an index of his maturity that he should have applied the theme to a Negro couple, in the realization that blacks and whites share the same hopes and the same disillusionments.

Unhappily, Fitzgerald had few illusions about the kind of man he was. And what kind was that? Obviously far too complex to be forced into any psychological pigeonhole, he corresponded in his behavior rather closely to what psychologist Avodah K. Offit has described as the "histrionic personality." Drama is the essence of life to such people, Offit points out. They covet attention and become actors to get it. Their "primary art" is seduction, but since some resist seduction, the histrionic often "turns to less artful but more direct maneuvers for attention," such as bemoaning cruel fate. Often the histrionic personality plays the role Samuel Johnson's dictionary defined as that of a "seeksorrow," one who is certain that no one else has ever suffered so much and determined that others should realize this. No amount of sympathy or attention or love is ever enough to satisfy such a person.

Generally, according to Offit, histrionics tend to be women. Whatever the sex, however, the pattern was much the same: an opening attempt to please others with one's lovableness, and, should that fail, insistence "on the limelight for [one's] black vapors." But how could such people—seductive, demanding, manipulative, shallow or overemotional, time-consuming, and unrewarding—manage to seem attractive? The answer, Offit believes, lies in their "uncanny ability to make sensitive and perceptive observations about others," their "intuitive insight into the ways of engaging other people."

Fitzgerald's compulsion to attract women fits into this description, and so too do his frequent attempts to enlist sympathy for the (admittedly harsh) blows life had dealt him. That's the whole programme of "The Crack-Up" articles. The closest tie of all, though, lies in the area of performance. Throughout his life Fitzgerald thought of himself as a dramatist. At ten, he was making up shows and assigning himself parts where he could wear his red sash and tricornered hat. During teen-age years, he wrote, produced, and acted in four different plays for an amateur dramatic club in St. Paul. At Princeton, he wrote book and/or lyrics for several Triangle club shows. His 1922 play, *The Vegetable,* opened and closed in Atlantic City, but he continued to think he had a particular gift for the theater. "If I ever get out of debt," he wrote Ober in 1935, "I want to try a second play. It's just possible I could knock them cold if I let go the vulgar side of my talent." And as late as February 1939 he and Sheilah Graham entered into a 50–50 contractual agreement to write a play that was never completed.

Moreover, he loved to show off. As a boy he learned Mark Antony's speech, and would spout "Friends, Romans, Countrymen" to whatever audience of admiring middle-aged ladies his mother could muster. Sometimes he'd recite without being asked. Zelda's similar streak of exhibitionism was one of the things that appealed to him about her. Together—at least during the first years of their marriage—they demonstrated a virtual "genius for imaginative improvisations" to delight their guests. The gaiety, of course, was not always sincere. He recognized the actor in himself as Rosemary did in Dick Diver. "I am an actor," he'd say. Or "I have two sides: the worker and the showoff. I like to show off."

When he wasn't playing the lover or the entertainer, he'd descend into highly public melancholy. Near the end of her long, painful stay at Prangins, Zelda wrote trying to cheer *her husband* up. "Can't you possibly be just a little bit glad that we are alive and that all the year that's coming we can be to-gether and work and love and get some peace for all the things we've paid so much for learning? Stop looking for solace: there isn't any, and if there were life would be a baby affair." But he did not change. As Arnold Gingrich observed, Fitzgerald was "melodramatic and always in the middle of a tragedy." Admittedly, he suffered tragic blows in his life, but if he hadn't, Gingrich thought, he would have gone looking for them. He "had a queer Keltic tendency to enjoy ill-luck as some people enjoy ill-health. He liked to dramatize to himself the inevitability of both his latest and his next defeats."

However it could be gotten, what he wanted—what he demanded—was attention. He would tell Laura Guthrie how to act: do this, sit here, don't talk. Once he startled her by commanding, "Take that necklace off." She did so immediately; she'd been thinking of doing it when he spoke. One function he demanded of Laura and of several nurses was that of rubbing his head. Fitzgerald was particularly fond of such massage. He liked sitting in the barber chair, "rather happy and sensually content at the strong fingers on his scalp." The experience relaxed him. On one occasion he fell asleep while Laura was rubbing his head. When he'd been drinking, though, mere rubbing wasn't enough. His scalp would itch so badly that he'd plead with her to scratch it. "As hard as I could claw," she remarked, "I never got him to say it was hard enough." No such service could be too much.

For Fitzgerald as for the histrionic personality, the goal was to attract the admiration of others. During most of his life he measured success in terms of popularity and approbation rather than accomplishment. Though he disliked or even scorned its members, he wanted to be accepted into a social elite that kept its doors shut against him. As a youth, he fantasized about gaining entrance as a great athlete or a war hero, but physical capabilities and circumstances militated against him there. As a writer, he found the door opened a crack, then shut again once his fame began to fade. It was primarily as an actor, an eternally charming entertainer, that he commanded the approval and admiration he needed. Almost everyone who knew him was struck by his obvious—even painfully obvious—desire to please.

In the army, Fitzgerald had been at best an indifferent officer. The most distinctive thing about him, fellow officer Devereux C. Josephs recalled, was that he "was eager to be liked and almost vain in seeking praise." Twenty years later, he struck Margaret Culkin Banning in much the same way. "He wanted everyone to like him," she said, "and was afraid they wouldn't." *Everyone* included children as well as adults: usually they were easier to please. One day in Antibes, Robert Benchley remembered, Fitzgerald got down on his stomach and crawled around all afternoon playing tin soldier with a lot of kids. Anyone who'd do that shouldn't be unhappy, he wrote Scott after reading *Tender Is the Night*. When Fitzgerald visited his cousin Cecilia Taylor in Norfolk, he would bring a small corsage for each of her three little daughters. "Naturally they thought he hung the moon," a friend of theirs observed. He even courted the good opinion of servants. "I must be loved," he told Laura Guthrie in 1935. "I tip heartily to be loved. I have so many faults that I must be approved of in other ways."

As that last remark suggests, his insatiable quest for popularity sprang from a basic insecurity about himself. In company he would try to conceal the insecurity through "a constant effort to be brilliant, amusing and inventive." Often the effort succeeded in charming people, but not always. Perhaps he was most winning, where women were concerned, when he simply listened, for—as Margaret Turnbull has said—he "had this extraordinary quality of giving you his undivided attention." At the beginning of their romance, Sheilah Graham wrote, Scott made her feel that simply dancing with her was "the most extraordinary privilege." He directed his words to her alone ("You can stroke people with words," he wrote in his notebooks) and above all gave "rapt attention" to everything she said. Like Gatsby, Fitzgerald had a way of "concentrating on *you* with an irresistible prejudice in your favor." "As far as I know," Margaret Egloff observed, "everyone who was really exposed to him loved him. He simply couldn't bear it if they didn't." Nora

Flynn, keenly aware though she was of his self-centeredness, still admired Fitzgerald's special charm. "Some people waltz with rubbers on and some as if they were walking on air," she said. "That's the way talking with Scott was, and being with him at its best."

Trying hard to be at his best sapped Fitzgerald's energy and left him drained and exhausted. Then the effort began to show, as Marjorie Kinnan Rawlings, author of *The Yearling*, detected during their meeting in 1936. "He was not interested in me as a writer or as a woman, but he turned on his charm as deliberately as a water-tap, taking obvious pleasure in it. The irony was there, too, as though he said, 'This is my little trick. It is my defiance, my challenge to criticism, to being shut out.'" He had overspent his quota of charm and was left "emotionally bankrupt," as he called it in "The Crack-Up." He was left as well with an inner awareness that approached self-disgust. He wrote about that feeling too, in "The Crack-Up" and elsewhere.

Intellectually, he was fully aware of the dangers inherent in seeking popularity. Hollywood's Elsa Maxwell, he observed in his notebooks, "was a social impressario of considerable ability but her ambition had driven her to please so many worthless people that she had become, so to speak, a sort of lowest common denominator of all her clients." The same thing, he feared, might happen to him. He resolved not to go around "saying I'm fond of people when I mean I'm so damned used to their reactions to my personal charm that I can't do without it. Getting emptier and emptier." At one time in the past, he wrote Perkins in May 1940, he had thought he could "make people happy and it was more fun than anything. Now even that seems like a vaudevillian's cheap dream of heaven, a vast minstrel show in which one is the perpetual Bones." The self-contempt in that remark Fitzgerald managed, to some degree, to transplant to his fiction.

As Henry Dan Piper, one of Fitzgerald's most perceptive critics, has commented, his fictional heroes "are destroyed because they attempt to fulfill themselves through their social relationships. They cannot distinguish between social values like popularity, charm, and success, and the more lasting moral values." Their creator did make that distinction, however, and so was constantly surrounding his characters with a mist of admiration and then blowing it away. In *This Side of Paradise,* Amory Blaine attempts to change himself from a "personality" into a "personage." A personality, as the book defines it, depends for his self-image on the approval of others. A personage, on the other hand, "is never thought of apart from what he's done." It is the difference between the charmer and the achiever, and at the end of the novel Fitzgerald rather unpersuasively announces that Amory has at last become a personage.

Presumably he has progressed further than Basil Duke Lee, another autobiographically based character whom Fitzgerald follows only through the high school years. In "The Perfect Life," Basil begins to think of himself as a leader of men, one who can influence younger boys for good or ill, and then drifts off into romantic visions of climbing the heights of society and receiving applause as he goes. When in his daydream he is tapped last man for Skull and Bones and turns it down, instead pointing to another man who wanted it more, "a burst of sobbing would break from the assembled crowd." At his inauguration as president (at 25!), "all around him his people would lift up their faces in admiration and love." Fitzgerald then underlines the ridiculousness of the dreams by bringing Basil back to earth, where he is consuming crackers and milk stolen from the school pantry. In *Tender Is the Night,* however, the hero's plight is much more poignant because he realizes but cannot abandon his shoddy ambition to court the love of others at all costs. Basil is amusing, Amory unconvincing, Dick Diver painfully to the life.

Tender Is the Night is a book about charm. Immediately after the appearance of *The Great Gatsby,* Fitzgerald began considering a novel on the topic. An April 1925 letter from Willa Cather served as a catalyst. Anyone swept away by personal charm, she observed, was likely to be amazed that the effect was so much greater than the cause, and in writing it was much easier to describe the effect than the person who produced it. Fitzgerald repeated the thought in describing Diver: "He won everyone so quickly with an exquisite consideration and politeness that moved so fast... that it could be examined only in its effect." That effect, or rather those effects, were what he set about to explore in his novel, though he was worried—rightly, as it turned out—that the book would not be properly understood or appreciated. "About five years ago I became, unfortunately, interested in the insoluble problems of personal charm and have spent the intervening time on a novel that's going to interest nobody and probably alienate the remaining half dozen who are kind enough to be interested in my work," he commented.

The first hundred pages of *Tender,* as Piper has pointed out, constitute "one of the best guides ever written on the theory and practice of charm." Diver presents himself to Rosemary with ingratiating wit. "It's not a bad time," he says on first meeting. "It's not one of the worst times of the day." The next time they speak, he asks her to lunch with his party, his voice promising "that he would take care of her, and that a little later he would open up whole new worlds for her." He introduces her smoothly, without reference to her film success. He is considerate, and moves the beach umbrella to "slip a square of sunlight" off her sunburned shoulder. With his reddish hair and complexion, bright, hard blue eyes, and somewhat pointed nose, "there was never any doubt at whom he was looking or talking—and this is a flattering attention, for who looks at us?... His voice, with some faint Irish melody running through it, wooed the world, yet she [Rosemary] felt the layer of hardness in him, of self-control and of self-discipline, her own virtues." In Paris she walks a step behind to admire and adore him:

> His step was alert as if he had just come from some great doings and was hurrying on to others. Organizer of private gaiety, curator of a richly incrusted happiness. His hat was a perfect hat and he carried a heavy stick and yellow gloves. She thought what a good time they would all have being with him tonight.

Superlatively, Dick Diver has the gift of making others happy; he also has a compulsion to exercise this gift. At the very beginning of his career as a doctor, he has supper with Franz Gregorovius and his bride, and goes out of his way to charm Kaethe Gregorovius, though she smells of cauliflower and he hates himself for taking the trouble. There was "a pleasingness about him that simply had to be used," a charm that he cannot help dispensing.

In considering personal charm, Fitzgerald is most concerned about the consequences for Doctor Diver himself. In the end his obsessive need to please leads to ruination. Baby Warren initially thinks Dick "toothsome," yet in her Anglophilia decides that he "put himself out too much to be really of the correct stuff." In time even those who loved him to begin with develop similar reservations. Toward the end Nicole analyzes her husband dispassionately as he starts "to play with Rosemary, bringing out his old expertness with people, a tarnished object of art." And Rosemary herself sees that the game of love between them is really only a charade. "Oh, we're such *actors*—you and I," she says at the moment of their deepest intimacy. "When people have so much for outsiders," she wonders, "didn't it indicate a lack of inner intensity?"

A greater loss to Dick than that of women's love was the loss of his vitality. To the extent that *Tender Is the Night* can be regarded as a psychological novel, the most interesting case study is not of Nicole, or of the poor artist, tortured by eczema, who was modeled on Zelda, but of Dick Diver himself. He transfers his energy and wholeness not only to Nicole but to everyone else as well, giving up a piece of himself here and a crumb there until there is nothing left with which to work his magic. "I guess I'm the Black Death," he tells Rosemary in Rome. "I don't seem to bring people happiness any more." A hollow man, he fades away in the towns of upstate New York, bereft even of self-respect.

During his young manhood Diver had gone through "a heroic period" when "he had no idea that he was charming, that the affection he gave and inspired was anything unusual among healthy people." Such innocence did not last; eventually Diver dispenses his charm mechanically or even cynically. In the last scene of the book Diver summons up his old fatal pleasingness for Mary Minghetti. Though it's not yet noon on the beach he's been drinking anisette and has

> arrived at where a man should be at the end of a good dinner,
> yet he showed only a fine, considered, restrained interest in
> Mary. His eyes, for the moment clear as a child's, asked her

sympathy and stealing over him he felt the old necessity of convincing her that he was the last man in the world and she was the last woman.

. . .   .

His glance fell soft and kind upon hers, suggesting an emotion underneath; their glances married suddenly, bedded, strained together. Then, as the laughter inside of him became so loud that it seemed as if Mary must hear it, Dick switched off the light and they were back in the Riviera sun.

The laughter was not simply or entirely at Mary's expense. Much of it Dick directed at his own shallow self.

In the portrait of Diver, Fitzgerald came close to confronting what he most disapproved of in himself. Originally he had intended to model Diver on Gerald Murphy, but before long made the shift to what John O'Hara called "a tall Fitzgerald." This close identification of author and character accounts for a critical shortcoming in this brilliant novel. At the time the book came out, a number of reviewers thought Diver's decline and his rapid acceptance of it unconvincing. That was not precisely the problem: The problem is that one does not know how to respond to Diver. On the one hand, he emerges as a sympathetic character, well-intentioned, generous, exploited by the rich. On the other hand, during the course of his downfall he becomes progressively less admirable and likable.

Attempts to construct a successful play or film based on the novel have foundered on this point. Zelda suggested immediately after *Tender* was published that if Scott undertook to write a play version he should "make the man weak and charming from the first, always gravitating towards the center of things: which would lead him, when he was in the clinic, to Nicole and later to Rosemary." That was not at all what Fitzgerald had in mind. He thought, for example, that Mrs. Edwin Jarrett's adaptation failed to make Diver an attractive enough figure. Rosemary shouldn't express her distaste for the battlefield scene, he instructed Mrs. Jarrett in February 1938, since "she had a *good* time and it belittles Dick's power of making things fun . . . Dick's curiosity and interest in people was *real*—he didn't stare at them—he glanced at them and *felt* them." In fact, he insisted, Diver "is after all a sort of superman, an approximation of the *hero* seen in overcivilized terms—taste is no substitute for vitality but in the book it has to do duty for it." It was one thing for Fitzgerald to dissect the weakness in himself through Diver, and another to let others do it. He wanted only the good and kind and innocently charming doctor on the stage or screen.

12

"a writer only"

WITH A handsome contract from MGM in his pocket, Fitzgerald arrived in Hollywood in June 1937 determined to recoup his fortunes and straighten out his life. It was an unlikely place, this city of gilt and make-believe, for a man in his forties to achieve maturity, but that is what he managed to accomplish during the three and a half years left to him. He could not have made it without the love of an unusual woman.

Fitzgerald met Sheilah Graham less than a fortnight after coming to Hollywood at a party celebrating her engagement to the Marquess of Donegall. He saw her again a week later, at the Screen Writers Guild dance. On July 24 they had dinner together for the first time. Within a month they were lovers. Her engagement was called off, and, though they kept separate residences for propriety's sake, they began to spend their evenings together. The arrangement lasted until Fitzgerald's death.

In her blonde beauty, Sheilah resembled Zelda—that was what first attracted Scott—but she came from a totally different world. What's more, she pretended to a status in that world she did not have. According to her story, she had been born to an upper-class English family, but had become a showgirl and a journalist because she found society boring. Not entirely persuaded, Fitzgerald kept prying for details. Eventually she told him the truth. Her name was Lily Sheil. She'd been born in London's East End slums and raised in an orphanage. She'd been married before, to a much older man who urged her to go on the stage and did not object when wealthy men took her out, since it provided them both with an entree to the upper strata of society. Attractive and bright, Sheilah was soon moving in those circles; she was even presented at court. With her marriage failing, she came to America and landed a job writing a syndicated column on Hollywood for the North American Newspaper Alliance. She was twenty-eight, made $160 a week on her column, and only dimly understood what she was getting into as Fitzgerald's companion.

Sheilah was the only woman of humble beginnings he'd ever loved. At times, Fitzgerald was the tenderest of suitors, sending flowers and notes of endearment. He also played the role of knight-errant, defending his lady against real and imaginary enemies. In October, a pretentious British producer wrote Sheilah a nasty letter, accusing "Miss Mussolini Graham" of bad manners and poor sportsmanship in breaking a dinner date and not responding to his phone calls. "It is a matter of complete indifference whether I meet you or not," he added, but she might at least have communicated with him. Delighted at the opportunity, Fitzgerald answered the letter. When "a girl neglects two dozen phone calls," he pointed out, it was fair to assume that she wasn't interested. Perhaps the producer should try other phone numbers. In any event he could "always take refuge behind that splendid, that truly magnificent indifference."

Sheilah was less pleased on two other occasions when Scott attempted to support her career with his fists. Late in 1937 she signed to do a weekly radio show in Hollywood. The first broadcast went badly, and the sponsor thought an actress should be hired to read the copy. Sheilah disagreed and flew to Chicago in an attempt to make the broadcast herself. Scott went along and, under the influence of liquor, threatened to punch the executive who was stalling Sheilah, and made such a nuisance of himself at airtime that he had to be escorted from the studio. Two years later, when an editorial in the *Hollywood Reporter* accused Sheilah of being disloyal to the industry in the remarks she was making on a speaking tour, Scott rode to her defense once again. Though John O'Hara insisted it was a bad idea to hit a newspaper man and refused to go along, Fitzgerald presented himself at the paper and demanded to see the publisher. The publisher, wisely, did not emerge from his office. When Fitzgerald's indignation—and, probably, his alcoholic ardor—cooled, he left without forcing a confrontation.

With most of the women he'd known and admired—Ginevra, Zelda, Nora Flynn, Sara Murphy—Fitzgerald had felt himself a social inferior. With Sheilah it was different, yet she was not "poor Sheilah" in need of a champion at all, but a practical and—in Hollywood—powerful woman who could take care of herself very well. Her independence, like her background, fascinated Fitzgerald. When she first told him her story, he asked how many affairs she had had. Sheilah didn't know what to say. She was twenty-eight; she'd been on the stage. Finally she decided that "eight was a nice round figure." Eight affairs, she told him, and "he was really quite shocked," she recalls, and then intrigued, and then extremely jealous. In the course of her work she routinely met and talked to the leading actors and directors and producers in Hollywood. Some of them, finding her attractive, flirted or made passes at her. When this happened—when John Boles or Randolph Scott or Errol Flynn indicated their interest in her—Fitzgerald became furious and resorted to an old method to punish her. He got drunk.

Usually the punishment ran to a pattern. First Scott would abuse Sheilah verbally. A breakup would follow, and then he would apologize profusely. It was entirely his fault. He'd behaved terribly. She was right to send him away. It would be better if he were dead, and perhaps that could be arranged. Confronted by such elaborate signals (she knew he kept a pistol around the house), Sheilah would take him back. She didn't know what else to do; she had no experience in dealing with alcoholics. Besides, she loved him, despite the awful things he said and did in his drunken rages.

The insults he directed at her often focused on sex. Even in his poem "Beloved Infidel," Fitzgerald celebrates Sheilah's beauty in the context of her dubious past. "That sudden smile across a room/ Was certainly not learned from me," the poem begins. Each of its seven stanzas ends with the same two words: "other men," as in "lips once soft for other men," "the things you learned from other men," and "the tale you told to other men." It made for a curiously ambiguous love poem. Fitzgerald was grateful for whatever and whomever had made her what she was—"How can I hate him

Zelda and Scott Fitzgerald, when they were very young

Sheilah Graham, English chorus girl to Hollywood columnist;
Scott and Sheilah, together until the end

when/He did his share to fashion you?" he wrote—and still deeply troubled about her past. In this poem, as in less subtle ways, he touched his wound of jealousy and reminded her of the life she was trying to put behind her.

At the end of a Sunday afternoon party he and Sheilah gave, Scott drunkenly ordered everyone home and told the last guests— screenwriter Nunnally Johnson and his wife—that he knew they'd never come back, since he was living with his "paramour." It was a curiously stilted and old-fashioned word; on the back of his framed picture of her, he was more explicit: "Portrait of a Prostitute," he wrote. These devastating accusations have been interpreted as examples of Fitzgerald's puritanical streak, but he was also concerned about the impropriety of their relationship. He sometimes spoke to Sheilah of divorcing Zelda and marrying her. On one occasion, he went so far as to seek reassurance about this plan from Nora Flynn. Go ahead, she advised him. Nora was sure he was doing the right thing. The time had come for him to have a life of his own, and she had "a strange feeling" that Sheilah was the right person for him. He'd be of more use to Scottie if he were happy and "living, so to speak, again." But the mores of the times, his guilt feelings, and his sense of propriety all conspired against divorcing the woman who had once meant everything to him.

Meanwhile, Zelda was kept in the dark. Once or twice a year Scott would fly back East and they would take a vacation together. These reunions rarely worked out well. In April 1939 they went to Cuba where Scott got drunk and was beaten up while trying to stop a cockfight. Back in New York the drinking continued until he was taken to the alcoholic ward at Bellevue, and then to Doctors Hospital. Zelda returned to her Asheville sanitarium alone, and covered for him with the doctors there. "You are the finest, loveliest, tenderest, most beautiful person I have ever known," he wrote her in May. The way he had behaved would try anyone "beyond endurance." But they never saw each other again, and in their weekly correspondence Zelda seemed aware that some things were being kept from her. "What is your actual address?" she asked. "S'pose I wanted to phone you—or do something unprecedented like that?"

At the end of November 1939, his relationship with Sheilah

underwent its most severe crisis. *Collier's* had decided not to se-
rialize the novel about Hollywood he had just begun. Furious and
frustrated, he fell off the wagon precipitously. In the scene that
followed, he struck Sheilah and danced around the room shouting
"Lily Sheil! Lily Sheil!" She tried to end the relationship permanently, but Fitzgerald would not go quietly. Instead, he sent threatening notes to her, "Get out of town, Lily Sheil, or you will be
dead in 24 hours," and a meddling telegram to her boss at the
North American Newspaper Alliance, "SHEILAH GRAHAM TODAY
BANNED BY EVERY STUDIO STOP SHE IS RUINING NANA IN HOLLYWOOD
STOP SUGGEST YOU SEND HER BACK TO ENGLAND WHERE SHE BE-
LONGS STOP DO YOU KNOW HER REAL NAME IS LILY SHEIL?" Eventually
she forgave him in response to flowers and apologies and letters
like this one:

> I want to die, Sheilah, and in my own way. I used to have
> my daughter and my poor lost Zelda. Now for over two years
> your image is everywhere. Let me remember you up to the end
> which is very close. You are the finest. You are something all
> by yourself. You are too much something for a tubercular neu-
> rotic who can only be jealous and mean and perverse. . . . It's
> not long now. I wish I could have left you more of myself. You
> can have the first chapter of the novel and the plan. I have no
> money but it might be worth something. . . . I love you utterly
> and completely.

He'd had his last binge, Fitzgerald promised her. This time he was
going to stop drinking for good. This time he meant it.

Sheilah came back for the year that was left to them. During
this period they often went to films, but never to nightclubs and
rarely to parties. Sheilah sent her legman to cover Hollywood get-
togethers in order to stay home. Except when he was drinking—
about five months out of their three and a half years with each
other, she estimates—they had good times together. In Ping-Pong
matches he'd strike the ball, pirouette, and try to hit it again. They
acted out roles in films he was working on, once collapsing in
laughter as he played a comic Rhett Butler to her Scarlet O'Hara.
And during that last year especially, they conducted their "College

of One," with Fitzgerald the professor to an apt and eager classroom of one. Earlier Sheilah had found him a series of houses in Malibu and Encino to indulge his lifelong habit of moving frequently from place to place and to provide him with a quiet atmosphere, but now he was settled in a Hollywood apartment a 1403 North Laurel, a block from her own, The rent was only $110 a month. It was, he observed, the least expensive place he could live in without looking poor. There they held their evening seminars on the curriculum he devised: a mixture of the classics and modern books and poems, interspersed with art and music, politics and history. She made oral or written reports on the books she read, and was not always the reverent pupil. Her reaction to *This Side of Paradise*, for example, was "Well, it isn't Dickens." But that hurt Fitzgerald and she was immediately contrite. She had always been a quick study, but it was one thing to acquire the accent and manners of the British upper classes and quite another to tackle Proust and Mann, Dostoyevsky and Flaubert, Keats and Shakespeare, Beethoven and Leonardo. No other man had treated her mind with such respect, and for that she was deeply grateful. To please her instructor she memorized and recited the assigned poems, or listened to recordings, hard, and sang him the melodies at night.

There can be no question of Sheilah's devotion to Fitzgerald. Married or not, she wanted to have his child, but the idea frightened him, and though they took no precautions, nothing came to pass. Years later, when she met Rebecca West—who had borne a child by her lover H. G. Wells—Sheilah thought, *she was luckier than me*. In October 1939 she added a codicil to her will leaving all of her estate in the United States to him, and after he died she designated Scottie as beneficiary. Repeatedly she tried to soften the sometimes cruel letters that Fitzgerald sent his daughter at boarding school and Vassar. "What are you trying to do?" she asked him. "Help her or alienate her forever?" It was a question she must often have put to herself too, for his behavior when drunk seemed designed to destroy their relationship. "Why did he want to torture me?" she wonders, at the same time realizing that it was himself he was tormenting when he turned on those who loved him.

Alert and engaging in her seventies, Sheilah continues to be disturbed by biographical accounts that characterize her as taking care of Fitzgerald or functioning as his mistress. When he was drying out, Fitzgerald hired nurses to keep him under control, but Sheilah did not serve as his nurse, or as his housekeeper, or even, very often, as his cook. Usually they ate dinner out, since she worked all day long; sometimes he cooked crab soup or prepared a batch of fudge to reduce his craving for alcohol. What she did provide was common sense. Having emerged from poverty herself, she encouraged him to cut back on his reckless spending. He gave her presents, but mostly she paid her own way. The very word "mistress" conjures up for her penny-dreadful images of kept women lounging in sumptuous apartments. Obviously, it was not that way at all. "You were not Scott's mistress," Edmund Wilson told her after Fitzgerald's death. "You were his second wife."

But what was her particular appeal for him, besides her physical beauty? "You're a Fitzgerald hero, not a Fitzgerald heroine," Wilson also told her. In fact, Sheilah represented in some ways a female Gatsby, an outsider who had risen to a position of prominence (when Fitzgerald met her she was engaged to a marquess, and her column carried such authority in Hollywood that photographers used to take her picture and ignore her literary companion). As a young man who had strived for acceptance by the rich and powerful of St. Paul and Lake Forest and Princeton, he well understood her instinct to abandon the identity of Lily Sheil and adopt a more glamorous role.

Still more than Gatsby, however, Sheilah resembled a younger version of Fitzgerald's mother. Like the McQuillans, Sheilah had come from a poor if respectable background to earn a place in society. But as with Sheilah that place was not enough for Mollie Fitzgerald; instead she attempted to obliterate the humble origins and reach the very top by way of her talented son. That position was denied him, painfully. Fitzgerald inherited from his mother the vitality that made his career possible, but he also inherited from her his debilitating sense of social inferiority. Perhaps most of all, Sheilah and Mollie were alike in loving Fitzgerald enough to overlook his failings. According to Sheilah, "he despised his mother," yet he seems to have been searching all his life for some woman who, like his mother, would forgive him anything and attribute whatever outrages he committed to a temporary spell as a "bad brownie." Sheilah did not *forgive* him for what he did when drunk, she insists, but she did take him back. And unlike the dowdy and saturnine Mollie Fitzgerald, she was both pretty and educable. At last Fitzgerald found a beautiful woman who loved him, no matter what. He needed all her support, and more, as he made his assault on Hollywood.

He arrived there in 1937 in dire financial straits. His earnings, which had averaged nearly $35,000 from 1929 to 1931, dwindled to a mere $10,000 in 1936. The *Saturday Evening Post,* his primary source of income for years, was no longer buying his fiction. Meanwhile, his expenses had risen drastically through Zelda's institutional care and Scottie's private schooling. Desperate, Fitzgerald signed over portions of his life insurance benefits to Ober and to Scribner's. He pawned the silver. He even considered selling the books in his library, but they would only bring in about $300 and he needed much more than that. C.O. Kalman in St. Paul helped meet the need, loaning him $6,000 in October 1936 and another $1,500 in December. Fitzgerald repaid him by June 1937 out of the $20,000 he inherited from his mother's estate, but he was a long way from solvent. He still owed well over $20,000 to Scribner's and Ober and Perkins and Highland Hospital when he went to work for MGM.

The contract Ober had negotiated called for $1,000 a week until the end of 1937, with an option to renew for a year at $1,250 a week. Fitzgerald kept only $400 a week of the $1,000 salary, using the rest to pay off his agent and publisher and taxes. Out of the $400 he paid Zelda's bills at Highland and Scottie's at Miss Walker's, as well as his own life insurance. By the end of 1938, after MGM exercised its option, he managed to catch up on nearly all his debts. But during those first eighteen months on the job, he'd accumulated only one screen credit, and it surprised no one when the studio let him go.

On his brief visits to Hollywood in 1927 and 1931, Fitzgerald had thought he could sweep in and bewitch the film capital with his rhetorical legerdemain. When he didn't, it hardly mattered. But in 1937 he needed the money badly and set out to learn the craft. Budd Schulberg, the son of a film producer, was struck by Fitzgerald's dedication. He'd seen other well-known writers, like

John O'Hara and Dorothy Parker, take their huge weekly checks
and run. But Fitzgerald worked hard, taking notes on everything
he saw and heard and spending long hours in the screening room.
At the end of a day on the lot he could barely lift his chin off his
chest. Yet he felt a certain excitement at first, as a July 1937 letter
to his agent's wife, Anne Ober, indicated:

> I have seen Hollywood—talked with Taylor, dined with
> March, danced with Ginger Rogers (this will burn Scottie up
> but it's true), been in Rosalind Russel's dressing room, wise-
> cracked with Montgomery, drunk (gingerale) with Zukor and
> Lasky, lunched alone with Maureen O'Sullivan, watched Craw-
> ford act and lost my heart to a beautiful half-caste Chinese girl
> whose name I've forgotten. So far I've bought my own breakfasts.

Now the glamorous part was over, he went on. "From now on I
go nowhere and see no one because the work is hard as hell, at
least for me and I've lost ten pounds." Hollywood, he knew, represented a last chance to redeem his career and for a while he was
optimistic about his progress. "I like the work which is... most
often like fitting together a very interesting picture puzzle," he
commented in October 1937. "I think I'm going to be good at it."
Before long, however, he ran afoul of the Hollywood system of
multiple composition. One writer—or often, one team of writers—
would turn out a screenplay, another individual or group would
rewrite it, and a third or fourth would add or subtract from the
earlier versions. For *Three Comrades*, the prize-winning film that
earned Fitzgerald his only screen credit, producer Joe Mankiewicz
did the final polishing over Scott's vigorous objections. Mankiewicz
had removed "all shadows & rythm," he felt. Fitzgerald summed
up Hollywood policy toward writers in these terms: "We brought
you here for your individuality but while you're here we insist that
you do everything to conceal it." Subsequent assignments at MGM
did not change his opinion, as he was put on a couple of projects
that never reached the screen and pulled off others that did, notably
The Women. Fitzgerald was working on a film about Madame Curie
when the studio decided not to renew his contract in December
1938. "METRO NOT RENEWING TO MY GREAT PLEASURE BUT WILL FIN-

ISH CURIE THERES LOTS OF OTHER WORK OFFERED STOP HOWEVER
PLEASE SAY NOTHING WHATEVER TO PERKINS OR TO SCOTTIE WHO
WOULD NOT UNDERSTAND," he wired Ober. "Baby am I glad to get
out!" he added in a letter. "I've hated the place ever since Mon-
keybitch rewrote 3 Comrades!"

Fitzgerald's exhilaration was at least part bravado, for as a free-
lancer he could not count on regular paychecks. Early in 1939
Walter Wanger hired him to work on *Winter Carnival* with Budd
Schulberg. Later in the year, he spent a month on *Air Raid* and
a week on *Raffles* and for the year earned more than $21,000. He
could not make ends meet, however, and in July he applied to
Ober for an advance against future earnings. This time, the agent
refused. It was true that Fitzgerald had repaid his former debt,
Ober admitted, but he had mounting family expenses of his own
and could not take the risk. The decision was undoubtedly influenced by word of Scott's highly public benders in February and
April. Both hurt and defiant, Fitzgerald traced his difficulty instead
to the difference between the America of 1939 and that of 1929.
"I am amazed by the fact that there seems to be no credit abroad—
one can no longer borrow on one's capabilities or one's past record
as a money-maker." He fired Ober, and tried, with little success,
to negotiate with magazines on his own. He also switched Hollywood agents twice in the course of several months. The financial
strain showed in his correspondence. He complained to doctors
and nurses about their bills. He bargained down the rent on his
guest house in Encino. He stalled the insurance company, and told
the tax collector he'd have to wait. He would not, however, compromise on Zelda's care or Scottie's schooling. Scottie could have
attended public school. Zelda could have been institutionalized in
a state hospital. But he wanted Scottie to attend the best possible
school and he refused to suffer the indignity of placing his wife in
a public asylum for the mentally infirm.

Out of this crisis that reached its nadir with his failure to sell
Collier's the serial rights to his novel-in-prospect—out of the entire
disillusioning Hollywood experience—he developed a new and
effective approach to his profession. "I expect to dip in and out of
the pictures for the rest of my natural life," he wrote Scottie in the
winter of 1939, although "it is a business of telling stories fit for

children and this is only interesting up to a point." The money he made from films would go to finance the serious writing that he'd been placed on the earth to do. And even though Hollywood itself was a dump, a "hideous place... full of the human spirit at a new low of debasement," it generated the material for the first of those books. "My great dreams about this place are shattered," he wrote the Murphys in the spring of 1940, "and I have written half a novel and a score of satiric pieces that are appearing in the current *Esquires* about it." The satiric pieces focused on Pat Hobby, hack screenwriter; the novel on Monroe Stahr, producer and last tycoon.

Three years of observation and reflection went into *The Last Tycoon*, the novel he left half-completed at his death. Fitzgerald pumped Schulberg, a Hollywood insider by birth, for information about the place. Daily, Sheilah brought home bits of news and rumor and gossip she'd acquired for her column. On the job he learned about the system and came to know some of the major filmmakers. For background, character sketches, fragments of dialogue, and descriptions he had more than two hundred pages of notes to draw on. From the beginning of his career Fitzgerald kept notebooks; the notes became more copious, and more necessary, as he grew older. "Put it down," he insisted to Sheilah. "Make notes, always make notes." Then the notes had to be shaped into a plan; he devised at least five outlines to guide his progress on *Tycoon*. He was determined that the book should be "a *constructed* novel like *Gatsby*, with passages of poetic prose when it fits the action, but no ruminations or sideshows like *Tender*. Everything must contribute to the dramatic movement."

He set himself a difficult goal and began to fulfill it with the help of funds earned for an adaptation of "Babylon Revisited" in the spring of 1940, and for a Twentieth Century-Fox screenplay in the early autumn. These bonanzas, together with the $250 apiece he received for the Pat Hobby stories in *Esquire*, bought him time to work on the novel. Whether it would eventually have rivaled *Gatsby* cannot be determined, since Fitzgerald had only traversed about half the ground he meant to cover, and had not smoothed out even that half. *The Last Tycoon* as published consists of fragments stitched together by Edmund Wilson: a number of chapters in nearly finished form and a plan for the rest of the novel. Certain sections of the book, notably the chapters on the producer's day, are as good as anything he'd ever written. The part about Stahr, as even Hemingway acknowledged, was first-rate. "You can recognize Irving Thalberg, his charm and skill, and grasp of business, and the sentence of death over him."

At the same time, Hemingway felt that the love affair did not quite ring true: "In the things between men and women, the old magic was gone." The problem lay in Fitzgerald's dwindling capacity to feel. He had always written about his own emotional experience, if not always about the actual details of what had happened to him. In correspondence he advocated the virtues of composite characterization, but he himself was usually part of the composite. "My characters are all Scott Fitzgerald," he remarked in 1935. "Even the feminine characters are feminine Scott Fitzgeralds"—if not self-portraits, then portraits of close relations. "Books are like brothers," he wrote in his notebooks. "I am an only child, Gatsby my imaginary eldest brother, Amory my younger, Anthony my worry, Dick my comparatively good brother but all of them far from home. When I have the courage to put the old white light on the home of my heart, then—"

Then he was at his best. He borrowed story ideas from Zelda, and during the 1930s issued at least four brief contracts—promising to pay 10 percent, or 7½ percent, or $75 out of whatever he might earn—to people who supplied him with anecdotes he might turn into fiction. But such stories had to fit into his emotional range. He was not interested in anyone's "tales of being robbed by Brazilian pirates in a swaying straw hut on the edge of a smoking volcano in the Andes, with his fiancee bound and gagged on the roof." Such adventures lay beyond his ken. "I must start out with an emotion—one that's close to me and that I can understand."

This approach demanded a substantial personal investment and Fitzgerald repeatedly resorted to a financial metaphor in describing the artistic process. The "price for doing professional work," he insisted in a November 1938 letter to an aspiring writer, was extremely high. "You've got to sell your heart, your strongest reactions," not minor feelings that you could talk about at the dinner table, and that was particularly true of the beginner. As for the mature writer, Fitzgerald feared he'd spent so much of his emotional capital that his account had run dry. Writing *Tycoon* was "hard as pulling teeth," he complained to Zelda. "I feel people so much less intently than I did once." It showed in the part of the novel he was able to complete before his death. The golden girl had disappeared, and with her much of the emotional power of *Gatsby* and *Tender*.

Yet in important ways *Tycoon* represented a very real advance for its author. For the first time he shone his light on an entire industry, an industry that mirrored American civilization. While looking at motion pictures so closely he was also exploring facets of his nation's history. Both *Gatsby* and *Tender* had made connections between the time present of the plot and the time past of the United States. In *Tycoon* this historical emphasis—exemplified in repeated references to Abraham Lincoln and Andrew Jackson—became far more pervasive. Moreover, the novel-in-progress promised to be Fitzgerald's most politically sophisticated book through its examination of the de-personalization of business, of the growth of Communist-led labor unions, and of the class struggle. Influenced by his own study of Marxism, Fitzgerald intended to "analyze the class interests" of each of the characters in *Tycoon*, he told Budd Schulberg.

Above all, *The Last Tycoon* demonstrated what writer Nancy Hale has called Fitzgerald's "astonishing capacity to change and develop." His last novel, he wrote Zelda the month before he died, was "nothing like anything else" he'd ever done. And the changes, as Hale remarked, were "all in the direction of truth and away from illusion." In his young manhood Fitzgerald valued the capacity to dream above almost everything else. The middle-aged author, recognizing the dangers in harboring false views of the world, gave up the dreams in order to confront reality without a scrim. It was true of his work and true of the man himself. "I have made two rules in attempting to be both an intellectual and a man of honor simultaneously—" he confided to his notebooks, "that *I do not tell lies that will be of value to myself*, and secondly, *I do not lie to myself*."

Moreover, in *Tycoon* Fitzgerald established what John Dos Passos called "that unshakable moral attitude...that is the basic essential of any powerful work of the imagination." Throughout his life Fitzgerald was driven by a strong sense of right and wrong. Katharine Tighe, one of his oldest friends in St. Paul, always thought of him "as someone intrinsically and deeply good." When he engaged in what she called "divergences from norm," he tended to excoriate himself for them. As critic and editor Ernest Boyd put it in his 1924 sketch of Fitzgerald, his "confessions, if he ever writes any . . . will be permeated by the conviction of sin, which is so much happier than the conviction that the way to Utopia is paved with adultery." His early fiction is full of the horrors of evil. The devil confronts Amory, the would-be fornicator, in *This Side of Paradise*, and in a still earlier story, "Sentiment—and the Use of Rouge," a young Englishman returns from World War I to find moral standards in disrepair. "Damned muddle—" he reflects confusedly,

> everything a muddle, everybody offside, and the referee gotten rid of—everybody trying to say that if the referee were there he'd have been on their side. He was going to go and find that old referee—

Fitzgerald attacked the hypocrisy and stupidity of the older generation but not its basic values. Charlie Wales, the reformed playboy in "Babylon Revisited," wishes he could "jump back a whole generation and trust in character again as the eternally valuable element." So did Fitzgerald, for all around him he saw people who "had no principles," who were "never sure as their fathers or grandfathers had been."

In his college days he had displayed considerable talent at writing musical comedies. And he might have "gone along with that gang" (Rodgers and Hart, Cole Porter), he wrote his daughter in November 1939, "but I guess I am too much a moralist at heart and want to preach at people in some acceptable form, rather than to entertain them." One of the persons he was preaching to—the most attentive member of the congregation—was himself. "Again and again in my books," he wrote O'Hara in July 1936, "I have tried to imagize my regret that I have never been as good as I intended to be." His fiction served as a sort of confessional to replace the one he'd left behind with the Catholicism of his youth. Yet the greatest good of all, in his implicit code, derived from the Protestant ethic: the imperative of work.

Only Fitzgerald's least attractive protagonist, the indolent, procrastinating Anthony Patch of *The Beautiful and Damned,* dares challenge the primacy of work. "I want to know just why it's impossible for an American to be gracefully idle," he remarks, and then idles his way into alcoholism and decrepitude. In a newspaper interview published in the same year as the novel, Fitzgerald made it clear that Anthony did not speak for him. Rich young men "brought up to be absolutely helpless" could only learn to survive through work, he said. "Work is the one salvation for all of us—even if we must work to forget there's nothing worth while to work for, even if the work we turn out—books, for example—doesn't satisfy us. The young man must work. His wife must work—" One of the things he admired about Sheilah was that she was gainfully employed. Her occupation as gossip columnist was not an especially dignified one, but she did work, as Lois Moran had worked as an actress, and as Zelda Fitzgerald—partly in response to her husband's praise of Lois Moran—tried to do as dancer, writer, and artist.

Fitzgerald did not always follow his own advice, of course. Early in his career he tended to write in spurts, and to play the rest of the time. But then he castigated himself for his lack of production, as in an April 1924 letter to Perkins:

> It is only in the last four months that I've realized how much I've—well, almost *deteriorated* in the three years since I finished the Beautiful and Damned. The last four months of course I've worked but in the two years—over two years—before that, I produced exactly *one* play, *half a dozen* short stories and three or four articles—an average of about *one hundred* words a day. If I'd spent this time reading or travelling or doing anything— even staying healthy—it'd be different but I spent it uselessly, neither in study nor in contemplation but only in drinking and raising hell generally.

Ten years later, after an even more fallow period, he drafted an (unpublished) preface to *Tender Is the Night*. "This is the first novel the writer has published in nine years," he began, and went on to observe that during that time there had been scarcely a week when someone didn't ask him how the novel was going and when it would be published. At first he'd told them what he thought was the truth: "this fall," "next spring," "next year." But as time wore on, Fitzgerald admitted, "I lied and lied, announced that I had given it up or that it was now a million words long and would eventually be published in five volumes." On this subject his conscience was active, as *Tender* itself confirmed: it tells the story of a man who is ruined when he gives up his work for a career of pleasing others. In the correspondence of his last years he warned Scottie against succumbing to the same fate.

While at Princeton, he told her, he'd made the mistake of equating work with "something unpleasant, something to be avoided, something to be postponed." The solution was to start with the hardest things first. "Please work—" he pleaded, "work with your best hours." It was a lesson her mother had resisted to her cost. "She realized too late that work was dignity, and the only dignity, and tried to atone for it by working herself, but it was too late and she broke and is broken forever." Moreover, he urged Scottie to avoid Zelda's mistake of refusing to take responsibility for her actions. "All I believe in in life," he also wrote Scottie, "is the rewards for virtue (according to your talents) and the *punishments* for not doing your duty, which are doubly costly."

It followed that those granted a talent had an obligation to exercise it as well and as often as possible. When Fitzgerald didn't write, or wrote stories he called "trash," he expected punishment—and even tried to administer it himself. His two documented attempts at suicide, in the fall of 1936, came at the end of a long alcoholic period in which he'd let his talent, and hence his self-image, erode. "Even at killing myself I'm a failure," he told Baltimore newspaperman Louis Azrael. He also lamented his reputation as a basically frivolous writer. "I am the W. J. Locke of America," he wrote to author Herbert Agar, needing to be told that it was not true, that his work far surpassed that of Locke, the British author of gaily romantic early-1900 novels. During the worst moments of his Hollywood years, Sheilah Graham recalled, he even demanded reassurance from strangers. "I'm F. Scott Fitzgerald, the very well-known writer," he'd brashly announce, and hope for a glimmer of recognition. But that nonsense stopped with his last bender.

After December 1939 Sheilah never saw him take another drink. One by one his personal demons were exorcised along with the liquor. In the spring, Zelda was provisionally released from Highland Hospital and sent home to Montgomery to live with her mother. Scottie started getting better grades at Vassar. Most important, he began to think well of himself. If he hadn't succeeded in Hollywood, perhaps it was because it demanded a kind of talent he did not possess, or no longer possessed. It was not, he knew, for lack of effort. Besides, he had earned enough money there to pay off his debts and return, with firm resolve, to novel writing. Similarly, if the old ecstasy was gone from his romance with Sheilah, so was the compulsion to command women's admiration.

"He was a charmer," as his secretary, Frances Kroll, recalls, but Sheilah was his lady then and he was not in condition to have numerous affairs. There may have been one such affair, with a nurse in 1939. Sheilah recalls stopping at Fitzgerald's house in Encino and meeting a nurse who gave off a suspiciously proprietary air. This did not bother Sheilah very much. "When he was drunk," she said, "he would have had an affair with a tree." And when the drinking stopped, so did the womanizing. In his last months he lived happily and simply with Sheilah, drinking Cokes instead of gin and pursuing his craft. Growing up was "a terribly hard thing to do," he observed in his notes. "It is so much easier to skip it and go from one childhood to another." At the end he was growing up fast.

To guide the process he adopted what he called, in an October 1940 letter to Scottie, "the wise and tragic sense of life... the sense that life is essentially a cheat and its conditions are those of defeat, and that the redeeming things are not 'happiness and pleasure' but the deeper satisfactions that come out of struggle." In that letter, as in many others he sent his daughter during the last two years of his life, he was sending messages to himself. Don't play, work. Don't entertain, enlighten. Above all, don't please others, please yourself. "My God, Andrew!" he had thundered at young Turnbull, "Popularity isn't worth a damn and respect is worth everything and what do you care about happiness—and who ever does except the perpetual children of the world?"

At last he took these messages to heart and guided his life by them. He contemplated the future with ambition. On a handwritten sheet, he projected a 17-volume "Works of F. Scott Fitzgerald" that would include three new novels (one of them, based on his "Count of Darkness" stories, to be issued in two volumes), three additional books of stories, one volume of plays and poetry, and one of essays. Then—after the fashion of Henry James and his New York edition—he proposed spending the five years from 1955 to 1960 on a 12-volume revised edition. Eye cocked on posterity, he spelled out his goals. "I want to write scenes that are frightening and inimitable. I don't want to be as intelligible to my contemporaries as Ernest who as Gertrude Stein said, is bound for the Museums. I am sure I am far enough ahead to have some small immortality if I can keep well."

He decided, in short, to become "a writer only": the career he had promised to embark on five years earlier in "The Crack-Up" essays. Writing provided him with a vocation and constituted "the only dignity," as he'd told Scottie. It did not matter what others thought of him. The one good and valid and lasting way of pleasing them—and the only way he could please himself—was to develop the gift for darkening paper that had come down to him through whatever mysterious agency. Even in fragmentary form, *The Last Tycoon* testifies that Fitzgerald's ability had not deserted him. As James Thurber commented in 1951, Fitzgerald had once "thought of his talent as something that could be lost, like his watch, or mislaid, like his hat, or slowly depleted, like his bank account, but in his last year there it still was, perhaps surer and more mature than it had ever been." Living in the book as he had once with *Gatsby*, he sensed that creative surge returning.

Unfortunately, the years of dissipation had done their damage. His long-latent tuberculosis became active. Finding it difficult to sleep, he took seconal, nembutal, and barbitol to cure his insomnia, and benzedrine to get going in the morning. His nerves were on edge; the clatter of a neighbor's dog on the tin roof was driving him "gradually mad," he complained in July 1940. Very little time remained before the two heart attacks that were to kill him, but he continued his work on *Tycoon*, writing during his "best hours." Finally, a kind of peace settled over him. He died December 21 as content with himself as he'd ever been.

An early version of Fitzgerald's will called for a funeral "in accordance with my station." Toward the end he crossed that out and wrote "the cheapest possible funeral" instead. Appearances didn't matter. Besides, he didn't want to saddle his survivors with unnecessary expenses. He left $600 in an envelope for burial expenses, and the much borrowed-against insurance policy for Scottie and Zelda. John Biggs, his executor, thought there must be more money hidden away in a secret bank account or concealed in the kitchen furniture, but a search revealed nothing. Fitzgerald's only real legacy was his fiction. It has been enough.

Notes

These notes have two purposes: to document what is said in this book and to indicate where the documentation can be found. Hence there is no annotation to Fitzgerald's novels and stories that are readily available in standard editions. As much as possible I've tried to locate letters and notes originally read at Princeton in such recently published collections as *Correspondence of F. Scott Fitzgerald* and *The Notebooks of F. Scott Fitzgerald*, two of the several volumes of Fitzgerald's work made available through the dedicated scholarship of Matthew J. Bruccoli. Yet a good many letters cited here, both to and from Fitzgerald, have not been previously published anywhere; almost all of these are at Princeton. As a rule I've used such new material where it combines insight with freshness, and have preferred primary to secondary sources. Among secondary sources, however, particular acknowledgment is due to Arthur Mizener's *The Far Side of Paradise*, Henry Dan Piper's *F. Scott Fitzgerald*, Andrew Turnbull's *Scott Fitzgerald*, Nancy Milford's *Zelda*, and Sheilah Graham and Gerold Frank's *Beloved Infidel*. In addition, the files of Mizener and Piper—at Cornell and Southern Illinois, respectively—provided much important evidence. On a few occasions I've cited information from current biographies by Bruccoli (*Some Sort of Epic Grandeur*) and André LeVot (*F. Scott Fitzgerald*).

The following abbreviations are used:

FSF   F. Scott Fitzgerald
ZF (and ZS)   Zelda Fitzgerald (and Zelda Sayre)
SF (and SFS)   Scottie Fitzgerald (and Scottie Fitzgerald Smith)

MP	Maxwell Perkins
EW	Edmund Wilson
HDP	Henry Dan Piper
AM	Arthur Mizener
SD	Scott Donaldson
Firestone	Fitzgerald Collection, Firestone Library, Princeton University.

1. A Man with No People

1 son of "a king": FSF, "Author's House," *Afternoon of an Author* (New York: Scribner's, 1958), p. 185 (hereafter *Afternoon*).

1 *"Why shouldn't...Coolidge"*: FSF to MP, 20 February 1926, *The Letters of F. Scott Fitzgerald*, ed. Andrew Turnbull (New York: Scribner's, 1963), p. 199 (hereafter *Letters*).

2 *"Dolly Madison"*: *The Notebooks of F. Scott Fitzgerald*, ed. Matthew J. Bruccoli (New York: Harcourt Brace Jovanovich, 1978), p. 267 (hereafter *Notebooks*).

2 *family tree*: FSF to EW, late 1920, *Correspondence of F. Scott Fitzgerald*, ed. Matthew J. Bruccoli and Margaret M. Duggan (New York: Random House, 1980), p. 76 (hereafter *Correspondence*).

2 *audience...Pope*: Archbishop Dowling to Monsignor O'Hearn, 3 June 1921, Firestone.

2–3 *"half black Irish..."*: FSF to John O'Hara, 18 July 1933, *Letters*, p. 503.

3 *"just missed"*: AM, interview with Richard Washington, 19 December 1947.

3 *Mollie...not beautiful*: C. N. B. Wheeler to HDP, 22 March 1945; Mrs. Herbert Lewis to HDP, n.d.; Elizabeth Beckwith MacKie memoir, Firestone; SD, interview with Norris and Betty Jackson, 8 August 1978.

3 *outspoken..."mourning"*: AM, interview with Mrs. Lorena McQuillan and David McQuillan, 3 January 1948; Andrew Turnbull, *Scott Fitzgerald* (New York: Scribner's, 1962), p. 66 (hereafter Turnbull).

3–4 *rather literary..."knew more"*: Lloyd Hackl, "Fitzgerald in St. Paul: An Oral History Portrait," *Fitzgerald/Hemingway*

Annual 1976, p. 120; FSF, "An Author's Mother," *The Price was High: The Last Uncollected Stories of F. Scott Fitzgerald*, ed. Matthew J. Bruccoli (New York: Harcourt Brace Jovanovich, 1979), pp. 736–739 (hereafter *Price*); *F. Scott Fitzgerald's Ledger* (Washington: NCR/Microcard, 1972), p. 174 (hereafter *Ledger*); "Auction," *Fitzgerald Newsletter*, ed. Matthew J. Bruccoli (Washington: NCR/Microcard, 1969), p. 164 (hereafter *Newsletter*); FSF to Alfred Dashiell, Christmas 1933, *Letters*, p. 238; FSF to Margaret Turnbull, 11 November 1936, *Letters*, p. 442.

5   *he drank...*"*back yard*": C. N. B. Wheeler to HDP, 13 February 1945; FSF, *Ledger*, p. 160.

5   *make excuses*: FSF, typescript of "Early Success," Firestone, pp. 10–11.

5   "*tired old stock*": FSF, "The Death of My Father," *The Apprentice Fiction of F. Scott Fitzgerald*, ed. John Kuehl (New Brunswick: Rutgers University Press, 1965), pp. 66–68 (hereafter *Apprentice*).

5   *Poe and Byron*: FSF to Mrs. Edward Fitzgerald, June 1930, *Letters*, pp. 495–96.

6   "*only moral guide*": FSF, "Death," *Apprentice*, p. 67.

6   "*cut the pie*": AM, interview with Paul Ballion, 3 January 1948.

6   "*He misses me...*": FSF to Harold Ober, May 1926, *As Ever, Scott Fitz——*, ed. Matthew J. Bruccoli and Jennifer M. Atkinson (Philadelphia: Lippincott, 1972), p. 91.

6–7   "*My father...resents...*": FSF, *Notebooks*, p. 151.

8   "*Just a boy...*": FSF, *Notebooks*, pp. 129–30.

8   *discouraging...visit...*: FSF to Mrs. Edward Fitzgerald, 18 July 1907, *Letters*, p. 449.

9   *gaucheries*: FSF, *Notebooks*, pp. 172, 202; Turnbull, p. 27.

9   *overprotectiveness...*"*chief clerk*": Henry Dan Piper, *F. Scott Fitzgerald: A Critical Portrait* (New York: Holt, Rinehart and Winston, 1965), pp. 8–9, 182 (hereafter *Piper*); telegram, Mrs. Edward Fitzgerald to Scribner's, 21 January 1926, and cable, FSF to Scribner's, January 1926, Firestone; FSF to Mrs. Edward Fitzgerald, June 1930, *Letters*, p. 496.

9   *DePinna...*"*bad brownie*": Turnbull, pp. 12–13; John J. Koblas, *F. Scott Fitzgerald in Minnesota: His Homes and Haunts* (St. Paul: Minnesota Historical Society, 1978), p.

12; Sheilah Graham and Gerold Frank, *Beloved Infidel* (New York: Henry Holt, 1958), p. 284 (hereafter *Infidel*).

10   *"falling into . . . west"*: Thomas Boyd, "Literary Libels (One): F. Scott Fitzgerald," *St. Paul Daily News* (5 March 1922).

10   *"Complacency . . .":* Grace Flandrau, "The Untamable Twin," *The Taming of the Frontier*, ed. Duncan Aikman (New York: Minton, Balch, 1925), p. 152.

10   *three-generation town*: FSF, review of Grace Flandrau's *Being Respectable, F. Scott Fitzgerald in His Own Time: A Miscellany*, eds. Matthew J. Bruccoli and Jackson R. Bryer (Kent, Ohio: Kent State University Press, 1971), p. 141 (hereafter *Miscellany*).

10–11   *early draft . . .*: FSF, *Notebooks*, pp. 267–68.

11   *"Tarkington says . . .":* FSF, Notes, Firestone.

11   *Kalman . . . "tracks"*: Lloyd Hackl, interview with Xandra Kalman, Minnesota Historical Society.

11   *Social Register*: St. Paul Social Registers for 1909, 1910, 1913, 1916, 1919, 1921, 1922, Minnesota Historical Society.

12   *"wholesale"*: FSF, Scrapbooks, Firestone: Fitzgerald's emendation was noted by John M. Allen, *Candles and Carnival Lights: The Catholic Sensibility of F. Scott Fitzgerald* (New York University Press, 1978), p. 146.

12   *city directories . . . moved . . .*: St. Paul city directories for 1890–98 and 1909–17, Minneapolis Public Library.

13   *599 Summit*: FSF to Alida Bigelow, 22 September 1919, *Letters*, p. 456.

13–15   *dream . . . of 1931 . . .*: FSF, "Mr. Consumer! Do you ever figure *Cost Plus*?", Firestone.

15   *Egloff . . . "Big Dream" . . .*: Margaret C. L. Gildea (Egloff), "Comments on the Dream," Firestone.

15   *"Up"*: FSF, *Ledger*, p. 151.

16   *"no habits of work"*: FSF, notes for "The Crack-up," Firestone.

16   *Aunt Annabel*: Turnbull, pp. 36–37; Arthur Mizener, *The Far Side of Paradise* (New York: Vintage, 1959), p. 4 (hereafter Mizener).

16   *"till 15"*: FSF to SF, summer 1935, *Letters*, p. 5.

16   *"unpopular"*: FSF, *Ledger*, pp. 158, 160, 161, 163, 166.

16   *"my mother lost . . .":* FSF, "Author's House," *Afternoon*, p. 184.

16–17 *death of...sisters*: Mrs. Edward Fitzgerald, "A Baby's Biography," Scrapbook on FSF, Firestone.

2. Princeton '17

18 *decided...made...opted*: Turnbull, pp. 13, 36; Robert Sklar, *F. Scott Fitzgerald: The Last Laocoön* (New York: Oxford University Press, 1967), p. 7; Donald Marsden, "F and the Princeton Triangle Club II," *Newsletter*, pp. 247–49.

18–19 *Yale..."American Life"*: Turnbull, p. 42; FSF to Ruth Sturtevant, May 1915, *Correspondence*, p. 10; Mizener, p. 41; FSF, "Princeton," *Afternoon*, p. 71.

19 *"Ralph Hale...poison"*: FSF to Ruth Sturtevant, n.d., University of Virginia Library.

19 *"local wit...girls"*: FSF to C. A. Wright, 24 April 1935, *Correspondence*, p. 409.

20 *"Began Spires"*: FSF, *Ledger*, p. 170.

20 *"For God's sake"*: John Peale Bishop to FSF, 2 January 1916, Firestone.

20–21 *academic record*: Princeton grades in Scrapbook, Firestone.

21 *"Math. school"*: FSF, "Popular Parodies—No. 1," *Miscellany*, p. 88.

21 *"English...brilliantly"*: John Biggs, Jr., "A Few Early Years: Recollections of F. Scott Fitzgerald and Princeton's Literary Past," *Princeton Tiger* (January 1957), p. 21.

21 *"pallid English"*: FSF, "Princeton," *Afternoon*, pp. 74–75.

22 *"books...in America"*: FSF, review of Charles G. Norris's *Brass*, *Miscellany*, p. 126.

22 *"graduate work"*: Piper, p. 26.

22 *poetry...Bishop*: FSF to SF, 3 August 1940, *Letters*, p. 88.

22 *"Gee but...Griffin..."*: Wilson M. Hudson, "F. Scott Fitzgerald and a Princeton Preceptor," 5 pages, Firestone.

22 *"simple bone-head"*: FSF to Alida Bigelow, 10 January 1917, *Letters*, p. 450.

23 *"A rugged...Frost"*: FSF, "Our American Poets," *Miscellany*, p. 98.

23 *"worst educated...blame"*: HDP, "Princeton and Fitzgerald," *Princeton Alumni Weekly*, 56 (9 March 1956), 10.

24   *"four months"*: FSF to SF, 17 September 1940, *Letters*, p. 94.

24   *"idiot . . . Triangle"*: FSF to SF, 18 April 1938, March 1939, and 12 April 1940, *Letters*, pp. 28, 52–53, 69–70.

24   *"year of terrible"*: FSF, *Ledger*, p. 170.

24–25   *"What on earth . . . quitting"*: FSF to ZF, 14 September 1940 and 19 December 1940, *Letters*, pp. 123–24, 133.

25   *"to play teacher"*: "College of One," *Newsletter*, pp. 253–54.

26   *"rather damns . . . country club"*: FSF to EW, 10 January 1918, *Letters*, p. 323; FSF, "Early Success," *The Crack-Up*, ed. Edmund Wilson (New York: New Directions, 1945), p. 88 (hereafter *Crack-Up*); Mizener, p. 59; John D. Davies, "Scott Fitzgerald & Princeton," *Princeton Alumni Weekly*, 66 (6 February 1966), 6.

26   *reply to . . . Hibben*: FSF to John Grier Hibben, 3 June 1920, *Letters*, pp. 461–63.

27   *"big four" . . .*: FSF, "Princeton," *Afternoon*, pp. 76–77.

27–28   *"gilded youth"*: FSF, "Princeton," *Afternoon*, p. 73.

28   *"signed all . . ."*: Telegram, Harry T. Dunn to FSF, spring 1916, Scrapbook, Firestone.

28   *satirical piece*: FSF, "The Diary of a Sophomore," *Miscellany*, pp. 89–90.

28–29   *"sober breath"*: FSF to Marie Hersey, May 1920, *Letters*, p. 460.

29   *banquet . . . Nassau Lit*: Mizener, pp. 120–21. The event is memorialized in verse by Edmund Wilson in "The Twenties," *The New Yorker* (28 April 1975), pp. 46–47.

29   *speech . . . Palmer*: Turnbull, pp. 174–75.

29   *nightmare . . . "spotlight"*: FSF, "Mr. Consumer! Do you ever figure *Cost Plus*?" Firestone.

29–30   *"give in the name"*: FSF to "Dear——ney," 12 February 1929, University Cottage Club, Princeton.

30–31   *letter . . . Turnbull*: FSF to University Cottage Club Elections Committee, 14 November 1939, *Correspondence*, pp. 560–61.

31   *"a little better" . . . best*: FSF to Margaret Turnbull, 13 November 1939, *Letters*, pp. 444–45; FSF to SF, 15 March 1940 and 18 March 1940, *Letters*, pp. 65, 66.

32   *"boy . . . Huntley"*: FSF, lists of admissions including prep

school backgrounds, Firestone; FSF to SF, 11 March 1938, *Letters*, p. 24.

32   *poem ...."hanging there"*: FSF to W. F. Clarkson, 19 September 1933, *Correspondence*, p. 317; Frances Fitzgerald Lanahan, "Princeton & My Father," *Princeton Alumni Weekly*, 56 (9 March 1956), 8.

32–33   *"only healthy ...world"*: FSF to SF, March 1939, *Letters*, p. 53; FSF to Margaret Turnbull, *Letters*, p. 445.

33   *"I hope ...victim"*: FSF to Ralph Church, *Letters*, p. 605; EW to Christian Gauss, *Papers of Christian Gauss*, eds. Katherine Gauss Jackson and Hiram Haydn (New York: Random House, 1957), p. 340.

33   *football ...heart attack*: Turnbull, p. 321.

33–34   *tears well up*: Turnbull, p. 249.

34   *new football song*: "F Football Song," *Newsletter*, pp. 201–202.

34   *Bowman ..."Glee Club"*: FSF to Brooks Bowman, 16 January 1935, *Fitzgerald/Hemingway Annual 1974*, pp. 9–10.

35   *"Keep the watch"*: FSF, typed song, "Literary Notes," Firestone.

35   *spring ..."in May"*: FSF, "The Bowl," *Price*, p. 265; John Peale Bishop to FSF, 11 November 1918, Firestone.

35   *"old way of things"*: John Peale Bishop to FSF, 27 December 1917, Firestone.

35   *"by way of ...poet"*: EW to FSF, 7 October 1917, Firestone.

35–36   *1917 poem*: FSF, "Princeton—The Last Day," *Poems 1911–1940*, ed. Matthew J. Bruccoli (Bloomfield Hills, Mich., and Columbia, S.C., 1981), p. 68 (hereafter *Poems*).

36   *"grassy parade ...minute"*: F. Scott and Zelda Fitzgerald, "'Show Mr. and Mrs. F. to Number ———,'" *Esquire* (June 1934), 23; the quotation about Princeton, as amended by FSF, appears on pp. 15–16 of the manuscript in the ZF papers, Firestone.

37   *"class elections"*: *Newsletter*, p. 6.

37   *"most perfect ...prettiest"*: Laura Guthrie Hearne journal, summer of 1935, Firestone (hereafter Guthrie).

37   *"greatest writers"*: EW, "Thoughts on Being Bibliographed," *Princeton University Library Chronicle*, 5 (February 1944), 54.

37   *"T. Scott ..."*: *A Book of Princeton Verse II*, ed. Henry Van

Dyke, Morris William Croll, Maxwell Struthers Burt, and James Creese, Jr. (Princeton University Press, 1919). The initial is wrong in the index and at the bottom of each of the three Fitzgerald poems included.

37 *"sense to spot him"*: Interview with Gregg Dougherty, *New York Times*, 31 July 1977, Section 11, New Jersey Weekly, pp. 1–4.

38 *lectures . . . The Club*: FSF to Christian Gauss, 7 September 1934 and 26 September 1934, *Letters*, pp. 386–87; Turnbull, pp. 250–51; Davies, "Scott Fitzgerald & Princeton," p. 14.

38 *underground library*: FSF to Asa Bushnell, 27 April 1936, *Letters*, p. 534.

38–39 *class notes*: FSF to Harvey H. Smith, Fall 1938 and 28 November 1940, Firestone; Stanley Olmsted, "Fitzgerald Sets Things Right about His College: Princeton a Hard Place to Get Into, F. Scott Insists," newspaper article, Scrapbook, Firestone.

39 *official . . . condolence*: University Cottage Club, Harold H. Short, secretary, to ZF, 14 February 1941, Firestone: hardly a Valentine.

39–40 *"I celebrated"*: FSF, Note, "Sequence of Events," Firestone.

40 *taxied out*: Interview with Gregg Dougherty, *New York Times*: this visit probably occurred in March 1935.

40 *"Princeton . . . proud"*: Lanahan, "Princeton & My Father," pp. 8–9.

40 *no obligation*: *The Romantic Egoists: A Pictorial Autobiography of Scott and Zelda Fitzgerald*, ed. Matthew J. Bruccoli, Scottie Fitzgerald Smith, and Joan P. Kerr (New York: Scribner's, 1974), p. 240 (hereafter *Egoists*).

40 *"most Princetonian"*: "On the Cover," *Princeton Alumni Weekly* (9 March 1956), p. 7; "The Issue of F. S. Fitzgerald," *Princeton Alumni Weekly* (13 April 1956), Letters section.

41 *"mind boggles"*: "Between the halves . . . ," *Princeton Alumni Weekly* (20 November 1959), 15.

41 *posthumous degree*: John Kuehl to SD, January 1983.

41 *fiftieth reunion*: "Reunion," *Newsletter*, pp. 276–77.

41 *"student . . . writing"*: "Writing Award Set Up," *New York Times*, 21 November 1955, p. 31.

3. "I Love You, Miss X"

42   *mother . . . manners*: SD, interview with Norris and Betty Jackson, 8 August 1978.

42   *"eternal homage"*: FSF to Robert R. Dunn, summer 1936, *Letters*, p. 536.

42   *"a lonely boy"*: Ruth Sturtevant Smith to AM, 3 September 194?.

42   *"little boy . . . welcome"*: Dwight Taylor, "Scott Fitzgerald in Hollywood," *Harper's* 218 (March 1959), p. 68.

43   *"fell in love" . . . candy*: FSF, *Ledger*, pp. 160, 162.

43   *Violet . . . "lovely teeth"*: FSF, "Girls I Have Known," AM notes, Cornell.

43–44   *Marie . . . Margaret*: "Scott Fitzgerald's 'Thoughtbook'," introd. John Kuehl, *Princeton University Library Chronicle*, 26 (Winter 1965), 102–108.

44   *"Dancing School . . . sex"*: FSF, *Ledger*, p. 165.

44   *self-assessment*: Mizener, p. 23.

44   *"top girl"*: FSF, *Notebooks*, p. 205.

45   *"adorable"*: AM, interview with Richard Washington, 19 December 1947.

45   *"Very Dear Marie"*: FSF to Marie Hersey, 29 January 1915, *Correspondence*, p. 7.

45   *"Great Heart Breaker"*: Marie Hersey to FSF, n.d., Firestone.

46   *"crucial moment"*: Marie Hersey to FSF, n.d., Firestone.

46   *"To run over . . ."*: Marie Hersey to FSF, n.d., Piper, p. 59.

46   "GO . . . ASSEMBLY": Telegram, Marie Hersey to FSF, 22 November 1919, Scrapbook, Firestone.

46   *frills . . . furbelows*: Mizener, pp. 119-120.

46   *adjective . . . "nice girl"*: FSF to Ruth Sturtevant, May 1915, *Correspondence*, pp. 9–10; Ted (?) Eaton to AM, 28 July 1948.

47   *"'Miss' Helen"*: FSF to Helen Walcott, 18 May 1915, Scrapbook, Firestone.

47   *"a marvel"*: Helen Walcott to FSF, 21 May 1915, Scrapbook, Firestone.

47   *"cinched and harnessed"*: FSF, "Babes in the Woods," *Apprentice*, p. 125.

47   remarkable ... document: FSF, "Babes in the Woods," Apprentice, pp. 124–131.

48   the name: FSF, Ledger, p. 167.

48–49   light-hearted letter: Reuben Warner to FSF, early 1915, Firestone.

49   Ginevra ... "quantity not quality": Turnbull, pp. 54–60; Mizener, p. 52.

49   no more to blame: Marie Hersey to FSF, 15 May 1916, Firestone.

49–50   "Ginevra fired" ... Poor boys: FSF, Ledger, p. 170.

50   speaker ... Charles King: Richard D. Lehan, F. Scott Fitzgerald and the Craft of Fiction (Carbondale: Southern Illinois University Press, 1966), p. 92.

50   "most glamorous": FSF to SF, 12 July 1940, Letters, p. 84.

50   "After the game ...": Elizabeth Friskey, "Visiting the Golden Girl," Princeton Alumni Weekly (3 October 1974), pp. 10–11.

50   "never did think": Mizener, pp. 51–53, 62.

51   "Triangle pin": Ginevra King Pirie to HDP, 12 May 1946.

51   "haemophile": FSF to Frances Turnbull, 9 November 1938, Letters, p. 578.

51   "my first girl": FSF, "Comments on Stories," Miscellany, p. 177.

51   Santa Barbara: Telegrams, Ginevra King Mitchell to FSF, 9 October 1937 and 10 October 1937, FSF to Ginevra King Mitchell, 9 October 1937, Firestone; Mizener, p. 300.

51–52   society page piece: Martha Blair, "These Charming People," Scrapbook, Firestone.

52   "to see how far": Elizabeth Beckwith MacKie, memoir, Firestone.

52   "Are your breasts": Elizabeth Beckwith MacKie, Notes, Firestone.

53   Osa Munson: Elizabeth Beckwith MacKie, Notes, Firestone

53   "ALL MARRIED": Telegram, Dorothy Parker to FSF, 6 July 19??, Firestone.

53   Nora Joyce ... "bunk": Herbert Gorman, "Glimpses of F. Scott Fitzgerald," memoir, Firestone.

53   "I love you" ... Miss X: Carmel Myers, "Scott and Zelda," Park East (May 1951), p. 32.

54   jewelry ... boiled: Mizener, p. 222.

54 HOLLYWOOD...LOVE: Telegram, Lois Moran to FSF, 14 March 1927, Firestone.

54 *"Daddy...leading man"*: ZF to SF, 1927, quoted in Nancy Milford, *Zelda* (New York: Harper & Row, 1970), p. 129 (hereafter Milford).

54 *"Say hello ..."*: Arthur W. Brown to AM, 27 June 1951.

54 *"breakfast food"*: Quoted in Milford, p. 249.

54 *"Polo Balls"*: Tommy Hitchcock to FSF, 26 May 1928, Firestone.

55 *"Darling, dumbbell..."*: Lois Moran to FSF, n.d., Firestone.

55 *"Anyhow...always"*: FSF to Lois Moran Young, 8 March 1935, *Correspondence*, pp. 403–404.

55–56 *The secret..."precious"*: FSF, "Written with Zelda gone to the Clinique," summer (?) 1930, *Correspondence*, pp. 239–40.

56 *change husbands*: FSF to Margaret Turnbull, 21 September 1932, *Letters*, p. 434.

56–57 *Rebecca West...remembered*: Turnbull, p. 196.

57 *"too big a poisson"*: ZF to FSF, 1930, Firestone.

57 walked out...Vanderbilt: AM, Interview with Xandra Kalman, 13 December 1947.

57 *Bijou ..."gin"*: Hans Schmid, "Switzerland of Fitzgerald and Hemingway," *Fitzgerald/Hemingway Annual*, 1978, p. 262; FSF, *Notebooks*, p. 104.

58 *Egloff...mid-1930s*: Margaret C. L. Gildea to Andrew Turnbull, 16 December 1958; Margaret C. L. Gildea to SD, 20 September 1979.

58–59 *"easiest prey"*: FSF, "Last Kiss," in FSF and ZF, *Bits of Paradise* (New York: Scribner's, 1973), p. 378.

59 *"nurses...sleep"*: FSF, Notes, Firestone.

59 *"Enough, Enough"*: FSF, Notes, Firestone.

59 *"men...nicer"*: B. F. Wilson, "All Women Over Thirty-Five Should Be Murdered" (interview with FSF), *Miscellany*, p. 266.

59 *"lionized him ..."*: ZF to Elise ———, 1944–45, *Fitzgerald/Hemingway Annual 1975*, pp. 4–5.

4. Darling Heart

60   *"army experience"*: Michel Mok, "The Other Side of Paradise" (interview with FSF), *Miscellany*, p. 297.

60   *"fastest" girl*: C. Lawton Campbell to HDP, 18 August 1956 (?).

60   *"Isabelle"...Ginevra*: Piper, p. 40.

60–61   *three other girls*: FSF, *Ledger*, pp. 172–73.

61   *"frog...jumped"*: SD, interviews with Katherine Elsberry Haxton and Eugenia McGough Tuttle, 6 November 1980.

61   *"love my Charlie"*: Lurline Pierson Weatherby produced this jingle during an interview with SD, 6 November 1980.

61   *"old Dick...gasping"*: Milford, pp. 16–17; Turnbull, p. 89; interview with Haxton; Mizener, p. 81.

62   *"radiant night...all right"*: ZF to FSF, 1934–35 (two letters), Firestone.

62–63   *"elaborate self-consciousness"*: FSF, Notes, Firestone.

63   *"John Sellers"*: FSF to Marjorie Sayre Brinson, December 1938 (unsent), Firestone.

63   *phone booth*: AM, note for revision.

63   *"car to Auburn"*: ZS to FSF, 1919, Firestone.

63   *"pinkest-whitest"*: ZS to FSF, 1919, Firestone.

63   *"amour...helps then"*: ZS to FSF, 1919 (two letters), Firestone.

64   *ring..."fiancées"*: ZS to FSF, March 1919, Firestone.

64   *"princesses in towers"*: ZS to FSF, summer 1919, Firestone.

64   *"Georgia Tech"*: ZS to FSF, spring 1919, Firestone.

64   *"great tragedy"*: FSF to Ruth Sturtevant, 24 June 1919, *Letters*, p. 455.

64   *"sordid...existence"*: Quoted in Mizener, p. 96.

64–65   *"Zelda...cagey"*: Quoted in Mizener, p. 84.

65   *"holds...at bay"*: FSF, notes for "Count of Darkness," Firestone.

65   *"may be a wreck"*: FSF to Ludlow Fowler, 10 November 1919, *Correspondence*, pp. 48–49.

65   *"situation is now"*: FSF to EW, quoted in EW, "The Twenties," *The New Yorker* (28 April 1975), p. 46.

65   *pills..."wanted to"*...: ZS to FSF, February 1920, *Correspondence*, p. 50.

65–66   *"young authors"*: ZS to FSF, early 1920, Firestone.

66   *"fairy tale"*: ZS to FSF, February 1920, *Correspondence*, p. 51.

66   *"stewed in public"*: Quoted in Milford, p. 60

66   *tried to elope*: ZS to FSF, February–March 1920, Firestone.

66   *"perfect baby"*: FSF to Ruth Sturtevant, 26 March 1920, *Letters*, p. 459.

66   *"war in ... sky"*: FSF, Notes, Firestone.

66–67   *"dear little fusses"*: ZS to FSF, 1919, Firestone.

67   *"most enormous"*: FSF to EW, January 1922, *Letters*, p. 331.

67   *"perfectly happy"*: FSF, Notes, Firestone.

67   *self-centered*: Milton Hindus, *F. Scott Fitzgerald: An Introduction and Interpretation* (New York: Holt, Rinehart and Winston, 1968), p. 33.

67   *"dead ... five hours"*: FSF, "Does a Moment of Revolt Come Some Time to Every Married Man?" *Miscellany*, pp. 185–86.

67–68   *"disturbing element"*: Milford, p. 44.

68   *"a terrible thing"*: FSF, *Notebooks*, p. 64.

68   *"Scott's hot"*: ZF to Ludlow Fowler, 16 August 1920, Firestone.

68   *"Dear Misguided ..."*: George Jean Nathan to ZF, 13 September 1920, Firestone.

68   *McKaig ... diary*: Milford, pp. 80–81.

69   *"seasick, hungover ..."*: SD, telephone conversation with Mrs. Howard I. MacMillan, Sr., 28 June 1978.

69   *transfer any guilt*: Milford, pp. 89–90.

69   *"Zelda's abortions"*: Rosalind Sayre Smith to FSF, 21 November 1930, Firestone.

69   *"minor operation ... horribly sick"*: Milford, note 121, p. 394; ZF to FSF, late summer/early fall 1930, *Correspondence*, p. 247.

70   *"He drew her body ..."*: Milford, p. 110.

70   *"Big Crisis"*: FSF, *Ledger*, p. 178.

70   *"locked her up"*: Milford, p. 366.

70   *"Whatever ... she wanted"*: Milford, p. 112.

70   *"That September ..."*: FSF, *Notebooks*, p. 113.

70   *"Her affair ... and mine"*: Milford, p. 222.

71   *"silent for a while ..."*: FSF, "Image on the Heart," *Price*, p. 678.

71   *regretted having flirted:* HDP, Interview with ZF, 13–14 March 1947.

71   *various flirtations:* ZF to FSF, late summer/early fall 1930, *Correspondence*, pp. 245–51.

71–72   *steps . . . clothes . . . wristwatch:* Sheilah Graham, *The Real F. Scott Fitzgerald Thirty-Five Years Later* (New York: Grosset & Dunlap, 1976), p. 68; Milford, pp. 127, 129.

72   *suspicion . . . "Creole":* ZF to FSF, November 1931, *Correspondence*, p. 271; ZF to FSF, fall 1931, Firestone.

72   *In fifteen minutes . . . :* Milford, p. 268.

73   *sexual equipment:* Ernest Hemingway, *A Moveable Feast* (New York: Scribner's, 1964), pp. 189–93; AM, interview with Xandra Kalman, 13 December 1947; AM, interview with EW, n.d.

73   *"too pretty . . .":* Lloyd Hackl, interview with Xandra Kalman, who did not agree.

73   *looked like . . . a fairy:* Guthrie, p. 8.

73   *"half feminine":* FSF, Notes, Firestone.

73   *shocked . . . at Princeton:* Mizener, p. 179.

73   *"sex-in-the-raw":* FSF to John Peale Bishop, 30 January 1935, *Letters,* p. 366.

73   *refused . . . blurb:* John O'Hara to David Brown, 9 December 1961, *Selected Letters of John O'Hara,* ed. Matthew J. Bruccoli (New York: Random House, 1978), p. 380.

73   *Frank Harris:* Turnbull, p. 69.

74   *sex scene . . . provocative:* Graham, *The Real F. Scott Fitzgerald,* p. 180.

74   *"She saw the males . . .":* FSF, *Notebooks,* pp. 234–35.

75   *"really loved him":* FSF, *Crack-Up,* p. 99.

75   *"telling lies":* ZF to FSF, 1930, Firestone.

75   *"had . . . Forel convinced":* FSF to Dr. Adolf Meyer, 10 April 1933, *Correspondence,* p. 306.

75   *"My instinct . . . repeated":* FSF to ZF, 1930, Firestone.

75   *"idea began . . . Dolly Wilde":* FSF to ZF, 1930 (unsent?), Firestone.

75   *"believes herself in love":* "From the doctor at Malmaison," Firestone.

75   *"friend . . . Opera":* Milford, pp. 252, 373.

76   *sat her beside Dolly:* ZF to FSF, 1930–31, Firestone.

76   *"only one . . . cured":* ZF to FSF, 1930–31, Firestone.

76 *studio...Brooks*: André LeVot, *F. Scott Fitzgerald* (New York: Doubleday, 1983), pp. 235–36.

76 *On the boat*: ZF to FSF, late summer/early fall 1930, *Correspondence*, pp. 248–49.

76 *flower...flirted*: Milford, pp. 147–48.

76 "*I wanted...beautiful*": Milford, p. 168. The passage Milford omitted reads: "Perhaps it is depraved, but..."

77 "*everything of beauty*": Milford, p. 175.

77 "*wrong...to love my teacher*": ZF to FSF, late summer/early fall 1930, *Correspondence*, p. 249.

77 "*overly affectionate*": Dr. H. W. Trutman, "Mrs. Z. S. Fitzgerald—Rapport sur son Séjour à Val Mont du 22.5 au 4.6.1930," Firestone.

77 "*red-haired girl*": FSF to Dr. Oscar Forel, 29 January 1931, Firestone.

77 *one painting*: ZF to FSF, 1934, Firestone.

5. Genius and Glass

78 "*ambitious enough*": ZS to FSF, December 1919, Firestone.

78 "*comedy team*": Kenneth Tynan, "Profile (Louise Brooks)," *The New Yorker* (11 June 1979), p. 71.

79 "*Daddy...cul-de-sacs*": ZF to SF, c. 1944, *Egoists*, p. 237.

79 "*theory...genius*": Ibid.

79 "*consciousness raised*": Leslie Wayne, "Scottie's Childhood Undimmed by Shadows of Unhappiness," *Philadelphia Inquirer*, 21 November 1974, Section D, pp. 1B–2B.

79 "*no use killing*": Turnbull, p. 191.

80 *solo in* Aida: Julie Sedova to ZF, September 1929, Firestone.

80 "Please *write*...": ZF to FSF, June 1930, *Correspondence*, p. 237.

80 *too late...*"*tendrement*": Lubov Egorova to FSF, 9 July 1930, Firestone.

80 "*shimmy dancer*": FSF to Harold Ober, 8 February 1936, *Letters*, p. 402.

81 "*recognized...plagiarism*": ZF, "Friend Husband's Latest," *Miscellany*, p. 333.

81 *questionable...finance*: For a summary of FSF's practice in this regard, see W. R. Anderson, "Rivalry and Partnership: The Short Fiction of Zelda Sayre Fitzgerald," *Fitzger-*

ald/Hemingway Annual 1977, pp. 19–42.

81 *"dark middle"*: Turnbull, p. 194.

81 *"teach me ...everything"*: ZF to FSF, fall 1931 (two letters), Firestone.

82 *"changed address"*: Dr. Mildred T. Squires to FSF, 17 March 1932, Firestone.

82 *"job on ...paper"*: ZF to FSF, 9 March 1932, *Correspondence*, p. 288.

82 *"scathing criticism"*: Milford, p. 220.

82 *"École Fitzgerald"*: ZF to FSF, early March 1932, *Correspondence*, p. 286.

82 *"one whole section"*: Milford, p. 216.

83 *"beautiful gossamer ..."*: ZF to FSF, April 1932, *Correspondence*, p. 291.

83 *fold her hands*: ZF to FSF, spring 1932, *Correspondence*, pp. 293–94.

83 *"like ...something"*: ZF to FSF, 1932 (?), Firestone.

83 *"praise ...restraints"*: FSF to MP, before 2 May 1932 and c. 14 May 1932, *Letters*, pp. 266–29.

84 *"indebtedness" ...$5,000*: Milford, p. 226.

84 *"Possibly ...genius"*: FSF to Dr. Adolf Meyer, 10 April 1933, *Correspondence*, p. 308.

84 *elaborate strategy*: FSF, Notes, Firestone.

84 *confrontation*: The transcript of this meeting is printed in Matthew J. Bruccoli, *Some Sort of Epic Grandeur: The Life of F. Scott Fitzgerald* (New York: Harcourt Brace Jovanovich, 1981), pp. 349–53 (hereafter *Grandeur*).

85 *sixteen states ...divorce*: E. A. Poe to FSF, 1 June 1933, Firestone.

86 *"KEEP COOL" ...custody*: FSF, Notes, Firestone.

86 *chilling document*: FSF, Notes, Firestone.

86–87 *two ...alternatives*: FSF, Notes, Firestone.

87 *"great artist"*: ZF to FSF, March 1934, *Correspondence*, p. 334.

87 *"self-expression"*: FSF to ZF, 1932 (?), *Correspondence*, p. 300.

87 *"I do not think ..."*: Dr. Mildred T. Squires to FSF, 9 March 1932, Firestone.

87 *exhibited ...sales*: Milford, pp. 289–90; Cary Ross to FSF,

4 May 1934, *Correspondence*, pp. 359–60.

87–88   *O'Keeffe...“dormant feelings”*: ZF, letter about O'Keeffe show in New York, February–March 1934, Firestone.

88   *screens...tempera*: ZF to FSF, winter 1939–40 (two letters), Firestone.

88   *glass...eggshell*: Milford, pp. 232–33, 326; FSF to Judge and Mrs. A. D. Sayre, 1 December 1930, *Correspondence*, p. 254; FSF to Rosalind Sayre Smith, 19 July 1934, *Correspondence*, p. 373; Mizener, p. 254.

88   *“don't write...blame”*: ZF to FSF, late 1930, *Correspondence*, p. 238.

89   *“blaming yourself”*: FSF to Judge and Mrs. A. D. Sayre, 1 December 1930, *Correspondence*, p. 255.

89   *how much...to blame*: Guthrie, p. 114.

89   *wedding...champagne*: SD, interview with SFS, 21 May 1978.

89–90   *vase...nosebleed*: Milford, p. 140.

90   *“rather she die”*: Rosalind Sayre Smith to FSF, 8 June 1930, Firestone.

90   *“upset and harrowed”*: FSF to Rosalind Sayre Smith, after 8 June 1930, *Correspondence*, p. 236; FSF to Marjorie Sayre Brinson, December 1938 (unsent), Firestone.

90   *“bitch person”*: FSF to SF, July 1939, *Letters*, p. 61 (identification of Rosalind and the word *bitch* are deleted in the printed letter).

90   *“hiding in closets”*: FSF, Notes, Firestone.

90–91   *“syllables...parrot”*: FSF, *Notebooks*, pp. 88, 151.

91   *“decent...suave”*: FSF to Rosalind Sayre Smith, 1938 (unsent?), Firestone.

91   *Rosalind...Forel*: Milford, p. 162.

91   *Mrs. Sayre...melancholia*: Mrs. A. D. Sayre to FSF, 16 July 1930, Firestone.

91   *liver...suicide*: Mrs. A. D. Sayre to FSF, 26 February 1934, Firestone; Milford, p. 280.

91   *“Morgan blood”*: Mrs. A. D. Sayre to FSF, 31 July 1933, Firestone.

91–92   *“wheels...backward”*: FSF, *Notebooks*, p. 205.

92   *“putrid...rot”*: Mrs. A. D. Sayre to FSF, 18 January 1939, Firestone.

92 *"handsome . . . not good"*: Helen F. Blackshear, "Mama Sayre, Scott Fitzgerald's Mother-in-Law," *Georgia Review*, 19 (Winter 1965), 467.

92 *"ulterior motives"*: FSF to Marjorie Sayre Brinson, December 1938 (unsent), Firestone.

92 *"illness . . . wrecked"*: FSF, *Notebooks*, p. 203.

92 *"cross over"*: Mrs. A. D. Sayre to FSF, 13 June 1939, Firestone.

92 *"my family . . . thinks"*: ZF to FSF, 1932 (?), Firestone.

92–93 *joint case . . .*: Milford, pp. 302–303; Thelma Nason, "Afternoon (and Evening) of an Author," *Johns Hopkins Magazine*, 21 (February 1970), 12.

93 *"committed Mencken"*: FSF, Notes, Firestone.

93 *"carried off . . ."*: Milford, p. 270.

93 *hotel . . . "madman"*: FSF to Dr. Robert S. Carroll and Dr. R. Burke Suitt, 7 April 1938, *Correspondence*, p. 492.

93 *"tucked into . . ."*: Dr. Robert S. Carroll to FSF, 30 September 1939, Firestone.

93–94 *"Do you remember . . ."*: FSF, "Lamp in a Window," *The New Yorker* (23 March 1935), *Poems*, p. 95.

94 *"never believed me"*: ZF to FSF, 1935 (?), Firestone.

94 *"lady . . . royal darling"*: ZF to FSF, 1930–31, Firestone.

94–95 *"erotic aberrations"*: ZF to FSF, 1930–31, *Correspondence*, p. 257.

95 *"faithful St. Bernard . . ."*: ZF to FSF, November 1931, Firestone.

95 *"crazy people" . . . in Phipps*: ZF to FSF, 1932, Firestone.

95 *"need anything . . . hope"*: ZF to FSF, 1936 (?), Firestone.

96 *"today by the sea . . ."*: ZF to FSF, 1936 (?), Firestone.

96 *"long delay . . ."*: FSF, "Form Letter II," *Correspondence*, p. 621.

96 *"open suitcase"*: Sara Mayfield, *Exiles from Paradise: Zelda and Scott Fitzgerald* (New York: Delacorte, 1971), p. 99.

96 *"was crazy . . . America"*: ZF to SF, 1927, Firestone.

97 *"a room to paint . . . Sundays"*: ZF to FSF, summer 1930, Firestone.

97 *"75,000!"*: ZF to FSF, November 1931, *Correspondence*, p. 277.

97 *kind of house*: ZF to FSF, November 1931 and February 1932, *Correspondence*, pp. 277, 283.

97   *"sycamore...cigar bands"*: ZF to FSF, June 1935, *Correspondence*, p. 414.

98   *"abnegatory skies...soon"*: ZF to FSF, late 1930s, Firestone.

98   *"Oh, Do-Do..."*: ZF to FSF, late 1930s, Firestone.

6. The Glittering Things

99   *"love...main concern"*: FSF to Van Wyck Brooks, 13 June 1925, *Correspondence*, p. 170.

99   *"nothing else...counts"*: Guthrie, p. 140.

99   *"two or three...experiences"*: FSF, "One Hundred False Starts," *All the Sad Young Men* (New York: Scribner's, 1926), p. 65.

100   *"a poor boy...lived it"*: Turnbull, p. 150.

100   *"nine girls out of ten"*: FSF, *Apprentice*, p. 126.

100   *"Those wealthy goats"*: FSF, *Notebooks*, p. 135.

100–101   *"lack of money...my girl"*: FSF, *Crack-Up*, p. 77.

101   *"go mad...debutante"*: FSF to MP, 31 December 1920, *Letters*, p. 145.

105   *"whole idea of Gatsby"*: Turnbull, p. 150.

108   *"never...real...emotional life"*: FSF, inscription in *The Great Gatsby*, in Matthew J. Bruccoli, *F. Scott Fitzgerald: A Descriptive Bibliography* (University of Pittsburgh Press, 1972), p. 255.

110   *"searching...perfect love"*: Guthrie, p. 82.

111   *"Distance...Savory"*: Emily Dickinson, poem 439, *Final Harvest* (Boston: Little, Brown, 1961), p. 103.

111   *"a beauty...inaccessible"*: John Berryman, "F. Scott Fitzgerald," *Kenyon Review*, 8 (Winter 1946), 106–107.

112   *Anson's increasing girth*: For this insight I am indebted to Vivian Breckenridge's unpublished 1978 paper, "Anson the Hunter."

112   *"The very rich..."*: For a fuller discussion of this topic see Scott Donaldson, *By Force of Will: The Life and Art of Ernest Hemingway* (New York: Viking, 1977), pp. 212–13.

112–13   *"riches...never fascinated"*: FSF to Ernest Hemingway, August 1936, *Letters*, p. 311.

113   *Jimmy Worthington*: FSP, "What Kind of Husbands Do 'Jimmies' Make?" *Miscellany*, pp. 186–92.

113 *leisure . . ."responsibility"*: Ibid.

113 *list of rich friends*: Turnbull, p. 315.

113 *"Dopey Sal . . ."*: FSF, Notes, Firestone.

114 *chew up . . . notes*: Calvin Tomkins, "Living Well is the Best Revenge," *The New Yorker* (28 July 1962), p. 57.

114 *"boom days . . . dollars"*: FSF, Notes, Firestone.

114 *"Money and alcohol . . ."*: Egoists, p. x.

114 *"richly poor . . ."*: FSF, draft of "Early Success," Firestone.

114 *"celestial bookkeeper . . ."*: Harold Ober to FSF, 21 June 1939 (unsent), *Egoists*, p. 223.

115 *sallied forth . . ."Kleenex"*: Mizener, pp. 104, 219.

115 *Zelda . . . extravagant*: HDP, interview with MP, 22 June 1945; McKaig diary, Turnbull, p. 114.

7. War Between the Sexes

116 *"opposite sex . . . an inch"*: Webster Schott, review of Wilfrid Sheed's *The Good Word & Other Words, Washington Post Book World* (24 December 1978), p. 4.

117 *Life promises . . ."dope"*: FSF to Mr. and Mrs. Eben Finney, 16 March 1938, *Letters*, pp. 574–75.

118 *"receding chins . . ."*: FSF, *The Beautiful and Damned* (New York: Scribner's, 1922), p. 28.

118 *a woman's country*: Harry Salpeter, interview with FSF, *Miscellany*, p. 276.

118 *"No Englishman . . ."*: Marguerite Mooers Marshall, interview with FSF, *Miscellany*, p. 256.

118 *"advantage of politeness . . ."*: FSF, *Notebooks*, p. 192.

8. Running Amuck

125 *"As to women . . . amuck"*: Father Fay to FSF, n.d. (1915–17), Firestone.

125 *"Goes a-courting . . ."*: FSF, *Notebooks*, 285.

125 *Parker . . ."acrobats"*: LeVot, pp. 293–94.

126 *"Women and liquor . . ."*: FSF to Arnold Gingrich, 11 May 1935, *Letters*, p. 524.

126 *"woman crazy"*: FSF to H. L. Mencken, c. 6 August 1935, *Correspondence*, pp. 421–22.

126   *"What I gave up . . .":* FSF to Dr. Oscar Forel, summer (?) 1930, *Correspondence*, p. 243.

126   *"no good women":* Guthrie, p. 133.

126   *"better women . . . made":* FSF, *Notebooks*, p. 336.

126   *O'Hara . . . movie stars:* John O'Hara to William Maxwell, 16 May 1933, *Selected Letters of John O'Hara*, ed. Matthew J. Bruccoli (New York: Random House, 1978), p. 429.

126–27   *one girl . . . Gish . . . Basso's wife:* Guthrie, pp. 119, 100, 131.

127   *"life . . . cycle":* Guthrie, p. 101.

127   *1935 . . . pursuit of women:* FSF, *Ledger*, 1935 (unpaginated).

127   *"spacious grace":* FSF to MP, 30 July 1934, *Letters*, pp. 250–51.

127–28   *Elizabeth asked him down . . . :* For documentation of the visits to Welbourne in 1934 and 1935 see A. Scott Berg, *Max Perkins: Editor of Genius* (New York: Thomas Congdon/Dutton, 1978), pp. 231, 244–45, 260–61 (hereafter Berg); *Dear Scott/Dear Max: The Fitzgerald-Perkins Correspondence*, ed. John Kuehl and Jackson Bryer (New York: Scribner's, 1973), pp. 204–208, 276 (hereafter *Scott/Max*); FSF, *Ledger*, 1934–35 (unpaginated).

128   *meet Gertrude Stein:* FSF to MP, 26 November 1934, *Scott/Max*, p. 214.

128   *called . . . Bishop's novel:* FSF to John Peale Bishop, 30 January 1935, *Letters*, p. 364.

128   *"his girl . . . my God . . .":* Berg, p. 246.

128   *"the show-off":* Berg, p. 248.

128   *"all . . . in love with him":* AM, interview with Marjorie Kinnan Rawlings.

128–29   *repeated visits . . . Tryon:* FSF, *Ledger*, 1935 (unpaginated).

129   *"never . . . behind . . . any Pole":* FSF, *Notebooks*, pp. 77–78.

129   *try to cheer him:* Milford, p. 312.

129   *"loved her" . . . relationship:* HDP, interview with ZF, 13 March 1947.

129   *last bus . . . "passion lingers":* Guthrie, pp. 11, 6.

129–30   *"terribly in love . . . such fun":* HDP, interview with Nora Flynn, 10 February 1947.

130   *"Who's your girl now":* Guthrie, p. 91.

130   *Nora . . . lobby:* Marie Shank to AM, 20 November 1949.

130   *"strange get-out"*: HDP, interview with Nora Flynn, 10 February 1947.

130   *pointedly snubbed*: FSF, *Ledger*, December 1935 (unpaginated): "Tommy Phipps snubs me."

130   *Laura Millar Guthrie . . . infatuated*: Guthrie, pp. 1–9, 16.

131   *"reaches women through . . . minds"*: Laura Guthrie, "What I Learned This Week," Firestone.

132   *"placid sunshine . . . wayward passion"*: Laura Guthrie, "You and I" (poem), Firestone.

132   *absolute . . . obedience . . . rubbing*: Guthrie, pp. 17–18.

132   *"Beer . . . waterfall"*: Guthrie, p. 17.

132   *Friday the 13th . . . "less in love"*: Guthrie, pp. 138–40.

132   *"Sweet Laura" . . . things left*: FSF to Laura Guthrie, 20 October 1935, Firestone.

132   *"your magic . . . yet"*: Laura Guthrie to FSF, fall 1935, Firestone.

132   *flowers . . . pay*: FSF to Laura Guthrie, 28 July 1936, Firestone; Laura Guthrie to FSF, 2 June 1936, Firestone: "If you did send me any fabulous sum it evaporated on the way here."

133   *"lived on . . . love"*: Guthrie, p. 118.

133   *"arrange something"*: FSF to MP, 15 April 1935, *Scott/Max*, p. 220.

133   *forget Zelda*: Guthrie, p. 96.

133   *stutter . . . Huckleberry*: Guthrie, p. 82; FSF to Beatrice Dance, August 1935, *Correspondence*, p. 419.

133   *father . . . "somebody"*: Guthrie, p. 122.

133–36   *affair . . . never saw her again*: The story of the Beatrice Dance–FSF affair has been reconstructed from the Laura Guthrie memoir.

135   *song about dogs*: EW, "The Twenties," *The New Yorker* (28 April 1975), p. 58.

136–37   *"awfully upset . . ."*: Guthrie, p. 90.

137–38   *writ of* habeas . . . : FSF to Beatrice Dance, late August 1935, *Correspondence*, pp. 420–21.

138   TAKE YOUR MEDICINE: Telegram, FSF to Beatrice Dance, 20 August 1935, *Correspondence*, p. 423.

138   *harsh letter*: FSF to Beatrice Dance (not so designated), September 1935, *Letters*, pp. 529–30.

138   *"Don't let Beatrice . . ."*: Guthrie, p. 150.

138 "FIND OUT WHY S....": Telegram, Beatrice Dance to Laura Guthrie, 10 August 1935, Firestone.

139 *Dr. Cade..."gorilla"*: FSF to Beatrice Dance, 6 March 1936, *Correspondence*, pp. 427–28; FSF to Beatrice Dance, 15 May 1936, Firestone.

139 *"A lot...five years"*: FSF to Beatrice Dance, 6 November 1940, Firestone.

139 *No other man...*: Beatrice Dance to Laura Guthrie, 5 July 1964, Firestone.

139–40 *Bert Barr...*Bremen: Turnbull, pp. 197–98; Matthew J. Bruccoli, "Epilogue: A Woman, a Gift, and a Still Unanswered Question," *Esquire* (30 January 1979), p. 67.

140 *humorous notes*: FSF to Bert Barr, 29 January–6 February 1931, *Correspondence*, pp. 259–60.

140 *two assignations*: FSF to Bert Barr, 24 April 1935, *Correspondence*, p. 408; FSF to MP, c. 25 June 1935, *Scott/Max*, p. 224.

141 *Hergesheimer..."I bet if Joe..."*: FSF to Margaret Case Harriman, August 1935, *Letters*, pp. 526–27; Margaret Case Harriman to FSF, August 1935, Firestone.

141 *"Margaret Case episode"*: FSF, Notes for *The Last Tycoon*, Firestone.

141 *"'Infidelity'...a subject"*: FSF to Beatrice Dance, 4 March 1938, *Correspondence*, p. 489.

141–42 *write about her*: FSF to Beatrice Dance, after 15 May 1936, *Correspondence*, p. 433.

142 *"Tragic July...Too Bad"*: FSF, Notes, Firestone.

142 *"I have just emerged..."*: FSF to James Boyd, August 1935, *Letters*, pp. 528–29.

142 *"girl's point of view"*: FSF, Notes, Firestone.

142 *For Esquire...badge..."Time Lapse"*: FSF, *Notebooks*, pp. 111, 104, 112.

143–44 *Antibes again..."Utopias"*: ZF to FSF, summer 1935 (two letters), Firestone.

9. Cracking Up

145 *one more favor..."kid out of school"*: Guthrie, pp. 138–43.

146 *"ratty old bathrobe"*: Arnold Gingrich, "Publisher's Page—

Will the Real Scott Fitzgerald Please Stand Up and Be Counted?" *Esquire*, 62 (December 1964), 12, 16.

146   "*...don't be depressed...*": ZF to FSF, 1931, Firestone.

146   "*Hemingway's..."melancholy*": FSF to Beatrice Dance, 15 September 1936, *Correspondence*, p. 543.

146   "*letters from all over*": FSF to Arnold Gingrich, 20 March 1936, *Letters*, pp. 533–34.

146–47   *O'Hara..."temptation*": John O'Hara to FSF, April 1936, *Selected Letters of John O'Hara*, ed. Matthew J. Bruccoli (New York: Random House, 1978), p. 115.

147   "*Please write me...*": FSF to MP, late February 1937, *Scott/Max*, p. 235.

147   "*sad...in middle life*": "Notes and Comment," *The New Yorker*, 12 (14 March 1936), 11.

147   "*a little too sorry...*": "Between the Lines," *San Francisco Chronicle*, 20 March 1936.

147   "*mental snapshot...*": Margaret Turnbull to FSF, 12 February 1936, Firestone.

147–48   "*Cheer up...more complicated*": Marie Hersey Hamm to FSF, 5 October 1936, Firestone; FSF to Marie Hersey Hamm, 28 October 1936, *Letters*, p. 545.

148   "*interested...himself*": HDP, interview with Nora Flynn, 10 February 1947.

148   "*life...dominated...*": Sara Murphy to FSF, 3 April 1936, in Linda Patterson Miller, "'As a Friend You Have Never Failed Me': The Fitzgerald-Murphy Correspondence," *Journal of Modern Literature*, 5 (September 1976), 375–76.

148   "*Christ, man...*": John Dos Passos to FSF, October (?) 1936, *Crack-Up*, p. 311.

148–49   "*Katy & I...*": John Dos Passos to FSF, n.d., Firestone.

149   "*nothing...wasted...*": Marjorie Kinnan Rawlings to FSF, n.d., Firestone.

149   *Forget...tragedy...*: Quoted in Mizener, pp. 259–60.

149   "*Maxie Baer*": Quoted in Berg, p. 302.

149   *open season*: FSF to Beatrice Dance, 15 September 1936, *Letters*, p. 542.

149   *Pegler's...obituary*: Westbrook Pegler, "Fair Enough," *New York World-Telegram* (26 December 1940), p. 17, partly quoted in Jackson R. Bryer, *The Critical Reputation of F.*

Scott Fitzgerald: A Bibliographical Study (Hamden, Conn.: Archon Books, 1967), p. 206.

149–50 *"indecent invasion . . .":* John Chamberlain, "The New Books," *Harper's,* 191 (September 1945), unpaginated; Matthew J. Bruccoli, "The Perkins-Wilson Correspondence," *Fitzgerald/Hemingway Annual 1978,* p. 65.

150 *"reconsider" . . . replied tactfully:* FSF to MP, 25 March 1936, and MP to FSF, 26 March 1936, *Scott/Max,* pp. 227–28.

150 *damage . . . reputation:* Harold Ober to FSF, 21 August 1936, *As Ever, Scott Fitz——,* ed. Matthew J. Bruccoli and Jennifer M. Atkinson (Philadelphia: Lippincott, 1972), pp. 279–80; FSF to Beatrice Dance, 15 September 1936, *Letters,* p. 542.

150 *"indiscreet" . . . Basso . . . Graham:* FSF to Corey Ford, April 1937, *Letters,* p. 549; Hamilton Basso to EW, 14 October 1944, Firestone; *Infidel,* p. 237.

150 *"hated it . . . real . . . record":* EW to MP, 16 February 1941, in EW, *Letters on Literature and Politics 1912–1972,* ed. Elena Wilson (New York: Farrar, Straus and Giroux, 1977), pp. 337–38.

151 *"Glenway . . . work":* EW to John Biggs, 3 June 1943, Ibid., p. 348.

151 *Trilling . . . Wescott . . . Wanning:* Lionel Trilling, "F. Scott Fitzgerald," *The Nation,* 166 (25 August 1945), 182; Glenway Wescott, "The Moral of F. Scott Fitzgerald," *Crack-Up,* pp. 323–27; Andrews Wanning, "Fitzgerald and His Brethren," *Partisan Review,* 12 (Fall 1945), 545.

151 *Kazin realized . . . :* Alfred Kazin, "Fitzgerald: An American Confession," *Quarterly Review of Literature,* 2 (1945), 342.

151 *"can't drink . . . impotent . . .":* John V. A. Weaver to FSF, 17 February 1936, Firestone.

152 *"From the stuff . . . everything":* George Martin to FSF, 20 January 1937, Firestone.

152 *"Certainly . . . rationalizations . . .":* George Martin to FSF, February (?) 1937, Firestone.

153 *"so convincing . . . depressions":* Mrs. E. H. Tyson to FSF, n.d., Firestone.

154 *third . . . "Handle . . .":* The titles of the second and third articles of *The Crack-Up* were transposed during the movement from *Esquire* to the book. The original and presumably

the correct order is this: "Pasting It Together" is the second article, "Handle with Care" the third.

155–56   *Didion . . . theme . . .* : Joan Didion, *Slouching Towards Bethlehem* (New York: Simon and Schuster, 1979), pp. 147–48.

156   *Rascoe . . . Street*: Burton Rascoe to FSF, 10 February 1936, Firestone; Julian Street to FSF, 12 February 1936, Firestone.

156   *"a hopeless mess"*: FSF, Notes, Firestone.

156   *slip of . . . pen*: Robert Sklar, *F. Scott Fitzgerald, The Last Laocoön* (New York: Oxford University Press, 1967), p. 309.

156–57   *"breakdown . . . 'change of life'"*: FSF to Mrs. Laura Feley, 20 July 1939, *Letters*, p. 589.

10. Demon Drink

158   *two tests*: SD, interview with SFS, 21 May 1978.

158   *"American literary drunks"*: Alfred Kazin, "'The Giant Killer': Drink & the American Writer," *Commentary*, 61 (March 1976), 44.

159   *"Writing . . . relaxes"*: Dr. Donald Goodwin, "The Alcoholism of F. Scott Fitzgerald," *Journal of the American Medical Association (JAMA)*, 212 (6 April 1970), quoted by Ralph Tyler, "The Muse in the Bottle," *Bookviews* (September 1978), pp. 14–19.

159   *"drive for success"*: Kazin, *Commentary*, p. 50.

159   *Millay . . . "sitting-down"*: Charles Foster told this anecdote sometime during 1963–66.

159–60   *"drunk . . . great fun"*: Lewis Hyde, "Alcohol and Poetry: John Berryman and the Booze Talking," *American Poetry Review*, quoted by Tyler, *Bookviews*, p. 18.

160   *suicide . . . "celebrate"*: Donald Hall, *Remembering Poets: Reminiscences and Opinions* (New York: Harper & Row, 1978), pp. 28–29.

160   *"kindliness . . . gaieties"*: FSF, *The Beautiful and Damned* (New York: Scribner's, 1922), p. 417, FSF, *Notebooks*, p. 35.

160   *beset with guilt*: SD, interview with SFS, 21 May 1978.

160–61   *copied out . . . fragment*: AM, Notes.

161   *"pay and pay and pay"*: FSF, Notes, Firestone.

161   *meticulous recording* . . . : Mizener, p. 20; FSF, *Ledger*, pp. 167–68; FSF, "A Short Autobiography (With Acknowledgments to Nathan)," *The New Yorker* (25 May 1929), pp. 22–23.

161–62   *boast about* . . . *"most notorious"*: Goodwin, *JAMA*, p. 87; FSF to MP, 25 August 1921, *Letters*, p. 148; Ring Lardner to FSF, 25 March 1922, Firestone; John Chapin Mosher, "That Sad Young Man," *Miscellany*, p. 443.

162   *omit* . . . *"liquor thing"*: FSF to EW, January 1922, *Letters*, p. 330.

162   *"pass out cold* . . .*"*: Ernest Hemingway to Harvey Breit, 18 August 1954, *Selected Letters 1917–1961*, ed. Carlos Baker (New York: Scribner's, 1981), p. 834.

162   *"One cocktail* . . . *off"*: AM, Notes.

162   *"very bad drinker"*: "The Reminiscences of Carl Van Vechten," Oral History Office, Columbia University, 1960.

162   *Wilson* . . . *Dos Passos*: EW, "The Twenties," *The New Yorker* (28 April 1975), p. 52.

163   *beer* . . . *gin*: Guthrie, p. 56; Marie Shank to AM, 26 October 1949.

163   *gill at a time*: AM, Notes.

163   *bottles* . . . *canyon*: Frances Ring, "My Boss, Scott Fitzgerald," *Los Angeles Magazine*, 7 (January 1964), 34–35.

163   *"twisted its arm"*: James Thurber, "Scott in Thorns," *Credos and Curios* (New York: Harper & Row, 1962), pp. 157–60.

163   *no trace of conviviality*: Max Eastman, *Love and Revolution—My Journey through an Epoch* (New York: Random House, 1964), p. 465.

163   *"furniture antiqued* . . .*"*: Kazin, *Commentary*, p. 45.

163   *car into a lake*: FSF, *Ledger*, p. 177.

163   *"candelabras* . . .*"*: Anita Loos, *Cast of Thousands* (New York: Grosset & Dunlap, 1977), p. 128.

164   *cat from* . . . *bed*: John Dos Passos to AM, 30 April 1950.

164   *tray of nuts* . . . : Turnbull, p. 165.

164   *ashtrays* . . . *wineglasses*: Calvin Tomkins, "Living Well Is the Best Revenge," *The New Yorker* (28 July 1962), pp. 60–61; Turnbull, p. 167.

164   *The gambit* . . . : John Dos Passos, *The Best Times* (New York: New American Library, 1966), p. 128.

164 *Sara . . . scathing . . .*: Sara Murphy to FSF, June 1926, *Correspondence*, pp. 196–97.

164–65 *overcome . . . remorse . . .*: AM, interview with Mr. and Mrs. C. O. Kalman, 13 December 1947; Loos, *Cast*, p. 129.

165 *warned Ludlow . . .*: Turnbull, p. 168.

165 *ledger . . . shorthand . . .*: FSF, *Ledger*, pp. 182–83.

165 Zelda . . . account . . .: ZF to FSF, late summer/early fall 1930, *Correspondence*, p. 248.

165 *"wrecked" himself*: FSF, *Ledger*, p. 182.

166 *"In the dark time . . ."*: FSF, poem fragment, Firestone: apparently these lines were deleted from "Lamp in a Window."

166 *insult . . . humiliated*: Ernest Hemingway to Harvey Breit, 18 August 1954, *Selected Letters*, p. 835.

166 *"no real . . . fellas . . ."*: Ring Lardner to Francis R. Kitchell, 15 June 1923, reprinted in Benjamin Lease, "An Evening at the Scott Fitzgeralds': An Unpublished Letter of Ring Lardner," *English Language Notes* (September 1970), pp. 40–42.

166 *Norfolk . . . stomach*: Joseph A. Howell, Jr., to AM, 12 January 1949.

166 *crime . . . Southerners*: Guthrie, p. 118.

166 *flattering . . . girl*: Infidel, p. 209.

166–67 *"had to get drunk . . ."*: FSF to ZF, summer (?) 1930, *Correspondence*, p. 239.

167 *"she who wanted . . . drink"*: FSF to Dr. Oscar Forel, summer (?) 1930, *Correspondence*, pp. 242–43.

167–68 *"potential . . . patient"*: Dr. Adolf Meyer to FSF, 18 April 1933, Firestone.

168 *discriminate . . . "schizophrene"*: FSF to Dr. Adolf Meyer, spring 1933, *Correspondence*, pp. 309–11.

168 *Ober . . . "apologia"*: FSF to Harold Ober, 8 December 1934, *As Ever, Scott Fitz——*, ed. Matthew J. Bruccoli and Jennifer M. Atkinson (Philadelphia: Lippincott, 1972), pp. 209–10.

168 *"without drink . . . survived"*: FSF to MP, 8 November 1934, *Scott/Max*, p. 210.

168 *Zelda's tragedy . . . morale*: FSF to Margaret Turnbull, June 1935, and FSF to C. O. Kalman, 10 October 1936, *Letters*, pp. 429, 544–45.

168–69   *Thurber...reasons*: Thurber, "Scott in Thorns," pp. 157–58.

169   *narcotics...deadening*: Thomas Boyd, "Literary Libels (One): F. Scott Fitzgerald," *St. Paul Daily News*, 5 March 1922.

169   *Ellerslie...liquor...work*: Milford, p. 141.

169   *"single American artist..."*: FSF to Marya Mannes, 21 October 1925, in Matthew J. Bruccoli, *F. Scott Fitzgerald: A Descriptive Bibliography* (University of Pittsburgh Press, 1972), p. 265.

169   *writer's vice..."heightens feeling..."*: Goodwin, *JAMA*, p. 88; Turnbull, p. 259.

169   *compare...Grant*: See, for example, FSF to Rosalind Sayre Smith, 19 July 1934, *Correspondence*, p. 374.

169   *"A short story...stimulant"*: FSF to MP, 11 March 1935, *Letters*, pp. 259–60.

169–70   *wagon...telling people*: FSF to MP, c. 1 July 1928, 11 March 1935, 19 January 1933, *Letters*, pp. 210, 260, 230; FSF to Arnold Gingrich, 8 May 1935, *Letters*, p. 523.

170   *"Pimlico...drunk"*: Elizabeth Beckwith MacKie, "Fitzgerald Notes," Firestone.

170–71   *tea dance...embarrassment*: FSF to SF, 12 December 1936, *Letters*, pp. 13–14; Turnbull, p. 283.

171   *slapped...inkwell*: Guthrie, p. 97; SD, interview with SFS, 21 May 1978.

171   *resolved to stop drinking*: FSF to Beatrice Dance, early 1937, *Correspondence*, p. 471.

171   *"Everyone...nice"*: FSF to MP, before 19 July 1937, *Letters*, p. 274.

172   *"Wherever you go..."*: Clifton R. Read to Ann Schilling, 12 February 1970, St. Paul Academy.

172   *"Just when somebody's..."*: FSF, *Notebooks*, p. 148.

172   *stand...people..."regime"*: FSF, *Notebooks*, pp. 222, 53.

172–73   *"You annoyed me..."*: FSF to "Dick" (Myers?), 29 September 1932, Firestone.

173   *"Drunk at 20..."*: FSF, *Crack-Up*, p. 196.

173   *North Pole...*: FSF to Margaret Turnbull, spring 1937, *Letters*, p. 443.

173   *"Parties...suicide"*: AM, Notes.

173   *grisly...organs*: Goodwin, *JAMA*, p. 88; Margaret C. L.

Gildea to Andrew Turnbull, 16 December 1958.

173 *"Then...drunk...died"*: FSF, Notes, Firestone.

176 *Bishop...memorial poem*: John Peale Bishop, "The Hours," *New Republic* (3 March 1941), p. 313.

11. The Worst Thing

177 *"Egyptian Proverb..."*: FSF, *Notebooks*, p. 10.

177 *small animals...*: Turnbull, p. 14.

177 *lost causes*: FSF, *This Side of Paradise* (New York: Scribner's, 1920), p. 25.

177–78 *"Physically..."*: Mizener, p. 23.

178 *"yellow"...cars*: Guthrie, pp. 61, 146, 12; *Infidel*, p. 235.

178 *"one real bad driver"*: John Sherwood, "'A Beautiful Time, Baby,'" *Baltimore Sun*, 18 September 1960, Sec. A, p. 3.

178 *killed...dissipation*: Guthrie, p. 99.

178–79 *"Ship as a sailor..."*: FSF to MP, 25 August 1921, *Letters*, p. 148.

179 *"salient points of character..."*: FSF, "Confused Romanticism," letter to *Princeton Alumni Weekly* (22 April 1932), pp. 647–48.

179 *feet..."Freudian"*: FSF, *Ledger*, p. 157; Mizener, p. 12.

179 *"refused to take off..."*: Sheilah Graham, *The Real F. Scott Fitzgerald Thirty-Five Years Later* (New York: Grosset and Dunlap, 1976), p. 33.

179 *women's feet...erotic*: SD, interview with Sheilah Graham, 7 February 1983.

179 *vain of...looks*: Turnbull, p. 40.

179 *"Perfection..."*: FSF, *Ledger*, p. 169.

179 *weakness...mouth*: Ernest Hemingway, *A Moveable Feast* (New York: Scribner's, 1964), p. 149.

180 *"About the army..."*: FSF to Mrs. Edward Fitzgerald, 14 November 1917, *Letters*, p. 451.

180 *social success abroad...*: Father Fay to FSF, 6 June 1918, Firestone.

180 *St. Mark's...Groton*: FSF, *Notebooks*, pp. 204, 302.

181 *family charades*: FSF, "Imagination—and a Few Mothers," *Ladies' Home Journal* (June 1923), pp. 21, 80–81.

181 *"unstable middle class"*: John Kuehl, *Apprentice*, pp. 46–57.

181 *"split social . . . almost vulgar"*: Elizabeth Beckwith MacKie, "Fitzgerald Notes," Firestone; Lloyd Hackl, interview with Xandra Kalman, Minnesota Historical Society; HDP, interview with Nora Flynn, 10 February 1947.

181 *Emily Post's . . . "a play . . ."*: Noted by EW in *Classics and Commercials* (New York: Farrar, Straus, 1950), p. 374.

181 *second-rate champagne*: FSF, *Crack-Up*, p. 216.

181 *never angrier . . .*: Mizener, pp. 181–82.

181 *lists of snubs*: FSF, Notes, Firestone: partly encompassed in FSF, *Notebooks*, pp. 103, 259.

181–82 *turned down . . . invitations*: Henry Wales, "N.Y. '400' Apes Chicago Manners; Fails; So Dull," *Chicago Daily Tribune*, 7 December 1925, p. 12.

182 *"impressed, but not very"*: FSF to MP, c. 27 December 1925, *Letters*, p. 195.

182 *ridiculous . . . squire*: HDP, interview with Michael Fisher, 24 May 1950.

182 *"Aghast, Caroline . . ."*: FSF, "Flight and Pursuit," *Price*, p. 309.

182 *"never wanted anything" . . . Vassar*: HDP, interview with Margaret Culkin Banning, 7 April 1947.

182 *man divided*: SD, interview with SFS, 21 May 1978.

183 *Irish . . . "romantic, but . . . cynical . . ."*: EW, "F. Scott Fitzgerald," *The Shores of Light* (New York: Farrar, Straus, 1952), p. 31.

183 *mother's side alone*: FSF to EW, January 1922, *Letters*, p. 331.

183 *"hollow, cheerless pain"*: FSF to EW, 25 June 1922, *Letters*, p. 337.

183 *"intense social self-consciousness"*: FSF to John O'Hara, 18 July 1933, *Letters*, p. 503.

184 *private utterances . . . Jews . . .*: FSF to Thomas Boyd, March 1923, *Correspondence*, pp. 126–27; FSF, Note, Firestone; FSF to Harold Ober, 8 February 1936, *Letters*, p. 402.

184 *"Semite . . . Goldwyn"*: FSF to James Branch Cabell, 23 February 1920, Firestone.

184–85 *"Hell, the best friend . . ."*: FSF, *Notebooks*, p. 333.

185 *"a moron's game"*: Quoted in Milton R. Stern, *The Golden Moment: The Novels of F. Scott Fitzgerald* (Urbana: University of Illinois Press, 1970), p. 20.

185   *At five ... six ...*: FSF, *Ledger*, pp. 156–57.

185   *Negro clergyman ...*: Turnbull, p. 232.

185   *Aquila ... "lisp"*: Turnbull, p. 236; Robert Forrey, "Negroes in the Fiction of F. Scott Fitzgerald," *Phylon*, 28 (Fall 1967), 293–98; Thelma Nason, "Afternoon (and Evening) of an Author," *Johns Hopkins Magazine* (February 1970), p. 5.

186   *"They shook their heads ..."*: FSF, "The Cruise of the Rolling Junk," *Motor* (March 1924), p. 58.

186–87   *Melarky ... antipathy*: Mizener, pp. 198–99, 206.

187   *"When things get so bad ..."*: FSF, "One Hundred False Starts," *Afternoon*, p. 135.

187   *Smith ... putting*: Turnbull, p. 304.

187   *"negro nurses ..."*: FSF to Helen Hayes, 16 September 1957, *Letters*, pp. 554–55.

187   *"Must all male ..."*: Earl W. Wilkins to FSF, 23 July 1934, Firestone.

187–88   *"Dearly Beloved ..."*: FSF, "Dearly Beloved," *Fitzgerald/Hemingway Annual 1969*, pp. 1–3.

188–89   *"histrionic personality"*: Avodah K. Offit, *The Sexual Self* (Philadelphia: Lippincott, 1977), pp. 57–64.

189   *making up shows ...*: FSF, *Ledger*, p. 161.

189   *"out of debt ... vulgar side"*: FSF to Harold Ober, before 2 July 1935, *Letters*, p. 399.

189   *contractual agreement*: Document, 28 February 1939, Firestone.

189   *"genius ... improvisations"*: EW to AM, 3 March 1950, *Letters on Literature and Politics 1912–1972*, ed. Elena Wilson (New York: Farrar, Straus and Giroux, 1977), p. 478.

189   *"actor ... show off"*: Guthrie, pp. 6, 130.

190   *"Can't you possibly ..."*: Milford, p. 191.

190   *"melodramatic ... defeats"*: HDP, interview with Arnold Gingrich, 29 March 1944; Arnold Gingrich, "Editorial: Salute and Farewell to F. Scott Fitzgerald," *Miscellany*, p. 479.

190   *"necklace off ..."*: Guthrie, p. 12.

190   *rubbing ... "hard enough"*: William Katterjohn, "An Interview with Theodora Gager, Fitzgerald's Private Nurse," *Fitzgerald/Hemingway Annual 1974*, pp. 79, 84; FSF, "Afternoon of an Author," *Afternoon*, p. 181; Guthrie, pp. 18, 106.

191 *"eager to be liked"*: Devereux C. Josephs to HDP, 1 May 1947.

191 *"wanted everyone..."*: HDP, interview with Margaret Culkin Banning, 7 April 1947.

191 *playing tin soldier*: Robert Benchley to FSF, 29 April 1934, *Correspondence*, p. 358.

191 *"hung the moon"*: Frances M. Martin to SD, 7 February 1978.

191 *"must be loved"*: Turnbull, p. 261.

191 "a constant effort...": Brian Way, *F. Scott Fitzgerald and the Art of Social Fiction* (New York: St. Martin's, 1980), p. 20.

191 *"undivided attention"*: Nason, *Johns Hopkins Magazine*, p. 7.

191 *Sheilah...Scott made her feel...*: *Infidel*, pp. 177–78; FSF, *Crack-Up*, p. 207.

191 *"simply couldn't bear it"*: Margaret C. L. Gildea to Andrew Turnbull, 16 December 1958.

192 *"rubbers...air..."*: HDP, interview with Nora Flynn, 10 February 1947.

192 *"not interested...shut out"*: Mizener, p. 291.

192 *"social impressario..."*: FSF, *Crack-Up*, p. 171: Elsa Maxwell's name is deleted in this volume.

192 *He resolved not...*: FSF, *Notebooks*, p. 17.

192 *"make people happy..."*: FSF to MP, 20 May 1940, *Letters*, p. 288.

192 *heroes "are destroyed..."*: Piper, p. 297.

193 *swept away by...charm*: Willa Cather to FSF, 28 April 1925, Firestone. See this idea expressed in FSF, *Tender Is the Night* (New York: Scribner's, 1934), p. 35: "He· won everyone..."

194 *"About five years ago..."*: FSF to Betty Markell, 16 September 1929, *Letters*, p. 495.

194 *"one of the best guides..."*: Piper, p. 214.

196 *"a tall Fitzgerald"*: John O'Hara to Gerald Murphy, 30 July 1962, *Selected Letters of John O'Hara*, ed. Matthew J. Bruccoli (New York: Random House, 1978), p. 402.

196 *"make the man weak..."*: ZF to FSF, n.d., Firestone.

196–97 *instructed Mrs. Jarrett...*: FSF to Mrs. Edwin Jarrett, 17 February 1938, *Letters*, pp. 566–67.

12. "a writer only"

198   *Fitzgerald ... Graham ... lovers*: *Infidel*, pp. 172–82.

198–99   *Lily Sheil ... Alliance*: *Infidel*, pp. 185–86, 190–95.

199   *flowers ... notes*: *Infidel*, pp. 188, 221.

199   *producer wrote ... Fitzgerald answered ...* : Sheilah Graham, *The Rest of the Story* (New York: Coward-McCann, 1964), pp. 240–41.

199   *nuisance ... at airtime ...* : *Infidel*, pp. 203–205.

199–200   *editorial ... confrontation*: *Infidel*, pp. 293–94.

200   *"nice round figure"*: SD, interview with Sheilah Graham, 7 March 1983.

200–201   *poem ... jealousy*: The poem is quoted in full in *Infidel*, pp. 194–95.

201   *"paramour"*: *Infidel*, p. 275.

201   *reassurance ... Nora ...* : Nora Flynn to FSF, n.d., Firestone.

201   *"finest, loveliest ..."*: FSF to ZF, 6 May 1939, *Letters*, p. 105.

201   *"actual address"*: ZF to FSF, 1939 (?), Firestone.

202   *struck ... shouting ...* : Turnbull, pp. 304–305.

202   *"I want to die ..."*: FSF to Sheilah Graham, 2 December 1939, *Correspondence*, p. 564.

202   *Ping-Pong ... comic Rhett ...* : SD, interview with Sheilah Graham, March 1983.

202–203   *"College of One"*: Sheilah Graham, *College of One* (New York: Viking, 1967).

203   *rent ... without looking poor*: Grandeur, p. 486.

203   *reaction to* This Side ... : SD, interview with Sheilah Graham, 7 March 1983.

203   *child ... Rebecca West*: SD, interview with Sheilah Graham, 7 March 1983.

203   *soften ... letters*: SD, interview with Sheilah Graham, 7 March 1983.

203   *"Why ... torture me?"*: SD, interview with Sheilah Graham, 7 March 1983.

204   *"not Scott's mistress ... hero"*: SD, interview with Sheilah Graham, 7 March 1983.

205   *earnings ... dwindled*: FSF, *Ledger*, pp. 65–77.

205–206   *Schulberg ... struck*: SD, interview with Budd Schulberg,

27 December 1978.

206   "*I have seen . . .*": FSF to Anne Ober, 26 July 1937, *Letters*, pp. 552–53.

206   "*I like the work . . .*": FSF to Allein Owens, 8 October 1937, *Letters*, p. 557.

206   "*We brought you here . . .*": FSF to MP, 25 February 1939, *Letters*, p. 284.

206–207   "METRO . . . Comrades!": Telegram, FSF to Harold Ober, 26 December 1938, and letters, FSF to Harold Ober, received 29 December 1938, *As Ever, Scott Fitz——*, ed. Matthew J. Bruccoli and Jennifer M. Atkinson (Philadelphia: Lippincott, 1972), pp. 379–80.

207   "*I am amazed . . .*": FSF to Dr. R. Burke Suitt, 16 August 1939, *Correspondence*, p. 542.

207–208   "*I expect to dip . . .*": FSF to SF, winter 1939, *Letters*, p. 48.

208   "*hideous place . . .*": FSF to Alice Richardson, *Letters*, p. 603.

208   "*My great dreams . . .*": FSF to Gerald and Sara Murphy, spring 1940, *Letters*, p. 429.

208   *two hundred pages*: Matthew J. Bruccoli, *"The Last of the Novelists": F. Scott Fitzgerald and The Last Tycoon* (Carbondale: Southern Illinois University Press, 1977), p. 129.

208   "*Make notes . . .*": *Infidel*, p. 315.

208   "constructed *novel . . .*": FSF to ZF, 23 October 1940, *Letters*, p. 128.

209   *part about Stahr . . ."old magic" . . .*: Ernest Hemingway to MP, 15 November 1941, *Selected Letters 1917–1961*, ed. Carlos Baker (New York: Scribner's, 1981), pp. 527–28.

209   *composite characterization*: FSF to Ernest Hemingway, 1 June 1934, *Letters*, pp. 308–309.

209   "*feminine . . . Fitzgeralds . . .*": Guthrie, p. 93.

209   "*Books . . . brothers . . .*": FSF, *Crack-Up*, p. 176.

209   *story ideas . . . contracts . . .*: Turnbull, p. 115; Julian Street to FSF, n.d., Firestone; Julian van Cortland to FSF, 25 April 1932, Firestone; contract signed by Dick York and FSF, 28 April 1936, Firestone; FSF to Marguerite Kennedy, 29 July 1939, Firestone.

209   "*start out . . . emotion*": FSF, "One Hundred False Starts," *Afternoon*, p. 132.

209 *"price . . . sell your heart . . ."*: FSF to Frances Turnbull, 9 November 1938, *Letters*, pp. 577–78.

210 *"hard as pulling teeth . . ."*: FSF to ZF, 2 November 1940, *Letters*, p. 129.

210 *politically sophisticated . . .*: For a thorough discussion of FSF's political beliefs, see SD, "The Political Development of F. Scott Fitzgerald," *Prospects VI* (New York: Burt Franklin, 1981), pp. 313–55.

210 *"class interests"*: AM, interview with Budd Schulberg, 7 August 1947.

210 *"astonishing capacity . . ."*: Nancy Hale, *The Realities of Fiction* (Boston: Little, Brown, 1962), pp. 203–209.

210 *"two rules . . ."*: FSF, *Crack-Up*, p. 197.

210–11 *"unshakable moral attitude . . ."*: John Dos Passos, "A Note on F. Scott Fitzgerald," *Crack-Up*, p. 339.

211 *"intrinsically . . . good"*: Katherine Tighe Fessenden to HDP, 30 April 1947.

211 *"confessions . . . adultery"*: Ernest Boyd, "F. Scott Fitzgerald," *Portraits: Real and Imaginary* (London: Jonathan Cape, 1924), p. 221.

211 *"had no principles . . ."*: FSF, *Notebooks*, p. 259.

211 *"moralist at heart . . ."*: FSF to SF, 4 November 1939, *Letters*, p. 63.

211 *"Again and again . . ."*: FSF to John O'Hara, 25 July 1936, *Letters*, p. 539.

212 *Rich . . . "brought up . . . helpless . . ."*: Marguerite Mooers Marshall, interview with FSF, *Miscellany*, p. 257.

212 *"It is only . . . raising hell"*: FSF to MP, c. 10 April 1924, *Scott/Max*, p. 69.

212–13 *(unpublished) preface . . .*: FSF, "A Preface," 1935, Firestone.

213 *"something unpleasant . . . doubly costly"*: FSF to SF, 18 April 1938, May 1938, and 7 July 1938, *Letters*, pp. 28–29, 31, 32.

213 *"Even at killing myself . . ."*: "Marked for Glory," *Newsletter*, p. 148.

213 *"W. J. Locke . . ."*: Herbert Agar, memoir of FSF, Newberry library.

213–14 *"I'm F. Scott . . ."*: *Infidel*, p. 202.

214   *"a charmer..."*: SD, telephone interview with Frances Kroll Ring, 13 March 1983.

214   *affair..."tree"*: SD, interview with Sheilah Graham, 7 March 1983.

214   *Growing up..."terribly hard"*...: FSF, Notes, Firestone.

214   *"wise and tragic..."*: FSF to SF, 5 October 1940, *Letters*, p. 96.

214–15   *"My God, Andrew..."*: Turnbull, p. 219; FSF to Andrew Turnbull, 8 August 1933, *Letters*, pp. 504–505.

215   *17-volume*...: FSF, Notes, Firestone.

215   *"I want to write..."*: FSF, Notes, Firestone.

215   *"a writer only..."*: FSF, *Crack-Up*, p. 83.

215   *"talent...mislaid..."*: James Thurber, "Scott in Thorns," *Credos & Curios* (New York: Harper & Row, 1962), p. 160.

216   *"cheapest...funeral"*: Lee Reese, *The House on Rodney Square* (Wilmington, Del.: The News Journal Company, 1977), p. 177: interview with John Biggs.

216   *$600...envelope*...: SD, interview with Sheilah Graham, 7 March 1983.

216   *money...search*: Reese, *The House on Rodney Square*, p. 177.

Index

SCOTT DONALDSON is one of the nation's leading literary biographers. He is the author of *By Force of Will: The Life and Art of Ernest Hemingway, John Cheever: A Biography, Archibald MacLeish: An American Life* (winner of the 1993 Ambassador Book Award for Biography), *Hemingway vs. Fitzgerald: The Rise and Fall of a Literary Friendship, Edwin Arlington Robinson: A Poet's Life* (named best biography of the year by Contemporary Poetry Forum), and *Fitzgerald and Hemingway: Works and Days*.